Book 2

OCR GCSE English Language

Jill Carter
Annabel Charles
Garrett O'Doherty

Assessment preparation for Component 01 and Component 02

OXFORD
UNIVERSITY PRESS

OXFORD
UNIVERSITY PRESS

Great Clarendon Street, Oxford, OX2 6DP,
United Kingdom

Oxford University Press is a department of the University of Oxford.

It furthers the University's objective of excellence in research, scholarship, and education by publishing worldwide. Oxford is a registered trade mark of Oxford University Press in the UK and in certain other countries

First published in 2015

British Library Cataloguing in Publication Data

Data available

ISBN 978-019-833279-4

10 9 8 7 6

Printed in India by Multivista Global Pvt. Ltd

Contents

OCR GCSE English Language specification overview

You are studying for a GCSE English Language qualification from OCR. The OCR GCSE English Language specification has been designed to help you explore communication, culture and creativity. You will have the opportunity to read a wide variety of literary and non-fiction texts from across a range of genres and time periods, developing your independent and critical reading skills and helping you to develop your voice as a writer.

The exam papers

The grade you receive at the end of your OCR GCSE English Language course is entirely based on your performance in two exam papers. The following provides a summary of these two exam papers:

Exam paper	Reading and Writing questions and marks	Assessment Objectives	Timing	Marks (and % of GCSE)
Paper 1: Communicating information and ideas	**Section A: Reading information and ideas** Exam text: • Two unseen non-fiction texts, including a text from the 19th century Exam questions and marks: • One short-answer question (1 x 4 marks) • Two medium-answer questions (1 x 6 marks and 1 x 12 marks) • One extended question (1 x 18 marks)	Reading: A01 A02 A03 A04	2 hours	Reading: 40 marks (25% GCSE) Writing: 40 marks (25% GCSE) Paper 1 total: 80 marks (50% of GCSE)
	Section B: Writing for audience, purpose and impact • Writing original non-fiction for different audiences and purposes Exam questions and marks: • Choice of two extended writing tasks (24 marks for content, 16 marks for technical accuracy)	Writing: A05 A06		
Paper 2: Exploring effects and impact	**Section A: Reading meaning and effects** Exam text: • Two unseen prose texts, one of which may be literary non-fiction Exam questions and marks: • One short-answer question (1 x 4 marks) • Two medium-answer questions (1 x 6 marks and 1 x 12 marks) • One extended question (1 x 18 marks)	Reading: A01 A02 A03 A04	2 hours	Reading: 40 marks (25% GCSE) Writing: 40 marks (25% GCSE) Paper 2 total: 80 marks (50% of GCSE)
	Section B: Writing imaginatively and creatively • Original creative writing Exam question and marks: • Choice of two extended writing tasks (24 marks for content, 16 marks for technical accuracy)	Writing: A05 A06		

Paper 1: Communicating information and ideas

This exam paper focuses on reading and writing non-fiction texts and has two sections:

- Section A: Reading information and ideas.
- Section B: Writing for audience, impact and purpose.

You will have two hours to complete this exam paper and it is worth 50% of your GCSE English Language grade.

Section A: Reading information and ideas

In Section A you will read and respond to two unseen non-fiction texts, one of which will be a text from the 19th century. The non-fiction texts included in the exam will be linked by theme and taken from a range of non-fiction genres including for example, essays, journalism, travel writing, speeches and biographical writing.

You are advised to spend one hour on Section A of the exam paper and should answer all the questions. The reading questions will assess the following assessment objectives:

- **AO1** Identify and interpret explicit and implicit information and ideas.
- **AO1** Select and synthesize evidence from different texts.
- **AO2** Explain, comment on and analyse how writers use language and structure to achieve effects and influence readers, using relevant subject terminology to support your views.
- **AO3** Compare writer's ideas and perspectives, as well as how these are conveyed, across two texts.
- **AO4** Evaluate texts critically and support this with appropriate textual references.

The reading questions are designed to increase in challenge, moving from short- to medium-answer response questions, focused on the writer's meaning and purpose, to a final, more detailed task that asks you to evaluate the two texts you have read. This section of the exam paper is worth 25% of your GCSE English Language grade.

Section B: Writing for audience, purpose and impact

In Section B you will write a piece of original non-fiction writing. You will be given a choice of two extended writing tasks, using an idea related to the reading theme, and have to answer one of these tasks. The writing tasks might ask you to:

- write in a range of non-fiction forms, for example, an article, speech or letter
- write for a specific purpose, for example, to describe, explain, inform, instruct, argue or persuade
- write for a specific audience.

You are advised to spend one hour on Section B of the exam paper and should answer only one of the writing tasks. Each writing task will assess the following assessment objectives:

- **AO5** Communicate clearly, effectively and imaginatively, selecting and adapting tone, style and register for different forms, purposes and audiences
- **AO5** Organize information and ideas, using structural and grammatical features to support coherence and cohesion of texts
- **AO6** Use a range of vocabulary and sentence structures for clarity, purpose and effect, with accurate spelling and punctuation

This section of the exam paper is worth 25% of your GCSE English Language grade.

Paper 2: Exploring effects and impact

This exam paper focuses on reading and writing narrative fiction and literary non-fiction and has two sections:

- Section A: Reading meaning and effects
- Section B: Writing imaginatively and creatively

You will have two hours to complete this exam paper and it is worth 50% of your GCSE English Language grade.

Section A: Reading meaning and effects

In Section A you will read and respond to two unseen prose from the 20th and 21st centuries. The texts included in the exam will be linked by theme and one text may be literary non-fiction.

You are advised to spend one hour on Section A of the exam paper and should answer all the questions. The reading questions will assess the following assessment objectives:

- **AO1** Identify and interpret explicit and implicit information and ideas.
- **AO2** Explain, comment on and analyse how writers use language and structure to achieve effects and influence readers, using relevant subject terminology to support your views.
- **AO3** Compare writer's ideas and perspectives, as well as how these are conveyed, across two texts.
- **AO4** Evaluate texts critically and support this with appropriate textual references.

The reading questions are designed to increase in challenge, moving from short- to medium-answer response questions, focused on the writer's meaning and effects, to a final, more detailed task that asks you to evaluate the two texts you have read. This section of the exam paper is worth 25% of your GCSE English Language grade.

Section B: Writing imaginatively and creatively

In Section B you will write a piece of original creative writing. You will be given a choice of two creative writing tasks, at least one of which will have a clear relation to the reading theme, and have to answer one of these tasks. The writing tasks might ask you to write in a range of forms, for example, short stories and autobiographical writing.

You are advised to spend one hour on Section B of the exam paper and should answer only one of the writing tasks. The following assessment objectives will be assessed in this section:

- **AO5** Communicate clearly, effectively and imaginatively, selecting and adapting tone, style and register for different forms, purposes and audiences
- **AO5** Organize information and ideas, using structural and grammatical features to support coherence and cohesion of texts
- **AO6** Use a range of vocabulary and sentence structures for clarity, purpose and effect, with accurate spelling and punctuation

This section of the exam paper is worth 25% of your GCSE English Language grade.

Grades

Your GCSE English Language grade will be awarded solely on the basis of your performance in these two exams and you will be awarded a grade from 1 to 9, with 9 being the top grade.

Introduction to this book

How this book will help you

Assessment preparation

The aim of this book is to prepare you for the questions and tasks you will face in the exam so that you can sit your final assessment with confidence. The book is structured around the two exam papers you will sit: Component 01 Communicating information and ideas and Component 02 Exploring effects and impact. The book provides a question-by-question approach to developing the skills you need to succeed.

Each section of the book begins with an overview of the relevant section of the exam outlining the content and focus of that section of the exam paper, guidance on how best to use your time in the exam and how your answers will be assessed.

Practise the types of questions and tasks you will face in the exams

Each section in the book shows you how to approach the relevant question or task in the exam and the key skills you need to demonstrate when writing your response. In each section you will find:

- a range of texts similar to those you will encounter in the exam (reading questions only)
- an extract from the mark scheme that examiners use to mark responses so that you can see exactly what skills are being assessed in each question
- sample questions with the key skills identified
- advice on how to demonstrate and combine the key skills in your response
- activities to practise and reinforce the key skills
- sample student responses
- opportunities for self-assessment and peer-assessment
- advice on how to improve your responses.

The book concludes with sample exam papers, in the style of the OCR exam papers, to enable you and your teacher to see how much progress you have made.

A note on spelling

Certain words, for example 'synthesize' and 'organize' have been spelt with 'ize' throughout this book. It is equally acceptable to spell these words and others with 'ise'.

Further OCR GCSE English Language resources

OCR GCSE English Language Student Book 1: Developing the skills for Component 01 and Component 02

Student Book 1 includes thematically-focused skills-based units to help develop key reading and writing skills in a motivational context. Structured around the Assessment Objectives, Student Book 1 provides the ideal preparation for students as they embark on this GCSE course.

The themes covered are:

- On the mind
- This life
- Friendship and family
- New horizons
- War and conflict
- Reflect and review

OCR GCSE English Literature Student Book

This student book provides comprehensive support for all components of the English Literature specification and focuses on key skills development, including:

- Support for the poetry anthology and unseen poetry
- Approaches to and guidance on Shakespeare, nineteenth-century prose and modern prose and drama
- Carefully structured activities to motivate and engage students
- Sample student responses at a range of levels and practice tasks
- Stretch and support features to ensure all students make progress
- Clear, student-friendly explanations of the Assessment Objectives and the skills required to meet them

OCR GCSE English Language Teacher Companion

The Teacher Companion provides holistic support for teachers to help them plan and deliver their GCSE programme, including:

- specification insight and planning guidance to aid planning and delivery of the specification
- teaching tips and guidance for effective lesson delivery to all students of the material in Student Book 1, with additional support for differentiation and personalization
- exam preparation guidance and planning with links to English Language Student Book 2
- guidance and support for delivering Spoken Language assessments
- links to, and guidance on, the additional resources on the accompanying OCR GCSE English Language Teacher Companion CD-ROM.

OCR GCSE English Language Teacher Companion CD-ROM

The Teacher Companion is accompanied by a CD-ROM containing the following resources:

- activity worksheets to support and extend activities in Student Book 1
- differentiated worksheets to support and stretch activities in Student Book 1
- Progress Check self-assessment and peer-assessment checklists
- mark schemes for end-of-chapter assessments in Student Book 1
- mark schemes for sample exam papers in Student Book 1
- short, medium and long term editable plans to aid the planning and delivery of the course.

Kerboodle Online Student Books

Kerboodle Online Student Books are available for separate access by teachers and students for all three OCR titles:

- English Language Student Book 1
- English Language Student Book 2
- English Literature Student Book

Component 01 Communicating information and ideas

Section A: Reading information and ideas

What is the content and focus of this section?

Component 01, Section A: Reading information and ideas assesses your ability to read and respond to non-fiction texts. In this section you will have to answer four questions based on two unseen non-fiction texts such as newspaper and magazine articles, speeches, travel writing, letters, diaries and biographical writing. One text will be from the 19th century and the other text from either the 20th or 21st century.

How to use your time in the exam

Section A of this exam is worth 40 marks and will form 25% of your total GCSE grade. The four reading questions will increase in challenge, moving from short- to medium-length response questions on either Text 1 or Text 2 to a final more detailed task which asks you to evaluate and compare the two texts you have read. You are advised to spend an hour on this section, although you might choose to spend longer on it. The grid below suggests how you might allocate your time.

Question and approach	Marks available	Suggested timing
Initial read of the texts and questions		Approximately 5–10 minutes
Question 1: Re-read the part of the text indicated in the question before answering.	4 marks	Approximately 5 minutes
Question 2: Skim and scan both texts before answering.	6 marks	Approximately 10–15 minutes
Question 3: Skim and scan the text indicated before answering.	12 marks	Approximately 15 minutes
Question 4: Skim and scan both texts before answering.	18 marks	Approximately 20–25 minutes

How will my reading be assessed?

The grid on the next page sets out the Assessment Objectives (AOs) that you will be assessed on in Section A of Component 01. An initial explanation of each Assessment Objective is provided as well as an indication of which question(s) will assess it, but a more detailed explanation is provided in the chapters that follow.

Assessment Objective		What does this mean?	Where you will apply this skill
AO1 (i)	Identify and interpret explicit and implicit information and ideas	Find specific information or ideas in the text. This information may be explicit or implicit. Where the information is implicit, you will have to infer and interpret this to show your understanding.	Question 1: you will be asked to identify specific words, phrases, quotations or examples from Text 1 and to explain what is suggested by them.
AO1 (ii)	Select and synthesize evidence from different texts	Identify information and ideas from both texts and draw this together.	Question 2: you will be asked to identify similarities between Texts 1 and 2 or summarize a common idea both texts share.
AO2	Explain, comment on and analyse how writers use language and structure to achieve effects and influence readers, using relevant subject terminology to support their views	Analyse how a writer uses language (i.e. words, phrases, language features and techniques) and structure (i.e. sentences, punctuation, paragraphs and structural features) to achieve specific effects and influence the reader. Use the correct terminology (e.g. metaphor, verb, etc.) when explaining how a writer uses these techniques.	Question 3: you will be asked to explore how language and structure are used in Text 2 to convey a particular idea or viewpoint.
AO3	Compare writers' ideas and perspectives, as well as how these are conveyed across two or more texts	Compare specific ideas, themes and viewpoints in both texts and how they are presented.	Question 4: you will be asked to compare how Texts 1 and 2 present a specific idea or viewpoint, identifying similarities and differences.
AO4	Evaluate texts critically and support this with appropriate textual references	Appraise texts in a considered and analytical way, quoting or referring closely to the texts to justify your ideas and provide a personal response.	Question 4: you will be asked to evaluate Texts 1 and 2 in response to a statement, exploring your impressions in relation to this and explaining the impact of the texts on a reader.

Mark scheme

For Question 1, worth 4 marks, the examiner will award marks for specific points or quotations listed in the mark scheme. However, for Question 2, 3 and 4 there is a level-based mark scheme describing the skills that will be shown in responses at different levels. For Question 2, there are three levels, Level 1 being the lowest and Level 3 the highest. For Questions 3 and 4, there are six levels, Level 1 being the lowest and Level 6 the highest. Each level descriptor contains key phrases summing up a typical answer at this level.

Level 6: Skilled analysis, sophisticated appreciation
Level 5: Analysis, perceptive understanding
Level 4: Developed explanation, secure understanding
Level 3: Clear explanation, general understanding
Level 2: Straightforward commentary, some understanding
Level 1: Descriptive response, limited awareness

As you work through this chapter, you will learn how to assess your own work and how to improve it to gain the highest mark that you can in the exam.

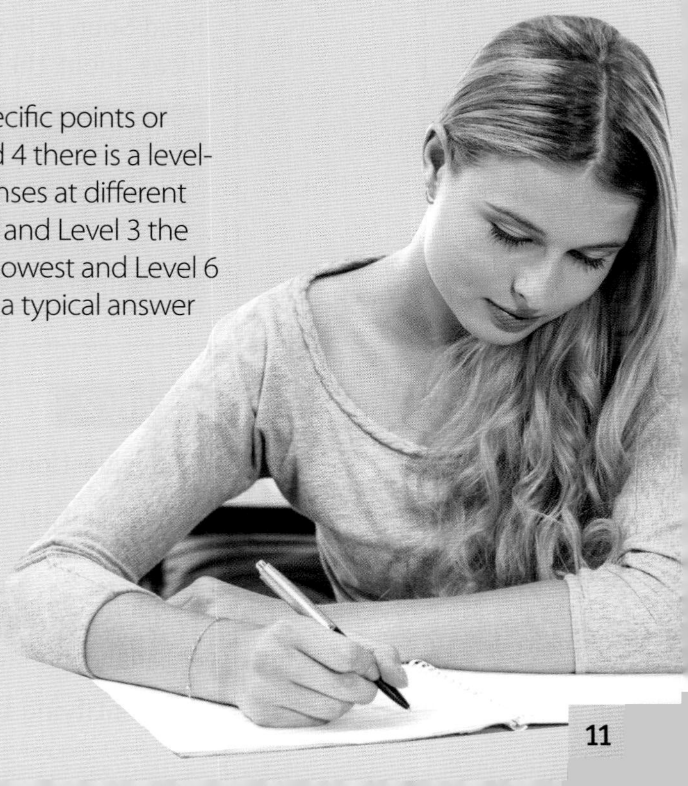

Reading an unseen non-fiction text

Tip

When you first read an unseen text in an exam situation, it can be helpful to work out its purpose and context, including the form or genre, when it was written and the approach it takes to its subject. Remember to look at the introduction to the text so you understand where it comes from, when it was written and by whom.

What to expect in the exam

In the exam you will be given a Reading Insert Booklet that contains two source texts. The texts will be non-fiction and will be referred to as Text 1 and Text 2. Each text will have a brief introduction explaining where it comes from, when it was written and by whom, with definitions for any difficult vocabulary provided at the end of each text. You cannot predict what these non-fiction texts will be and it is unlikely you will have read them before.

Developing your reading skills

Reading a wide range of non-fiction from the 19th, 20th and 21st centuries will help you to develop the skills you need to read and respond to the unseen non-fiction texts you will encounter in the exam. Try to make time to reflect on your reading and think analytically about the non-fiction texts you have read. You could use some of the following ideas to extend your reading experience.

- Read newspapers (print and online) to keep up to date with the latest news.
- Read magazines linked to your interests and hobbies.
- Ask teachers and the school librarian for recommendations of non-fiction books linked to the subjects and topics you are studying.
- Read non-fiction for pleasure, such as biographies of performers you like.

Activity 1

Read Source Text A. Copy and complete the grid below to record your initial ideas about the text.

Form	
Author	
Purpose	
Key ideas or information	

Activity 2

What questions could you ask about Source Text A?

With a partner, come up with at least one question for each of the following focuses:

- identifying explicit and implicit information and ideas
- analysing language and structure
- identifying the writer's ideas and perspective.

Source text A

In this account, Fanny Kemble describes going on the first train journey on the Liverpool to Manchester railway, with George Stephenson, on 25 August 1830.

We were introduced to the little engine which was to drag us along the rails. **She** (for they make these curious little fire horses all **mares**) consisted of a boiler, a stove, a small platform, a bench, and behind the bench a barrel containing enough water to prevent her being thirsty for fifteen miles.

This snorting little animal, which I felt rather inclined to pat, was then harnessed to our carriage, and Mr Stephenson having taken me on the bench of the engine with him, we started at about ten miles an hour. The steam-horse being ill-adapted for going up and downhill, the railway line was kept at a certain level, and appeared sometimes to sink below the surface of the earth, and sometimes to rise above it. Almost at starting it was cut through the solid rock, which formed a wall on either side of it, about sixty feet high. You can't imagine how strange it seemed to be journeying on thus, without any visible cause of progress other than the magical machine, with its flying white breath and rhythmical unvarying pace, between these rocky walls, which are already clothed with moss and ferns and grasses; and when I reflected that these great masses of stone had been cut asunder to allow our passage thus far below the surface of the earth, I felt as though no fairy tale was ever half so wonderful as what I saw.

Glossary

she the engine

mares female horses, used here to refer to the practice of describing the engine as female

Reading: Question 1

AO1 Identify and interpret explicit and implicit information and ideas

An overview of the question

Question 1 refers to the first text you will have read in your exam (Text 1) and is worth 4 marks. It assesses AO1 and requires you to show your understanding of information and ideas which are stated directly in the text and also implied or suggested indirectly. This question could be divided into two or more parts, e.g. 1a), 1b) and 1c).

In the question:

- You will be told to look again at a specific section or sections of the text, with line numbers given to guide you.
- You will be asked to identify key information, phrases, quotations or examples from this section of text which convey a certain idea or information.
- You may also be asked to explain, in your own words, how these phrases convey this idea or information.

The section of the text the question is about

Find explicit information, e.g. two quotations

The section of the text the question is about

1a) Look again at lines 1–7. Give **two** quotations which describe what the leech does. **[2]**

1b) Look again at lines 1–26. Explain how Redmond O'Hanlan's view of leeches changes during this passage. **[2]**

Interpret implicit information in your own words

How will my answer be assessed?

There are no levels in the mark scheme for answers to Question 1. You will be allocated up to a maximum of 4 marks for the correct information you identify and interpret.

Identifying explicit information

The first part of Question 1 will focus on **explicit** information, that is information and **ideas** that are stated directly. This should be quite a straightforward question but you should make sure you answer it carefully and precisely.

Look at Question 1a) below, which targets the first part of AO1, identifying explicit information and ideas. The key features of the question are highlighted in the annotations.

Key terms

ideas the information, experiences, opinions or arguments in a text

explicit stating something openly and exactly

This directs you to a specific section of text. It might be helpful to mark this on your copy of the text.

The command word 'Give' tells you that you have to identity/provide explicit information. You are not being asked to explain or elaborate your answer. 'Two features' tells you what your answer should comprise.

1a) Look again at lines 1–5. Give **two** features of the engine described in this section. **[2]**

____

____

This shows *which* features you are looking for – what they should relate to.

This is the number of marks awarded for this part of the question.

This is the space for you to answer the question.

An extract from the mark scheme that examiners would use to mark Question 1 is given below.

Award **one** mark for each of the following up to a maximum of **two** marks:

- 'little'
- 'a boiler'
- 'a stove'
- 'a small platform'
- 'a bench'
- 'a barrel of water'

Activity 1

1. a) Copy out and annotate the following question in the same way.

   b) Look again at lines 5–16. Give **two** quotations which tell you about the railway line they travelled along. **[2]**

2. Look back at Source text A on page 13 and note down the two quotations you would select to answer this question.
3. Compare your answer with a partner. Are there any differences between the quotations you have chosen?

Tip

You need to select the correct quotations to answer the question asked. You are not being asked to explain or elaborate your answer.

Improving your answer

Look at the mark scheme below. This is for the example Question 1a) in Activity 1 on page 15.

Award **one** mark for each of the following, up to a maximum of **two** marks:

- 'the railway line was kept at a certain level'/'appeared sometimes to sink below the surface of the earth, and sometimes to rise above it'
- 'it was cut through the solid rock, (which formed a wall on either side of it, about sixty feet high)'

Accept minor slips in quotations and quotations provided without quotation marks.

Candidates must show that each quotation has been separately identified. Do not accept indiscriminate copying of longer quotations with the correct answer(s) embedded.

Award **one** mark if a candidate identifies two correct quotations as one answer.

Activity 2

1. Use this mark scheme to mark your own answer to this question.
2. Now look at the student answers that follow and, using the mark scheme above, give each answer a mark.

Student A

1. It consisted of a boiler, a stove, a small platform and a bench.
2. It was cut through the rock.

Student B

1. The railway line was kept at a certain level.
2. The line appeared sometimes to sink below the surface and sometimes to rise above it.

Student C

1. Almost at starting it was cut through the solid rock, which formed a wall on either side of it, about sixty feet high. You can't imagine how strange it seemed to be journeying on thus, without any visible cause of progress other than the magical machine.
2. The line goes up and down.

3. Write feedback for each student. In your feedback you should:

- identify any problems with their answer
- give advice on how they could improve their answer to this type of question next time.

4. Create your own mark scheme for the following question.

> **1a)** Look again at lines 1–16. Give **two** quotations which tell you about the movement of the train. **[2]**

5. Compare your mark scheme with another person's. What differences can you find?

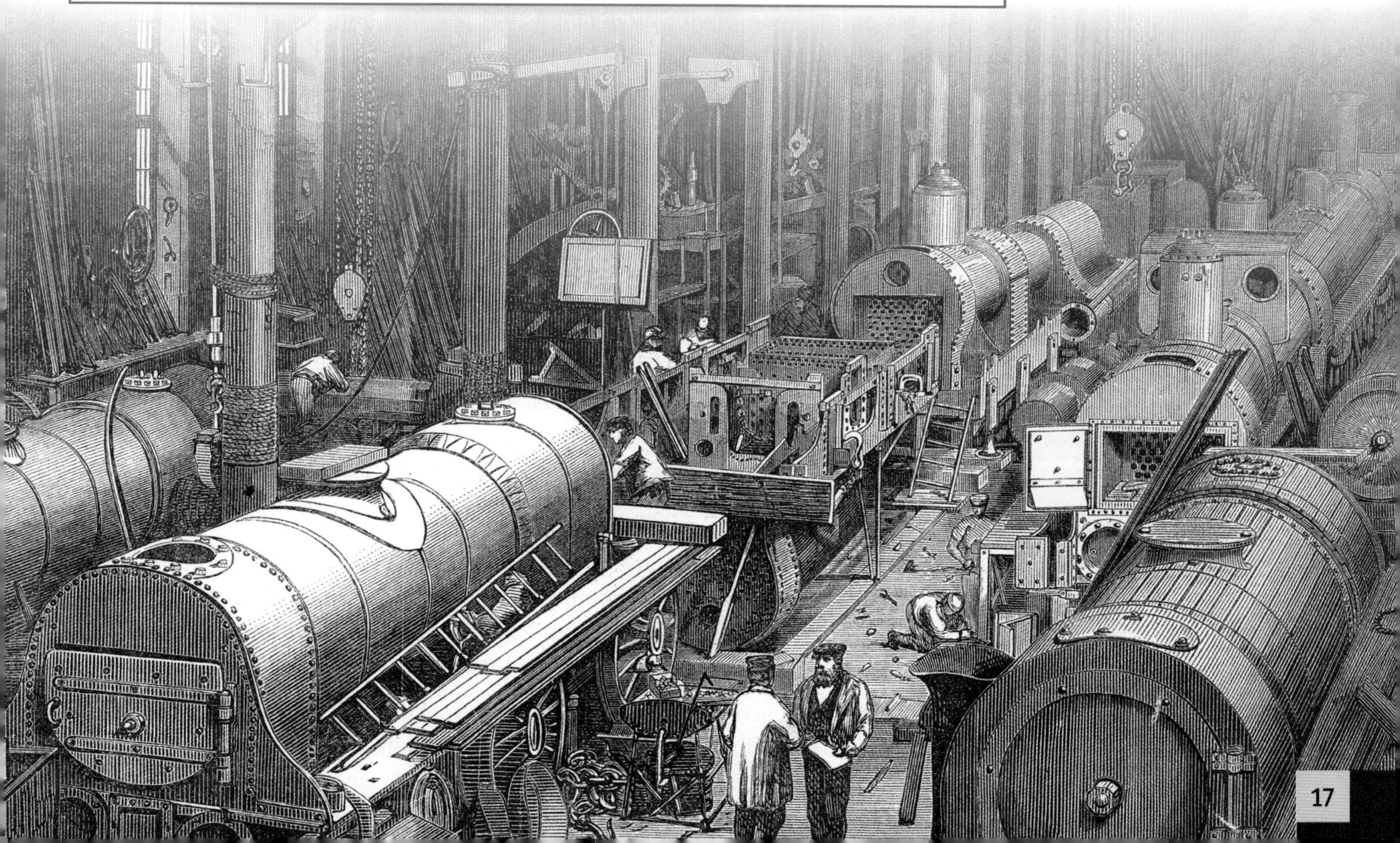

Interpreting implicit information

Key terms

implicit implied but not stated openly

interpret to explain the meaning of something said or written

The second part of Question 1 focuses on interpreting **implicit** information and ideas, that is information and ideas that are implied or suggested rather than stated directly and explicitly. As the reader, you have to **interpret** what the writer is implying or suggesting in the text and explain your interpretation in your own words.

Read Source text B, which begins below and then complete the Try it yourself activities that follow.

Source text B

The writer, Redmond O'Hanlan, is travelling through the jungle in Borneo, with his friend James and a number of local guides.

James sat on the tree trunk next to Dana, held his head in his hand – and then bounded up with a yell. There was a leech on his left arm. He pulled it off with his right hand, but the leech looped over and sunk its mouthparts into his palm. James began to dance, wriggling convulsively. He made a curious yelping sound. The Iban lay down and laughed. James pulled the leech out of his right palm with his left hand. The brown-black, tough, rubbery, segmented, inch long common ground leech, *Haemadipsa zeylanica*, then twisted over and began to take a drink at the base of James' thumb.

At this point, Leon obviously decided that the two had got to know each other well enough.

"Ah, my best friend, why you come so far to suffer so? Eh?"

James sat down trembling a bit and pulled out a cigarette.

I looked at my legs. And then I looked again. They were undulating with leeches. In fact, James' leech suddenly seemed much less of a joke. They were edging up my trousers, looping up towards my knees with alternate placements of their anterior and posterior suckers, seeming with each rear attachment, to wave their front ends in the air and take a sniff. They were all over my boots, too, and three particularly brave individuals were trying to make their way in via the air-holes. There were more on the way – in fact they were moving towards us across the jungle floor from every angle, their damp brown bodies half camouflaged against the rotting leaves.

"Oh God," said James, "they are really pleased to see us."

The Iban were also suffering and we spent the next few minutes pulling leeches off our persons and wiping them on the trees. Their bite is painless, but nonetheless it was unpleasant to watch them fill with blood at great speed, distending, becoming globular and wobbly.

Now that I had become accustomed to leech-spotting I discovered they were rearing up and sniffing at us from the trees, too, from leaves and creepers at face height. We covered ourselves with Autan jelly, socks and trousers,

Source text B (continued)

chests, arms and neck. Dana, Inghai and Leon put on their best (and only) pairs of long trousers, and I lent them pairs of socks (they were desperate). I took the opportunity to sidle off behind a bush and fill my boots and y-fronts with handfuls of zinc powder. Sitting down again, I was pleased to see that chemical warfare works: the leeches looped and flowed towards me and then stopped in mid-sniff, as disgusted by me as I was by them. They waved their heads about, thought a bit, decided they really were revolted, and reversed.

Try it yourself WITH SUPPORT

Now you are going to practise using the skills of inference and interpretation in response to Question 1b) below. The key features of the question are highlighted in the annotations.

This directs you to a specific section of text. It might be helpful to mark this on your copy of the text.

The command word 'Explain' tells you that you are being asked to make inferences using your own words to address the question.

1b) Look again at lines 1–8. Explain James' different reactions to finding a leech on his arm. **[2]**

This shows what your explanation should be about.

This is the number of marks awarded for this question.

Activity 3

1. **a)** Copy and complete the grid below to identify the key words and phrases from lines 1–8 that suggest James' reactions to finding a leech on his arm. The first two have been done for you.

   b) Using your own words, explain what your chosen word or phrase suggests about James' reaction.

Word or phrase from lines 1–8	What it suggests about James' reactions
'bounded up'	
'yell'	

2. Use your explanations from the second column to answer Question 1b), supporting your points with quotations from the first column.

Tip

Using your own words and supporting your points with very brief quotations (indicated with quotation marks) is the key to successfully answering 'interpretation' questions. Avoid simply repeating what is in the text without demonstrating inference.

Improving your answer

Look at the mark scheme for the example Question 1b) on page 19, below.

Award **one** mark for each explanation which shows understanding of James' reaction to finding a leech on his arm:

- James is **surprised/horrified** when he discovers the leech ('bounded up'/'yell')
- he is **desperate/does everything he can to get rid of it** ('dance'/'wriggling convulsively'/'curious yelping sound')

Activity 4

1. Look at the following student answers to the question above and give each one a mark. For each answer, write a brief comment explaining why you have given a particular mark.

Student A

James is obviously completely shocked when he discovers the leech. You can tell this because he 'bounds up'. He really wants to get it off him so he dances around and can't stop himself.

Student B

James bounded up with a yell. He tried to pull the leech off of his arm and made a curious yelping sound.

2. Share your marks and comments with a partner. Discuss what key piece of advice you would give to Student B.
3. Look back at your own answer to this question and decide what mark you would give it. What could you do to improve your answer?

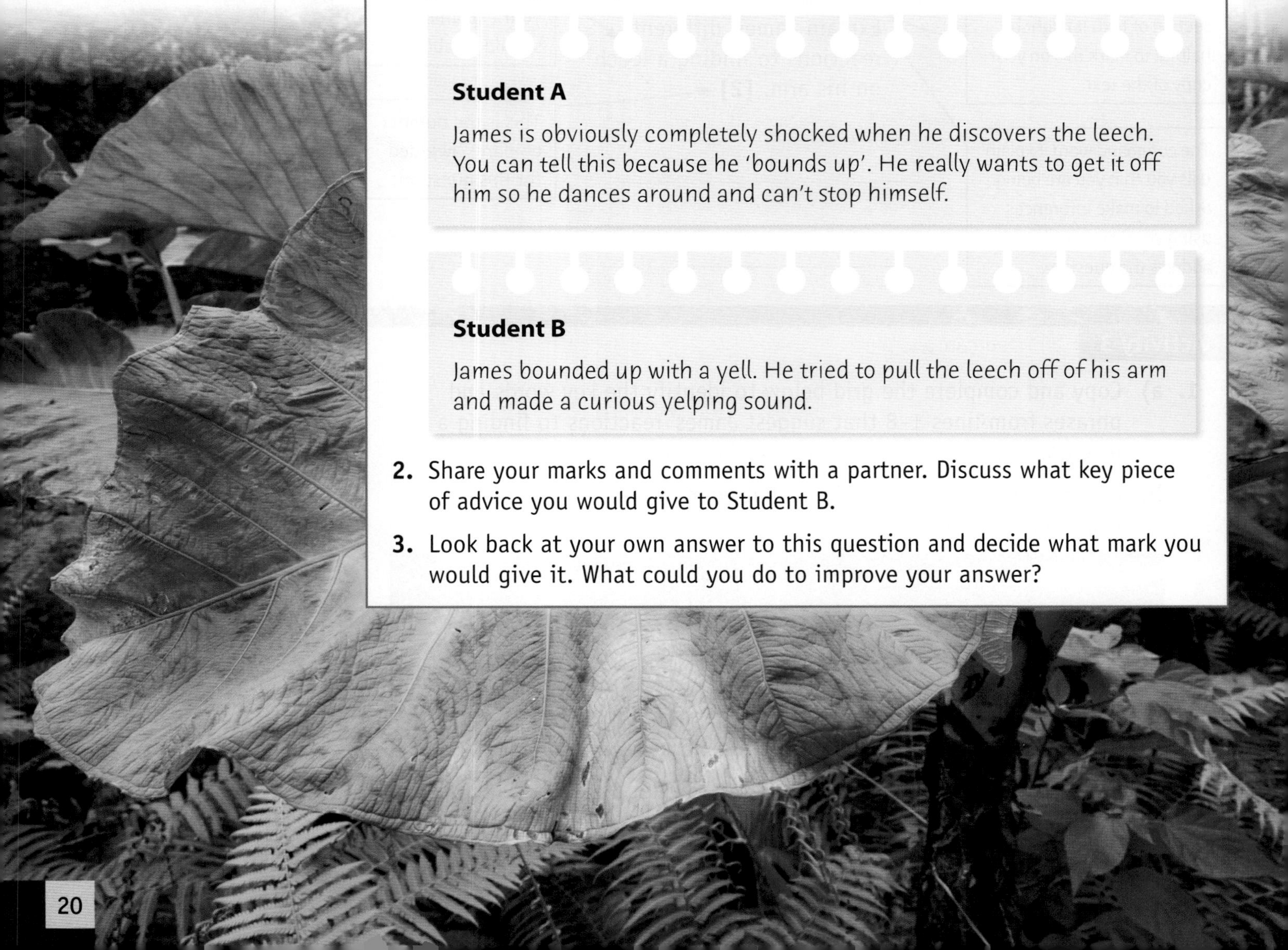

Try it yourself ON YOUR OWN

Look back at Source text B on pages 18 and 19, and write your response to the Question 1 task below, applying all the skills you have learned.

1a) Look again at lines 1–7. Give **two** quotations which describe what the leech does. **[2]**

1b) Look again at lines 13–26. Explain how Redmond O'Hanlon's view of leeches changes during this passage. **[2]**

Progress check

1. Write a mark scheme for this question. Compare your mark scheme with a partner's and agree a final version.
2. Using the mark scheme, mark each other's answers to Question 1. Give feedback on how your partner could improve their answer.
3. Which of the following questions assess:
   a. understanding of explicit information and ideas?
   b. understanding of implicit information and ideas?

   Identify the key words in each question which tell you what the question is targeting.

   Identify two aspects of the leeches' physical appearance.

   What impression do you get of the experience of dealing with leeches?

   Explain how you can tell travelling through the jungle is quite challenging.

   Give two features of the jungle landscape they are travelling through.

   How does Redmond O'Hanlan suggest that the leeches have almost human characteristics?

4. Copy and complete the following grid to assess how confident you are in using the skills required to answer Question 1. Reflect on the activities you have completed in this section and, for each skill, award yourself a confidence rating from one to five, with five being very confident.

Skill	Confidence rating (1–5)
Selecting phrases and quotations to identify explicit information and ideas	
Interpreting implicit information and ideas and explaining these in your own words	

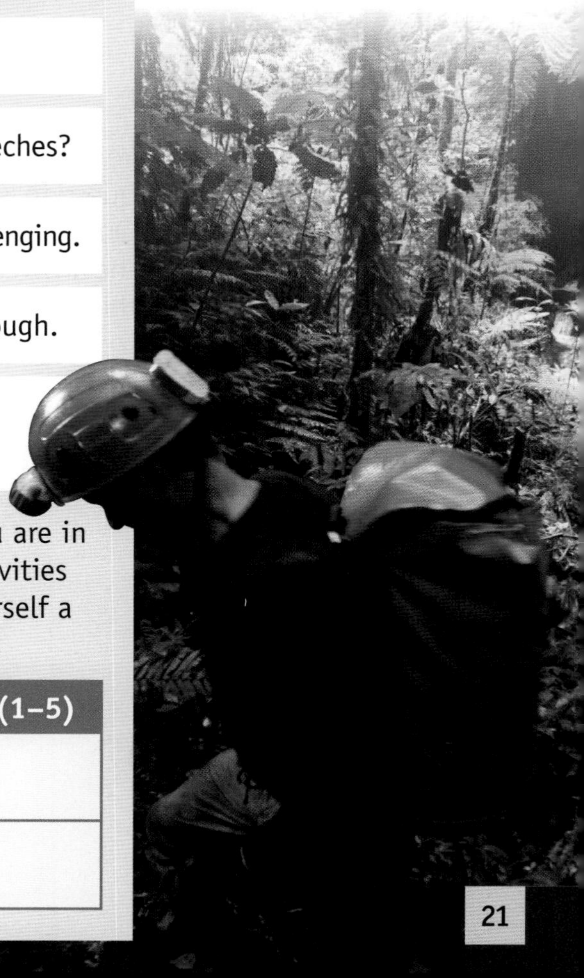

Reading: Question 2

AO1 Select and synthesize evidence from different texts

An overview of the question

Question 2 refers to both of the texts you will have read in your exam (Text 1 and Text 2) and is worth 6 marks. It assesses AO1 and is designed to test that you can recognize and **synthesize** information and ideas that the two texts have in common. This might be explicit and implicit information and ideas.

In the question:

- You will be presented with a statement identifying a similarity both texts share.
- You will be asked to identify other common ideas between the two texts.
- You will need to look at both texts in full, making connections between the texts in order to synthesize the information and ideas that they share.
- You will be asked to draw on supporting evidence from both texts to support your answer.

Key term

synthesize draw together information and ideas from both texts and explain this in your own words

> **2** These texts are both about people who show strong emotions toward snakes. What other similarities do these texts share?
> Draw on evidence from both texts to support your answer.

Statement identifying a link between the texts

The question you have to answer

Reminder to include quotations and textual references

You should re-read both texts before you answer the question. Remember this question is worth 6 marks, so you should spend less time on this question than on Questions 3 and 4, which are worth more marks. Use the blank lines provided in the answer booklet to guide you as to how much you should write in response to this question.

How will my answer be assessed?

An extract from the mark scheme that examiners use to mark Question 2 is shown below. There are three levels. For each level, the skills that you have to demonstrate in your response are shown in the right-hand column. The key words that identify the differences between each level are shown in bold and the annotations help to explain these more fully.

Level	Skills descriptor	
Level 3 (5–6 marks)	A **detailed** response which shows a **secure ability** to synthesize appropriate ideas and evidence from both texts, showing **perceptive understanding** of similarities, including **conceptual ideas.**	Developed, comprehensive Skill demonstrated throughout the response Insightful Abstract ideas that are presented implicitly in the texts
Level 2 (3–4 marks)	A response which shows **some ability to make connections** between ideas and evidence from both texts, showing **clear awareness of similarities.** The ideas and evidence selected **may not be equal** across both texts.	Demonstrates this skill, but not consistently Recognizes and explains common information and ideas Draws on evidence and ideas from one text more than the other
Level 1 (1–2 marks)	A response which shows **limited ability to select and make connections** between evidence from both texts, **showing little awareness of similarities.** The evidence selected is likely to focus on **more obvious, surface features** of the texts and may be **imbalanced** across the texts.	Few relevant connections made Few if any similarities identified Explicit information and ideas Draws on evidence and ideas from one text more than the other

Recognizing similarities

To answer this question successfully, you first need to have a clear overview of both texts. Read Source texts C and D on pages 25–26, then complete the activities below.

Activity 1

1. Copy and complete the grid below to build an overview of each text.

Overview	Source Text A	Source Text B
Author		
Genre		
Date published		
Key ideas		
Viewpoint		
Personal response		

2. Now summarize each text in one sentence. Try to focus your summary on the key ideas presented in each text.

To show you can recognize and explain the similarities between the two texts, you need to be able to bring together evidence from both and summarize this in your own words to demonstrate your understanding of the ideas and features they share.

Activity 2

1. Look back at the two sentences you wrote to summarize each text. Do these sentences suggest any similarities between the texts?
2. Look at the list of similarities suggested below. Put these in order of importance, with the most relevant similarity at the top of the list.
   - Both texts are about people facing difficulties in their lives.
   - There is a focus in both texts on the fear of having nothing, reaching rock bottom and having to throw oneself on the mercy of others.
   - Both texts explore the impact of poverty on people.
   - The importance of compassion and sensitivity to others' needs is examined in both texts.
   - Both texts are recounted from the point of view of someone experiencing deprivation.
   - The texts are similar because they consider the desperation and humiliation brought about by hunger.
   - Both texts focus on the importance of food.
3. Support each similarity in your list with evidence from both texts.
4. Using your own words, add any other similarities you can find to the list. Don't forget to support these with evidence from both texts.

Source text C

Some four million Irish people relied on potatoes as their main source of food in the mid-19th century. In 1845 and 1846, the crop was hit by blight. Around one million people died and 1,600,000 emigrated to the USA. This is an extract from the diary of Elizabeth Smith, who was the wife of an Irish landowner.

5 November 1846 Hal has just brought in two damaged potatoes the first we have seen of our own for on our hill few have been found as yet.

13 November Half the potatoes in this new field are tainted, some very badly.

12 January 1847 ... we make daily a large pot of soup which is served **gratis** to 22 people at present. It is ready at one o'clock and I thought it quite a pretty sight yesterday in the kitchen all the workmen coming in for their portion, a quart with a slice of beef; half of them get this one day for dinner with a bit of their own bread; the other half get milk and the cheap rice we have provided for them. Next day they reverse the order. The Colonel is giving them **firing** too; so they are really comfortable. There are twelve of them and ten pensioners, old and feeble men and women, or those with large families of children; some of them no longer living on our ground yet having been once connected with us we can't desert them. So far well; but beyond our small circle what a waste of misery; how are we to relieve it? Such a dense population squatted here and there upon neglected properties, dying with want, wretched every year but ruined this. At the Relief Committee yesterday it was resolved to institute soup kitchens at proper stations for general relief, to be supported by subscription, each subscription to have a certain number of tickets. I think the gentleman are doing this, the ladies must combine for a clothing fund. The rags are hardly coverings for decency; beds and bedding there are none, among the mob, I mean; such miseries crush hope, yet hope I will...

16 January We then went to Jem Doyle's. Most wretched it was though very clean, he must go to the poor house, he and his family. He has an ulcer on his leg, which will prevent his working for weeks and they will starve during this month that there is no relief going. Widow Mulligan is also starving. So are the Widow Quin and fifty more. They must be forced into the poorhouse for they cannot otherwise be supported.

Glossary

gratis free

firing firewood

Source text D

This is an extract from an article by Jack Monroe, written in 2014, about giving evidence at a parliamentary inquiry into food banks. Jack Monroe is a blogger and campaigner.

More than 'hunger hurts'

I gave evidence at the all-party parliamentary group inquiry into hunger and food bank use in the UK a few months ago, one of over 1000 pieces of evidence heard by the committee – expecting to recount a story told and retold at party conferences, charity events, radio interviews, to journalists, again and again and again over the past two and a half years. But the APPG wanted more than 'hunger hurts'. They asked, probed, dug, questioned, opening up the old wounds, and made notes as I trembled in my seat, recalling nights of wrapping a baby up in a vest and a babygro and a dressing gown before putting him down to sleep. Of going to bed shortly afterwards because there's nothing else to do, and it's dark, and cold, and you sold the telly, so you go to bed at 7pm and curl up beside him and hold him, because it feels like the only good thing you have. Of being asked, very quietly, by a member of staff at my local children's centre if a food bank referral form would help us out 'for a little while', as she noticed us having seconds at lunch, and thirds, and three or four sugars in endless cups of tea, of offering to wash up and boxing up the leftovers to take home, away from the eyes of the other mums in the group.

I talked about the unexpectedness of it all, of applying for flexible working hours and day work roles in the fire service before I resigned, of applying for every job I saw in the 18 months afterwards – care work, shop work, minimum wage work, apprenticeships at £80 a week to be told I was 'too old' at 23, when the 16-year-olds were cheaper to hire. Of the bank charges that mounted up when bills bounced, and the late payment charges, and how quickly a £6 water charge can spiral into hundreds of pounds in late fees and bank charges, and nobody will give you the smallest of overdrafts, to tide you over, because those charges and subsequent interest are worth far more to a high street bank.

I staggered out of parliament, clutching a friend, shaking and crying. I went home, phoned my partner at work, and wept down the line.

Try it yourself WITH SUPPORT

Now you are going to practise using these skills in a complete response to Question 2 below. The annotations give you further guidance on how to approach the question.

> Question 2 is about Source Text C and Source Text D.
>
> **2** These texts are both about people experiencing times of crisis.
>
> What other similarities do these texts share? Draw on evidence from both texts to support your answer. **[6]**

This directs you to the texts the question refers to.

This explains a link between the texts and gives you a focal point for identifying and exploring similarities between them.

This is the question you have to answer – the key word is 'similarities'. Although the word 'explain' isn't used, this question requires a developed explanation.

This is additional guidance which shows you need to support your answer by referring to both texts, including either close paraphrases or quotations.

This is the number of marks awarded for this question.

Tip

'Evidence' in this question means a quotation, paraphrase or reference to the text. You need to make sure you support each similarity with evidence from both texts, but it should be very brief or you will find yourself spending too long and writing too much on this question.

Activity 3

1. Look back at the list of similarities and supporting evidence you created in response to Activity 2 on page 24. Select the five most relevant similarities you could use to help you to answer this question.
2. Write your answer to this question. This should be no longer than ten lines long.

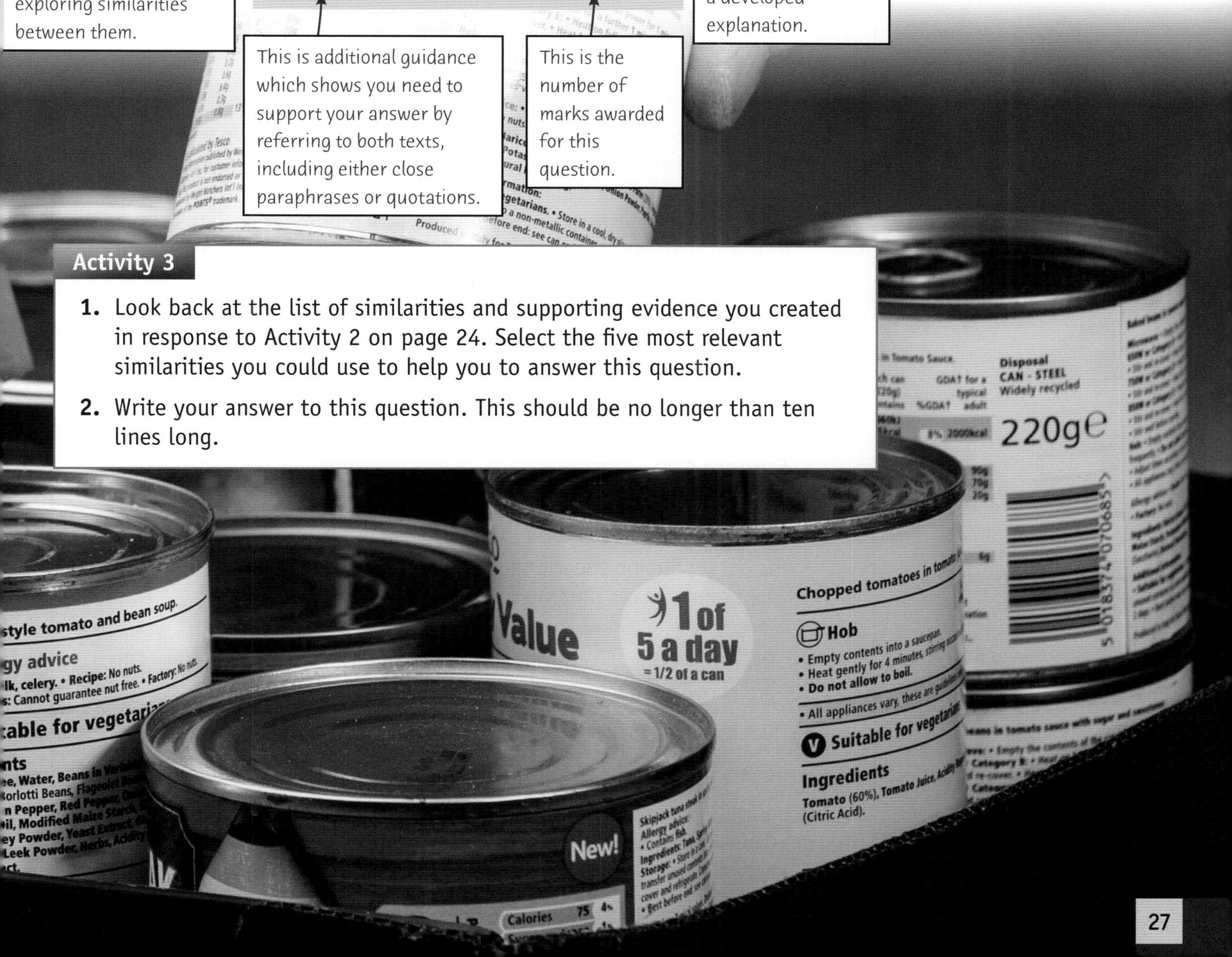

Improving your answer

Activity 4

1. Put the following responses to Question 2 in order of merit.

Student A

These two texts are about people experiencing times of crisis in their lives. The first text is about people in Ireland in 1846 and the potato blight and in the second text it's about someone who didn't have enough food because she didn't have a job and couldn't pay for any and had to go to a food bank. She tells people about what has happened to her and this is very difficult for her and she ends up crying which makes me feel sorry for her.

Student B

Both texts consider the impact of poverty on people, and in particular lack of food and the terrible despair ('crush hope'; 'wounds') and embarrassment that it can cause. In the first, people were reluctant to go to the poorhouse and, in the second, Jack Monroe tries to take home leftovers without anyone noticing. Both texts also explore the role of charity, the relief Committee and the member of staff at the children's centre, and food banks and the importance of compassion and understanding ('we can't desert them'; 'of being asked very quietly…').

Student C

Both texts are about people finding it difficult to get enough to eat and the effect this has on them. The first is about people in Ireland during the potato famine and the second in modern times is by Jack Monroe when someone is a parent and can't get a job.

2. **a)** Read the skills descriptors again and identify where different skills are shown in each response.

   b) Decide what mark each student should be given and why.

3. Re-read your own answer to this question. What mark would you award it?
4. Using the guidance in the mark scheme, rewrite your answer to this question to improve your mark.

Answer	Guidance
Where the candidate's answer consistently meets the criteria the higher mark should be awarded. **Level 3 (5–6 marks)** A detailed response which shows a secure ability to synthesize appropriate ideas and evidence from both texts, showing perceptive understanding of similarities between the two texts, including conceptual ideas. **Level 2 (3–4 marks)** A response which shows some ability to make connections between ideas and evidence from both texts, showing clear awareness of similarities between the two texts. The ideas and evidence selected may not be equal across both texts. **Level 1 (1–2 marks)** A response which shows limited ability to select and make connections between evidence from both texts, showing little awareness of similarities between the two texts. The evidence selected is likely to focus on more obvious, surface features of the texts and may be imbalanced across the texts. **0 marks** No response or no response worthy of credit.	Give credit for answers that synthesize evidence from both texts. Higher level responses will draw together and synthesize perceptive ideas, using appropriate evidence from both texts. Lower level responses will make straightforward connections between points and use some relevant evidence. Give credit for the quality of the response and the skills shown in the ability to synthesize appropriate ideas and evidence. Higher level responses will draw on conceptual ideas, such as the impact of poverty, humiliation and despair, whereas lower level responses will select and comment on more obvious features such as both texts being about people not having enough to eat/being helped by others in the community. Candidates may refer to some of the following points: • Both texts are about the impact of poverty on people/the sense of desperation it can engender. Examples of supporting evidence: Smith: *'waste of misery'/'such miseries crush hope'* Monroe: *'opening up the old wounds'/'feels like the only good thing you have'* • Both texts are about the powerlessness/humiliation experienced by people who are impoverished. Examples of supporting evidence: Smith: *he must go to the poor house, he and his family* Monroe: *'boxing up the leftovers to take home, away from the eyes of the other mums in the group'*

Synthesizing evidence and ideas

Key term

theme a key idea or issue that the text is concerned with

In order to gain the highest marks when you answer Question 2, you need to identify and explain conceptual ideas that connect the two texts as well as any factual links between them. Conceptual ideas could mean:

- **themes** that both texts share, such as change, hope, etc.
- characteristics or attitudes that characters in both texts display, e.g. courage, determination, etc.

Read Source text E on the facing page and then complete the activity below.

Activity 5

1. Identify two quotations that show what the snake looked like.
2. Explain how Ngouta reacted to the snake.
3. What impression do you get of Mary Kingsley's attitude towards snakes?

Now read Source text F on page 32 and complete the activity below.

Activity 6

1. Give two quotations which show that nobody knew exactly how the snake charmer managed to find and catch the snakes.
2. How can you tell there were some dangerous snakes in Egypt?
3. What impression do you get of Penelope Lively's attitude towards snakes?

You should refer to both texts in order to effectively synthesize the conceptual ideas and evidence you find. This could be by including quotations or paraphrasing information from the texts in your own words.

Activity 7

Look back at your answers to Activities 5 and 6. Synthesize the evidence you have found to explain one similarity both texts share. You could use some of the following sentence prompts in your explanation:

Both texts...

One similarity the texts share...

One theme the texts have in common...

For example in Source Text E... while in Source Text F...

Source text E

This text is taken from Travels in West Africa *by Mary Kingsley, an account of her journeys in the continent, which was published in 1897. Here she describes the experience of travelling in the African forest with her guide Ngouta and a Duke.*

The first day in the forest we came across a snake – a beauty with a new red-brown and yellow-patterned velvety skin, about three foot six inches long and as thick as a man's thigh. Ngouta met it, hanging from a bough, and shot backwards like a lobster, Ngouta having among his many weaknesses a rooted horror of snakes. This snake the Ogowe natives all hold in great **aversion.** For the bites of other sorts of snakes they profess to have remedies, but for this they have none. If, however, a native is stung by one, he usually conceals the fact that it was this particular kind, and tries to get any chance the native doctors might give. The Duke stepped forward and with one blow flattened its head against the tree with his gun butt and then folded the snake up and got as much of it as possible into his bag, while the rest hung dangling out. Ngouta, not being able to keep ahead of the Duke, his Grace's pace being stiff, went to the extreme rear of the party, so that other people might be killed first if the snake returned to life, as he surmised it would. He fell into other dangers from this caution, but I cannot chronicle Ngouta's **afflictions** in full without running this book into an old-fashioned folio size. We had the snake for supper, that is to say the Fan and I; the others would not touch it, although a good snake, properly cooked, is one of the best meats one gets out here, far and away better than African fowl.

Glossary

aversion strong dislike

afflictions problems

Glossary

galabiya robe

pergola arched structure covered with climbing plants

refuted denied

sybaritic luxurious or self-indulgent

admonitions warnings

Source text F

This text is taken from Oleander Jacaranda, *a memoir by the writer Penelope Lively, which describes her childhood in Egypt and was first published in 1994. Here she describes the visit of the snake charmer. Lucy is her nanny.*

He began with the garden. He walked ahead of us chanting softly, apparently to himself. He would pause, consider. He would continue, pause again. The chanting would get louder. Then he would shoot a skinny brown arm out of the sleeve of his **galabiya** up into the foliage of the **pergola**, or onto the overlapping branch of a tree, and there would be a snake, whipping and thrashing in his grasp. The snake would be encouraged to slash at his sleeve with its fangs – to drain the poison, I imagine – and was then dropped into the sack tied to his waist. And on we went, with everyone speculating sagely as to how it was done. He smelled them out, being endowed with some extra sense inconceivable to the rest of us. He mesmerized them with the chanting, forcing them to rustle and betray their presence. He was in collusion with the servants who had planted the snakes half an hour previously (this last suggested by cynical visitors and hotly **refuted** by my parents). I still don't know the secret of it, but it happened, and was vastly satisfying to all concerned. Except, I daresay, the snakes.

I was entranced by snakes and impervious to warnings. The most serious erosion of all freedoms, in my view, was the rule that you could never go barefoot in the desert because of sand-vipers. Even now, the feeling of sand on bare feet has an extra dimension of sybaritic delight. Many of our garden snakes would have been venomous to a greater or lesser degree, but I spent much time hunting for them – unsuccessfully for the most part – and yearned most of all for a sighting of a cobra, rumoured still to exist in small numbers in Lower Egypt. The ultimate treat of the snake charmer's visits was that I would be allowed to keep a small harmless snake. I would carry it about in the pocket of my dress for days, ignoring Lucy's revulsion and **admonitions**, until the poor thing escaped.

Try it yourself ON YOUR OWN

You are now going to apply the skills you have learned to answer the Question 2 task below.

This question is about Source text E and Source text F.

2 These texts are both about people who show strong emotions towards snakes.

What other similarities do these texts share? Draw on evidence from both texts to support your answer. **[6]**

Tip

Think about the similarity between the texts that is identified in the question. You need to make sure that the similarities you identify in your answer don't simply rephrase this, but express new ideas that both texts share.

Progress check

1. When you have completed your answer, swap it with a partner and mark each other's response using the mark scheme below. Give feedback to your partner, explaining the mark you have given them.

Level	Skills descriptor
Level 3 (5–6 marks)	A detailed response which shows a secure ability to synthesize appropriate ideas and evidence from both texts, showing perceptive understanding of similarities between the two texts, including conceptual ideas.
Level 2 (3–4 marks)	A response which shows some ability to make connections between ideas and evidence from both texts, showing clear awareness of similarities between the two texts. The ideas and evidence selected may not be equal across both texts.
Level 1 (1–2 marks)	A response which shows limited ability to select and make connections between evidence from both texts, showing little awareness of similarities between the two texts. The evidence selected is likely to focus on more obvious, surface features of the texts and may be imbalanced across the texts.
0 marks	No response or no response worthy of credit.

2. How confident are you now about answering Question 2? Use some of the sentence prompts below to write a brief evaluation of your skills in selecting and synthesizing evidence from different texts.

I understand how to…

I feel confident about…

I realize the important thing about answering this question is…

I need to focus more on…

I still need to practise how to…

Reading: Question 3

AO2 Explain, comment on and analyse how writers use language and structure to achieve effects and influence readers, using relevant subject terminology to support their views

An overview of the question

Question 3 refers to the second text you will read in your exam (Text 2) and is worth 12 marks. It assesses AO2 and is designed to test that you can analyse how writers use language and structure to create specific effects and have an impact on readers. It also requires you to use subject terminology to support your answer.

In the question:

- You will be asked to explore or analyse the way in which the writer presents a particular viewpoint, theme or idea.
- You will need to find relevant examples of vocabulary, language techniques and structural features that help you to answer the question.
- You will need to analyse the examples you find, demonstrating your understanding of their effects and using relevant terminology.
- You will need to refer to both language and structure in your response, striking a reasonable balance in your analysis.

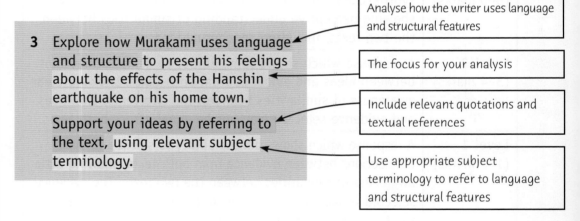

3 Explore how Murakami uses language and structure to present his feelings about the effects of the Hanshin earthquake on his home town.

Support your ideas by referring to the text, using relevant subject terminology.

- Analyse how the writer uses language and structural features
- The focus for your analysis
- Include relevant quotations and textual references
- Use appropriate subject terminology to refer to language and structural features

This question is worth 12 marks, so you need to make sure you allow enough time to write a detailed answer. Remember you can refer to the whole of Text 2 in your response and you should include relevant quotations and subject terminology to help you to answer the question.

Tip

In the exam, you need to make sure that any subject terminology you include helps to support the point you are making and enhance your answer. You will not gain marks for simply identifying the feature or technique. Remember to focus on the analysis of language and structure in your response.

How will my answer be assessed?

An extract from the mark scheme that examiners use to mark Question 3 is shown on the facing page. There are six levels. For each level, the skills that you have to demonstrate in your response are shown in the right-hand column. The key words that identify the differences between each level are shown in bold and the annotations help to explain these more fully. In each level you can be awarded a higher or lower mark; your answer will need to consistently meet the criteria set out in the skills descriptors to be awarded the higher mark.

Level	Skills descriptor	
Level 6 (11–12 marks)	• **A skilled analysis**, which demonstrates a **sophisticated appreciation** of how the writer has used language and structure to achieve effects and influence the reader. Candidates' analysis of both language and structure is **consistent** and **detailed**. • **Precisely selected** and **integrated** subject terminology **deployed to enhance the response**.	Highly effective exploration High-level knowledge and understanding Maintained throughout the response Explained fully Concise and very carefully chosen Embedded in the response Strategically used Shows insight
Level 5 (9–10 marks)	• An **analysis** which demonstrates a **perceptive understanding** of how the writer has used language and structure to achieve effects and influence the reader. Candidates' analysis of both language and structure is **reasonably detailed and balanced.** • **Well-chosen** subject terminology integrated into explanations.	Covers language and structure equally fully Relevant quotations support and enhance explanations
Level 4 (7–8 marks)	• A **developed explanation** which shows a **secure understanding** of how the writer has used language and structure to achieve effects and influence the reader. • Candidates **comment** on the effect of both language and structure, but the explanation **may not be entirely balanced.** • **Relevant terminology** should be used to develop ideas.	Elaborated with detail Sound overview Appropriate to the point being made
Level 3 (6–5 marks)	• A **clear explanation which shows a general understanding** of how the writer has used language and structure to achieve effects and influence the reader. Candidates **refer to language and structure but may not give a full explanation of the effects of both**. • **Some use of relevant subject terminology** to support ideas.	Shows straightforward understanding, but lacks detail Features identified but comments are undeveloped Some more obvious subject terminology used, e.g. sentence, paragraph, etc.
Level 2 (3–4 marks)	• A **straightforward commentary** which shows some understanding of how the writer has used language and structure to achieve effects and influence the reader. Candidates are likely to **refer more fully to either language or structure** and note some features **without explaining their effects.** • Some use of subject terminology, though it **may not always be relevant.**	Description of the text with some interspersed comments Unbalanced – more comments about either language or structure Aspects of language and/or structure identified but there are few or no comments Some use of terminology but it may be used incorrectly or inappropriately
Level 1 (1–2 marks)	• A **descriptive response** which shows **limited awareness** of how the writer has used language and structure to achieve effects and influence the reader. • **Little or no use of subject terminology.**	Paraphrasing or copying the text Some implicit understanding of aspects of language or structure but no explicit identification or comment Very little or no use of subject terminology or incorrect use
0 marks	No response or no response worthy of credit.	

Language features

When you answer Question 3, you need to identify and explain the effect of different language features and use subject terminology to support your explanations.

Language features include rhetorical techniques, stylistic and linguistic features, and grammatical aspects of language.

Some of the grammatical features you may want to refer to are listed below. Remember that simply identifying a word class or sentence type is not in itself worthy of credit.

Word class	Definition	Example
Noun	A word used to name a person, place or thing	The **pen** is mightier than the **sword**. We are fighting for **freedom**.
Adjective	A word which describes a noun	It was a **frightening** experience. The situation became more **serious**.
Verb	A word used to describe an action, feeling or state	I **feel** this is very important. **Take** a risk now! They **are defending** their position.
Tense	The tense of a verb tells you when the action of the verb takes place (present, past or future)	I **am speaking** to you today. I **spoke** to you yesterday. I **will speak** to you tomorrow.
Adverb	A word used with a verb, adjective or other adverb to describe how, when or where something happened	They worked **strenuously**. Training is **very** hard. She spoke **extremely** clearly.
Adverbial	A group of words that function as an adverb	**Last year**, the system was changed. The meeting will be held **in the library**.
Pronoun	A word used instead of a noun or noun phrase	**We** want **them** to listen to us. **Who** is responsible for **this**?
Conjunction	A word that links words, phrases and clauses	**Although** many won't agree, I think it is valid. They will go ahead with the cuts, **unless** we protest now.

SPAG

Activity 1

1. Look at the grid below to remind yourself of some of the most common rhetorical and stylistic techniques and add your own examples for each of these from your wider reading.
2. Try to add other techniques to this grid. Provide a definition and an example for any further techniques you can name.

Technique	Definition	Example
Alliteration	The repetition of consonants at the start of each word in a group for special effect	Creative, caring and characterful
Balanced sentence	A sentence where the two halves are parallel or balanced in structure. If the two halves are in contrast, it is called antithesis	In a year of good films, it is the film of the year. I was keen to get the job; they weren't so keen to have me.
Emotive language	Words and phrases that arouse emotion	The battle against poverty
Hyperbole	Deliberately exaggerated statement	The benefits are never-ending.
Imagery/ descriptive detail	Writing which creates a picture or appeals to other senses, including simile, metaphor and personification, and the use of vivid verbs, nouns, adjectives and adverbs	The factories are dimly lit places, like caves, with the constant thrum of machines, which creak and groan throughout the day and night.
Inverted sentence	A sentence where the verb comes before the subject	Never before have there been so many visitors to this town. Support them, I do not.
Metaphor	A comparison where one thing is said to actually be another	Exams are torture.
Minor sentence	A sentence which isn't complete but which makes sense as a unit of meaning in context	Disaster. Which was the worst possible outcome. No hope.
Onomatopoeia	Words which imitate the sound they represent	Explosion, clang, slither
Personification	A form of metaphor whereby an inanimate object is given living qualities	Time can take you by surprise.
Repetition	Words or phrases which are repeated for effect	Believe in yourself; believe in the future.
Rhetorical question	Question asked for dramatic effect and not intended to get an answer	Why should we put up with this?
Simile	A comparison where one thing is compared to another, using the words 'like' or 'as ... as'	Life is like a huge lottery As perfect as a snowflake
Tricolon	Groups of three related words or phrases placed close together	litter, vandalism and graffiti

Structural features

When answering Question 3, you also need to identify and explain the effect of different structural features and use subject terminology to support your explanation. Structural features include how a text begins and ends, how the material is sequenced, grouped and shaped, and how ideas are linked within and between paragraphs.

Activity 2

Look at the grid below to remind yourself of some of the most common structural features at sentence level.

Sentence type and structures	Explanation	Example
Statement	Gives information or tells you about something	Young people are not interested in politics.
Question	Asks about something and is marked by a question mark	Are young people interested in politics?
Command	An instruction, usually written in the imperative	Take an interest in politics.
Exclamation	Expresses surprise, shock or amusement and is marked by an exclamation mark.	Politics! What a terrible idea!
Clause	Part of a sentence with its own verb	After the training session was over
Simple sentence (single-clause sentence)	The most basic type of sentence consisting of a subject and a verb	Children need exercise.
Compound sentence (a type of multi-clause sentence)	A sentence containing two independent clauses linked by a conjunction	Independence is important and we will fight for it.
Complex sentence (a type of multi-clause sentence)	A sentence containing a main clause and one or more subordinate clauses linked by a **subordinating conjunction** or a relative pronoun.	Shakespeare, who was born in Stratford upon Avon, wrote many plays, including *Macbeth*.

Key term

subordinating conjunction a word used to join two clauses which are not equal, e.g. although, as, before, once, though, until

When you look at the structure of a text, you should also explore the following aspects:

- how the focus shifts, i.e. where the writer is directing the reader's attention
- the way the writer intersperses information, ideas, comments, personal experience and other features of content
- the coherence, i.e. the connections made between information, ideas, themes, etc.

The grid at the top of the next page shows some of the ways non-fiction texts can be structured.

Way of structuring a text	Explanation
Problem/solution	Explanation of a problem is followed by a solution
Cause and effect	Description of an event which then has an impact or effect on something else
Compare and contrast	Comparison of two events/ideas/viewpoints, showing the similarities and differences between them
Description/list	Presentation of a series of points, one after the other
Time order/sequence	Presentation of information or ideas in chronological order, often with dates or reference to years
Logical order/line of argument	Sequencing of ideas in order to build up an argument in a logical way, often using 'firstly', etc.
Topic grouping	Grouping of information or ideas according to subject, often with subheadings indicating what each section is about
Shifting focus between two or more ways of conveying information	Interspersing information with comment, personal experience, reflection, etc.

Activity 3

Use the questions in the grid below to help you to explore other aspects of structure in a non-fiction text that you are reading.

Aspect of structure	Questions to ask yourself
Sequence	• How is the information organized? • Is the information presented in chronological order, by topic or to support a line of argument? • How are the main ideas introduced? • Is there a key argument, idea or moment that the text builds up to? • Are ideas or patterns of language repeated or revisited in the text? • Can you spot any **motifs**?
Focus	• What is the viewpoint in the text? • Are there any other viewpoints acknowledged in the text? • What is the balance between different aspects of content, e.g. information, arguments, biographical details, anecdotes or comments? • Can you identify any contrasts or opposites within the text? • Are there any shifts in mood or tone?
Coherence	• What do you notice about the opening and how it introduces the topic? • What do you notice about the ending and how it rounds off the whole text? • Are different parts of the text (such as the opening and ending) connected in any way? • Can you identify any links within or across paragraphs? • Are any paragraphs particularly long, short or used to create a specific effect?

Key term

motif an element, idea or theme that is repeated throughout a text

Analysing language and structure

In Question 3, you might be asked to consider how the writer has used language and structure to convey their viewpoint about the information and ideas presented in the text. You could also be asked to think about the form and purpose of the text and to explore how language and structure have been used to influence the reader.

Read Source text G which begins on the facing page and then complete the activities below.

Activity 3

1. Discuss the ideas presented in Source text G. You should consider:
   - what the writer's viewpoint is
   - how effectively she presents this
   - any questions you want to ask
   - any points you wish to challenge.
2. Write a summary of the text in no more than three sentences. In your summary, you should include the form, purpose and viewpoint of the text.

You are now going to look at the different techniques Emma Watson has used to convey her ideas in this speech.

Tip

In the exam remember to read the introduction to the text. Check the date it was written and who the author is. These contextual details can help to develop your understanding of the text.

Activity 4

1. Re-read Source text G. Try to identify as many of the following features as you can.

   humour | anecdote | statistics

   common points of references, e.g. events, well known people, etc.

   historical information | scientific findings | case studies

   examples | quotations | personal experience | definitions

2. Choose one of the features you have identified and discuss why you think Emma Watson has chosen to include it.
3. How does Emma Watson use language and structure in this speech to present her views on feminism? Look back at the grids on pages 36–39 to remind yourself of some of the language and structural features you could find. Then create similar grids for this speech to explain the effects these create.

Source text G

This is an extract from a speech given by the actor Emma Watson at the United Nations on 20 September 2014 to launch an equality campaign called HeForShe.

For the record, feminism by definition is the belief that men and women should have equal rights and opportunities. It is the theory of political, economic and social equality of the sexes.

I started questioning gender-based assumptions a long time ago. When I was 8, I was confused for being called bossy because I wanted to direct the plays that we would put on for our parents, but the boys were not. When at 14, I started to be sexualized by certain elements of the media. When at 15, my girlfriends started dropping out of sports teams because they didn't want to appear 'muscly'. When at 18, my male friends were unable to express their feelings.

I decided that I was a feminist, and this seemed uncomplicated to me. But my recent research has shown me that feminism has become an unpopular word. Women are choosing not to identify as feminists. Apparently, I'm among the ranks of women whose expressions are seen as too strong, too aggressive, and too anti-men.

Why has the word become such an uncomfortable one? I am from Britain, and I think it is right I am paid the same as my male counterparts. I think it is right that I should be able to make decisions about my own body. I think it is right that women be involved on my behalf in the policies and decisions that will affect my life. I think it is right that socially, I am afforded the same respect as men.

But sadly, I can say that there is no one country in the world where all women can expect to see these rights. No country in the world can yet say that they achieved gender equality.

And if you still hate the word feminism, it is not the word that is important. It's the idea and the ambition behind it, because not all women have received the same rights I have. In fact, statistically, very few have.

In 1997, Hillary Clinton made a famous speech in Beijing about women's rights.

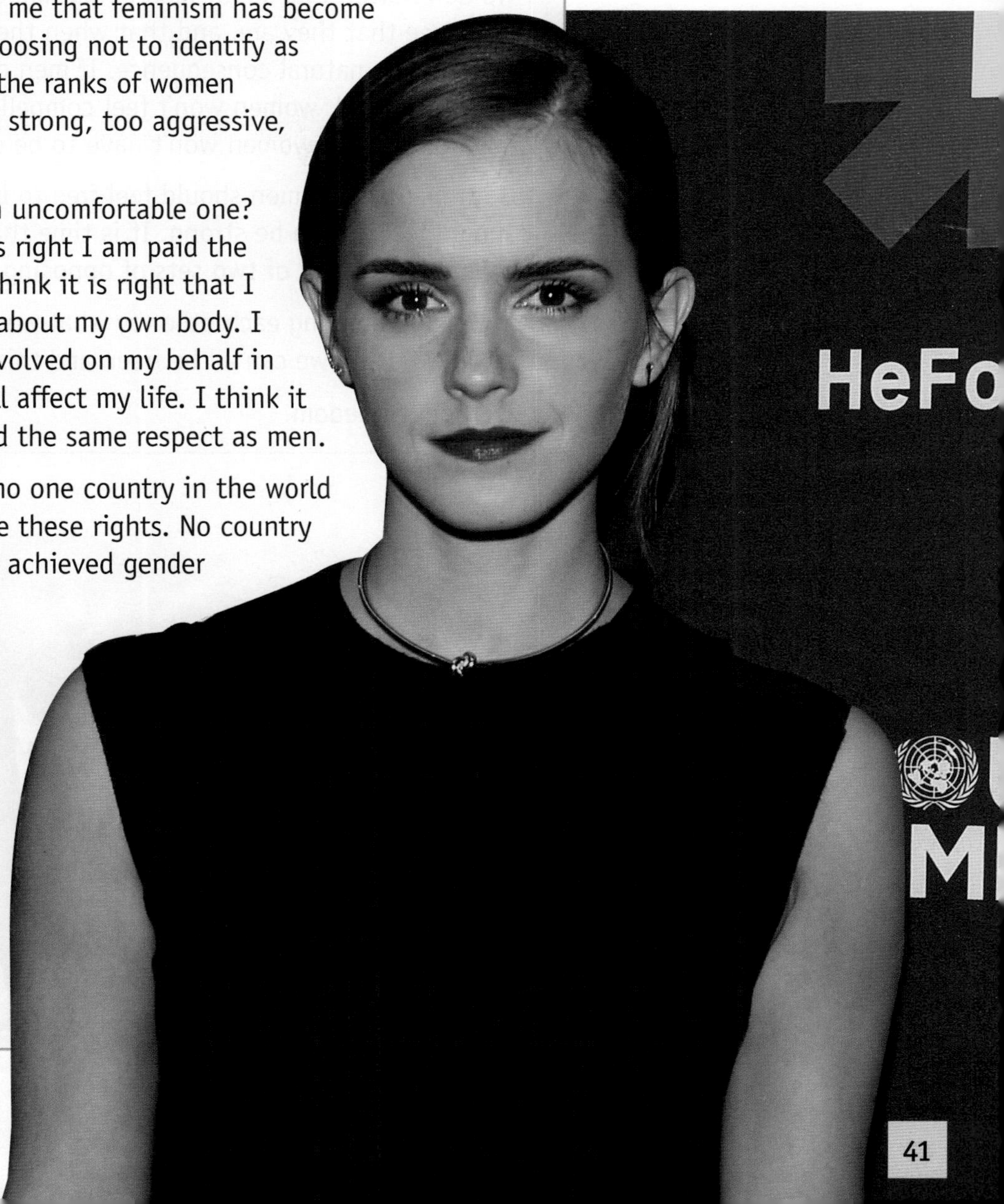

Source text G (continued)

Sadly, many of the things that she wanted to change are still true today. But what stood out for me the most was that less than thirty percent of the audience were male. How can we effect change in the world when only half of it is invited or feel welcome to participate in the conversation?

Men, I would like to take this opportunity to extend you a formal invitation. Gender equality is your issue, too. Because to date, I've seen my father's role as a parent being valued less by society, despite my need of his presence as a child, as much as my mother's. I've seen young men suffering from mental illness, unable to ask for help for fear it would make them less of a man. In fact, in the UK, suicide is the biggest killer of men between 20 to 49, eclipsing road accidents, cancer and coronary heart disease. I've seen men made fragile and insecure by a distorted sense of what constitutes male success. Men don't have the benefits of equality, either.

We don't often talk about men being imprisoned by gender stereotypes, but I can see that they are, and that when they are free, things will change for women as a natural consequence. If men don't have to be aggressive in order to be accepted, women won't feel compelled to be submissive. If men don't have to control, women won't have to be controlled.

Both men and women should feel free to be sensitive. Both men and women should feel free to be strong. It is time that we all perceive gender on a spectrum, instead of two sets of opposing ideals.

If we stop defining each other by what we are not, and start defining ourselves by who we are, we can all be freer, and this is what HeForShe is about.

It's about freedom.

Improving your answer

Read the following Question 3 and then look at Student A's answer below.

3 Explore how Emma Watson uses language and structure in her speech to present her views on feminism.

Support your ideas by referring to the text, using relevant subject terminology. **[12]**

Student A

In this text Emma Watson is giving a speech to the UN about her views on feminism. It was given on 20 September 2014 in the USA. Emma Watson is an actor who was in the Harry Potter films.

The speech starts by telling you what feminism is, which is helpful if you don't know what the word means.

Emma Watson uses the first person to show she is giving the speech. She says, 'I started questioning gender-based assumptions a long time ago. When I was 8, I was confused for being called bossy because I wanted to direct the plays that we would put on for our parents, but the boys were not. When at 14, I started to be sexualized by certain elements of the media.' There is a lot of repetition in this paragraph too which is very effective.

In this speech, Emma Watson uses the rule of three, rhetorical questions and personal pronouns, which are typical features of speeches and all help to make the speech good and show she is exploring her view on feminism for the audience.

The speech is in paragraphs which help to organize the ideas clearly for the audience and uses a variety of sentences to get her ideas over.

The speech ends with one short sentence which sort of sums up why she thinks it's important.

It is a really good speech and I think is interesting because she doesn't see feminism as being only for girls and women but includes men too.

Introductory sentence simply repeats the information given about the text. Instead this should sum up the purpose and viewpoint of the text to frame an exploration of Emma Watson's views on feminism.

This comment focuses on the opening of the speech – a structural feature – but needs to comment on the impact of starting with this definition of feminism.

Quotation is too long. The reference to 'first person' is sufficient evidence from the text – this point doesn't need a quotation as well.

Appropriate use of subject terminology but the comment needs to consider why Emma Watson has chosen to speak as 'I' here.

This point needs supporting with a brief quotation and explanation of how repetition is used to create a particular effect in this paragraph.

Identifies relevant features but these need to be supported by quotations and an explanation of their effect in this text.

Tries to link the comment back to the question but the comment needs to be less vague and more specific.

Further examples of different types and structures of sentences need to be identified and commented on.

Referring to paragraphs is beginning to identify a structural feature but the explanation needs to explain how they are used in this text and what the effect is.

This is an apt comment about the way the text ends. The comments could be developed to consider the impact of the simple structure of the sentence, the fact it is a single-sentence paragraph and the use of the abstract noun/ emotive word 'freedom'.

This personal response has been incorporated into a commentary on lines 33–49, where Emma Watson deliberately addresses men and so challenges the assumption that feminism is only about and for women.

Student A's answer on page 43 would be a Level 3 response because:

- the explanation shows a general understanding of how the writer has used language and structure
- the student refers to features of language and structure but doesn't give a full explanation of the effects these create
- the student refers to relevant subject terminology to support their ideas.

Activity 5

1. Look back at the mark scheme on page 35. Decide what mark you would give Student A's answer on page 43.
2. Rewrite Student A's answer to improve the level it would be given. Look at the mark scheme and the advice given in the annotations around the response to help you think about how you can improve the response.
3. Look at the following extracts from Student B and Student C's answers. Why is Student C's response better than the Student B's?

Student B

At the beginning of paragraph 4, Emma Watson uses a rhetorical question – 'Why has the word become such an uncomfortable one?' This is a question that doesn't expect an answer from the audience or reader and she is asking the audience to think about this idea.

Student C

In paragraph 4, Watson is challenging negative views of the word 'feminism' by asking a rhetorical question to make the audience think. She then argues in defence of her point of view and situation, emphasizing them through repetition ('it is right') while still being a bit tentative when she says 'I think'.

Tip

It is important to convey your ideas precisely and concisely. Incorporate brief quotations where relevant to support your points and use appropriate subject terminology to enhance your answer. Remember to ensure that your explanation focuses on how particular features create impact or achieve effects.

Try it yourself WITH SUPPORT

Now you are going to practise using these skills in a complete response to the example Question 3 below. Read Source text H and use the guidance on page 43 to answer the question below.

3 Explore how Stephen Emmott uses language and structure in this text to present his views about the way human beings use water.

Support your ideas by referring to the text, using relevant subject terminology. **[12]**

Source text H

This is an extract from an essay arguing that we are destroying the planet and our future is bleak. It is written by Stephen Emmott, Head of Computational Science at Microsoft Research, and was published in 2013. In this section he is talking about the shortage of water in the world.

Right now, over one billion people are living in conditions of extreme water shortage. Yet our consumption of water is accelerating rapidly. A staggering 70 percent of Earth's available fresh water is used for the irrigation of agriculture. Much of this water comes from underground water supplies called 'aquifers'. These are now being depleted faster – much faster – than they can be replenished. Yet we are going to have to increase irrigation significantly this century.

Our water use is increasing rapidly in other ways too. Take one important, yet little known, aspect of increasing water use: 'hidden water'. Hidden water is water used to produce things we consume but typically do not think of as containing water. Such things include chicken, beef, cotton, cars, chocolate and mobile phones.

For example: it takes around 3,000 litres of water to produce a burger. In 2012, around five billion burgers were consumed in the UK alone. That's 15 trillion litres of water – on burgers. Just in the UK. Something like 14 billion burgers were consumed in the United States in 2012. That's around 42 trillion litres of water. To produce burgers in the US. In one year.

It takes around 9,000 litres of water to produce a chicken. In the UK alone we consumed around one billion chickens in 2012. It takes around 27,000 litres of water to produce one kilogram of chocolate. That's roughly 2,700 litres of water per bar of chocolate. This should surely be something to think about while you're curled up on the sofa eating it in your pyjamas.

Source text H (continued)

But I have bad news about pyjamas. Because I'm afraid your cotton pyjamas take 9,000 litres of water to produce. It takes 100 litres of water to produce a cup of coffee. And that's before any water has actually been added to your coffee. We probably drank about 20 billion cups of coffee last year.

And – irony of ironies – it takes something like four litres of water to produce a one-litre plastic bottle of water. Last year, in the UK alone, we bought, drank and threw away nine billion plastic water bottles. That is 36 billion litres of water, used completely unnecessarily. Water wasted to produce bottles – for water.

It takes around 72,000 litres of water to produce one of the 'chips' that typically powers your laptop, Sat Nav, phone, iPad and your car. There were over two billion such chips produced in 2012. That is at least 145 trillion litres of water. On semiconductor chips.

In short, we're consuming water, like food, at a rate that is completely unsustainable.

Follow the guidance below to help you to draft your answer to Question 3 on page 45.

Starting your response

You could begin your answer with a brief introductory sentence summarizing the purpose and viewpoint of the text. You could use one of the following sentence prompts:

In this text, Stephen Emmott is arguing that...

The purpose of this text is... and Stephen Emmott's viewpoint is...

In this text, Stephen Emmott wants the reader to understand...

Analysing language features

Focus on the question you have been asked and remember to link the examples of language or stylistic features you identify to the purpose or effect of the writing. You might want to comment on how some of the following features are used in Source text H:

- statistics
- familiar examples
- the deliberately simple style
- repetition
- emotive language
- minor sentences
- connectives to show contrasting ideas
- personal pronouns.

Analysing structural features

When analysing Source text H, you could comment on:

- the way the opening of the text gains the reader's attention and outlines the topic
- how the second paragraph introduces the different examples he writes about
- how paragraphs are used to convey each chunk of information, how each one is developed and the way they are linked
- the impact of the final single-sentence paragraph, how it links back to the opening and rounds off the article.

Tip

When you have finished your response, read it through and count how many comments you have made about language features and how many about structural features. You need to try to ensure that there is a balance between the two, although usually there is more to say about language than structure.

Tip

You can write about language and structure separately. Alternatively, you can integrate your comments, which can be an effective approach as it enables you to link points – structural and language features often work together – and comment on the cumulative effect on the reader.

Try it yourself ON YOUR OWN

Write your response to the Question 3 task below, applying all the skills you have learned.

This question is about Source Text I.

3 Explore how Murakami uses language and structure to present his feelings about the effects of the Hanshin Earthquake on his home town.

Support your ideas by referring to the text, using relevant subject terminology. **[12]**

Source text I

In this piece of travel writing, Haruki Murakami describes returning to the place he grew up, Ashiya, near Kobe in Japan, to see what the place is like two years after the earthquake took place in 1995. This text was published in 2013 as part of a collection of writings about places.

Clad in rubber-soled walking shoes, shouldering a backpack with a notebook and small camera, I got off the train at Nishinomiya station and set off at a leisurely pace towards the west. The weather was so bright and sunny I wore sunglasses. The first place I came to was the shopping area near the south exit of the station. In elementary school, I often used to ride my bike over there to buy things. The city library was nearby, too, and whenever I had time I'd hang out there and pore over every young adult book I could lay my hands on. There was also a craft shop close by where I stocked up on plastic models. So this place brought back a rush of memories.

I hadn't been here for a long time and the shopping area had changed almost beyond recognition. How much of this was due to the normal changes over time, and how much was because of the physical devastation brought on by the earthquake, I really couldn't say. Even so, the scars left by the earthquake were plain to see. Where buildings had collapsed, vacant lots now dotted the area like so many missing teeth, with prefab temporary stores in between as if to connect them all. Summer grass grew in the roped off vacant lots, and the asphalt streets were filled with ominous cracks. Compared to the downtown shopping district of Kobe, which the world had focused on, and which had rapidly been rebuilt after the quake, the blank spaces here struck as somehow heavy and dull, with a quiet depth to them. Of course this wasn't only true of the Nishinomiya shopping district. There must be so many places around Kobe that still bear the same sort of wounds, but that are mostly forgotten.

Past the shopping district and across the main street is Ebisu Shrine. It's a very large shrine with thick woods within its precincts. When I was a small child, my friends and I loved to play here and it hurt to see the visible scars here now. Most of the large stone lights lining the Hanshin highway

Source text I (continued)

were missing the topmost lantern part. These were scattered on the ground below like heads lopped off by a sharp sword. The remaining bases had become a row of senseless, purposeless stone statues, solemnly silent, like symbols from a dream.

The old stone bridge across the pond where I used to catch shrimp as a child (using a simple technique: I would tie a string around an empty bottle, put in noodle powder as bait, lower it into the water and the shrimp would go into the bottle and then I would pull it up) had collapsed and remained that way. The water in the pond was dark and muddy and turtles of indiscriminate ages lay on the dry rocks, basking in the sun, their minds no doubt bereft of any thoughts. Terrible destruction was in evidence all around, as if the area was some ancient ruins. Only the deep woods were the same as I remembered from childhood, dark and still beyond time.

Progress check

1. Swap your response to Source Text I with a partner and mark each other's responses using the mark scheme on page 35.
2. Give feedback to explain the level and mark you have given. Identify ways your partner could have improved their answer.
3. Write three bullet point targets for the next time you answer Question 3.

Reading: Question 4

AO4 Evaluate texts critically and support this with appropriate textual references

AO3 Compare writer's ideas and perspectives, as well as how these are conveyed, across two or more texts

Key term

perspective viewpoint, e.g. a narrator's viewpoint or the viewpoint of the writer

An overview of the question

Question 4 refers to both of the texts you will read in your exam (Text 1 and Text 2) and is worth 18 marks. It assesses AO4 and AO3 and you will be expected to evaluate and compare the texts in response to a statement that links the two texts.

In the question:

- You will be given a statement that links the two texts, i.e. highlighting a common theme, idea or **perspective** in both texts or indicating a strength or feature they both share. This statement will give a focus for your evaluation and comparison of the texts.
- You will be asked how far you agree with this statement.
- You will be given three bullet points to help guide your response. The first two bullet points focus on evaluation of the texts (AO4) and the third bullet point focuses on comparison of the texts (AO3).
- You will be asked to use quotations from both texts to support your response.

This question is linked to both Text 1 and Text 2 and to both AO3 and AO4, with 6 marks available for AO3 and 12 marks available for AO4. The question overall is worth 18 marks, so it very important that you don't spend too long on Questions 1–3 and end up having to rush this question.

Look at the example Question 4 below. The annotations give you further guidance on how to approach the question.

> This question is about Text 1 and Text 2.
>
> **4** 'These texts show that it is difficult for women to achieve equality in the workplace.'
>
> How far do you agree with this statement?
>
> In your answer you should:
>
> - discuss what you learn about the role of women in the workplace and how it has changed over time
> - explain the impact of these ideas on you as a reader
> - compare the ways ideas about women's role in the workplace are presented.
>
> Support your response with quotations from both texts. **[18]**

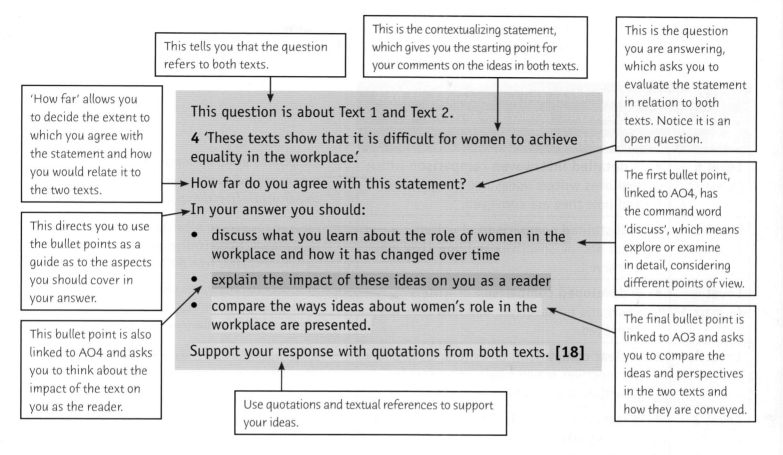

This tells you that the question refers to both texts.

This is the contextualizing statement, which gives you the starting point for your comments on the ideas in both texts.

This is the question you are answering, which asks you to evaluate the statement in relation to both texts. Notice it is an open question.

'How far' allows you to decide the extent to which you agree with the statement and how you would relate it to the two texts.

This directs you to use the bullet points as a guide as to the aspects you should cover in your answer.

The first bullet point, linked to AO4, has the command word 'discuss', which means explore or examine in detail, considering different points of view.

This bullet point is also linked to AO4 and asks you to think about the impact of the text on you as the reader.

The final bullet point is linked to AO3 and asks you to compare the ideas and perspectives in the two texts and how they are conveyed.

Use quotations and textual references to support your ideas.

How will my answer be assessed?

An extract from the mark scheme that examiners use to mark Question 4 is shown on the next page. The mark scheme is separated into the skills required for AO4 (evaluation) and the skills required for AO3 (comparison).

For each Assessment Objective there are six levels and the key words that identify the differences between each level are shown in bold with annotations provided to help explain these more fully. For AO4, you can be awarded a higher or lower mark for each level; your answer will need to consistently meet the criteria set out in the skills descriptors to be awarded the higher mark.

AO3: Compare writer's ideas and perspectives, as well as how these are conveyed, across two or more texts		
Level	**Skills descriptor**	
Level 6 (6 marks)	• A **detailed interwoven comparison** which **explores** writers' ideas and perspectives and how they are conveyed.	Comparative points are integrated and detailed, considering ideas and perspectives using well-chosen details from the texts
Level 5 (5 marks)	• A **sustained comparison** of writers' ideas and perspectives and how they are conveyed.	Focus on comparison is maintained throughout the response which covers ideas and perspectives using well-chosen details from the texts
Level 4 (4 marks)	• A **developed comparison** of writers' ideas and perspectives and how they are conveyed.	Some detailed comparative points evident in the response which covers ideas and perspectives using relevant details from the texts
Level 3 (3 marks)	• A **clear comparison** of writers' ideas and perspectives which **begins to consider** how they are conveyed.	Some straightforward comparative points made using details from the texts.
Level 2 (2 marks)	• A response which **identifies main points of comparison** between writers' ideas and perspectives.	Most obvious comparative points made with little or no consideration of relevant details from the texts
Level 1 (1 mark)	• A response which makes **simple points of comparison** between writers' ideas and perspectives.	One or two comparative points made with no consideration of relevant details from the texts

A04: Evaluate texts critically and support this with appropriate textual references

Level	Skills descriptor
Level 6 (11–12 marks)	• A **sustained critical evaluation** demonstrating a **perceptive and considered response to the statement** and a **full explanation of the impact of the texts on the reader.** • Comments are supported by **apt, skilfully selected and integrated textual references.**
Level 5 (9–10 marks)	• An **informed critical evaluation** showing a **thoughtful response to the statement** and a **clear consideration of the impact of the texts on the reader.** • Comments are supported by **persuasive textual references.**
Level 4 (7–8 marks)	• A response with **developed evaluative comments addressing the statement** and **some comments about the impact on the reader.** • Comments are supported by **well-chosen textual references.**
Level 3 (6–5 marks)	• A response with **clear evaluative comments** and **some awareness of the impact on the reader.** • Comments are supported by **appropriate textual references.**
Level 2 (3–4 marks)	• A response with **straightforward evaluative comments** and **a little awareness of the impact on the reader.** • Comments are supported by **some appropriate textual references.**
Level 1 (1–2 marks)	• A **limited description of content.** • Comments are supported by **copying or paraphrase.**

A focused and analytical appraisal of the texts maintained through the response
Shows insightful and reflective response to the given statement

Detailed consideration of the effect of the texts on you and other readers

Ideas supported by precise, relevant quotations or references, embedded in the response rather than given at the end of an explanation

A considered and focused appraisal of the texts
Shows some reflection in response to the given statement
Reasonably full explanation of the effect of the texts on you and other readers

Ideas supported by carefully selected quotations or references which enhance the evaluation

Thoughtful and detailed comments appraising the texts
Comments made in relation to the given statement
Some explanation of the effect of the texts on you and other readers

Ideas supported by quotations or references which have been chosen with some care

Appropriate comments appraising the texts, with little reference to the given statement
Some comments show implicit understanding of the effect of the texts on you or other readers
Ideas supported by apt quotations or references

Obvious points made to appraise the texts
Occasional implicit awareness of the effect on you or other readers

Some use of references or quotations, mostly appropriate

Mostly description, or paraphrase of the texts, without evaluative comments
Points supported by some evidence of unselective copying or paraphrase

Evaluating texts

When you evaluate texts you are being asked to make an individual and critical judgement about how effectively each text explores a specific theme, idea or perspective, and also to explain the impact this has on you as a reader. The key skills you need for this are the ability to:

- identify how a theme, idea or perspective has been presented
- explain how effectively this has been achieved and the impact of this on you as a reader
- select relevant quotations and textual references to support your comments.

Read Source texts J and K, which begin on the facing page, and then complete the activities below.

Activity 1

1. Look again at lines 1–4 of Source text J. Identify two things you learn about Patience's family.
2. Look again at lines 5–11 of Source text J. Explain two ways in which Patience's life is hard.
3. What was life like for women in the workplace at this time and what impact do these ideas have on you as a reader? Copy and complete the grid below to record your ideas.

What you learn about women in the workplace	Relevant quotations/ textual references	Impact on you as a reader
Suffer harassment from male workers	'the boys take liberties with me'	Shocking to learn about the powerlessness of women in the workplace at this time

4. Now look at Source text K. Copy and complete a grid like the one above to explore what you learn from this text about the treatment of women in the workplace. Remember to select quotations or textual references to support your points and comment on the impact of these on you as a reader.

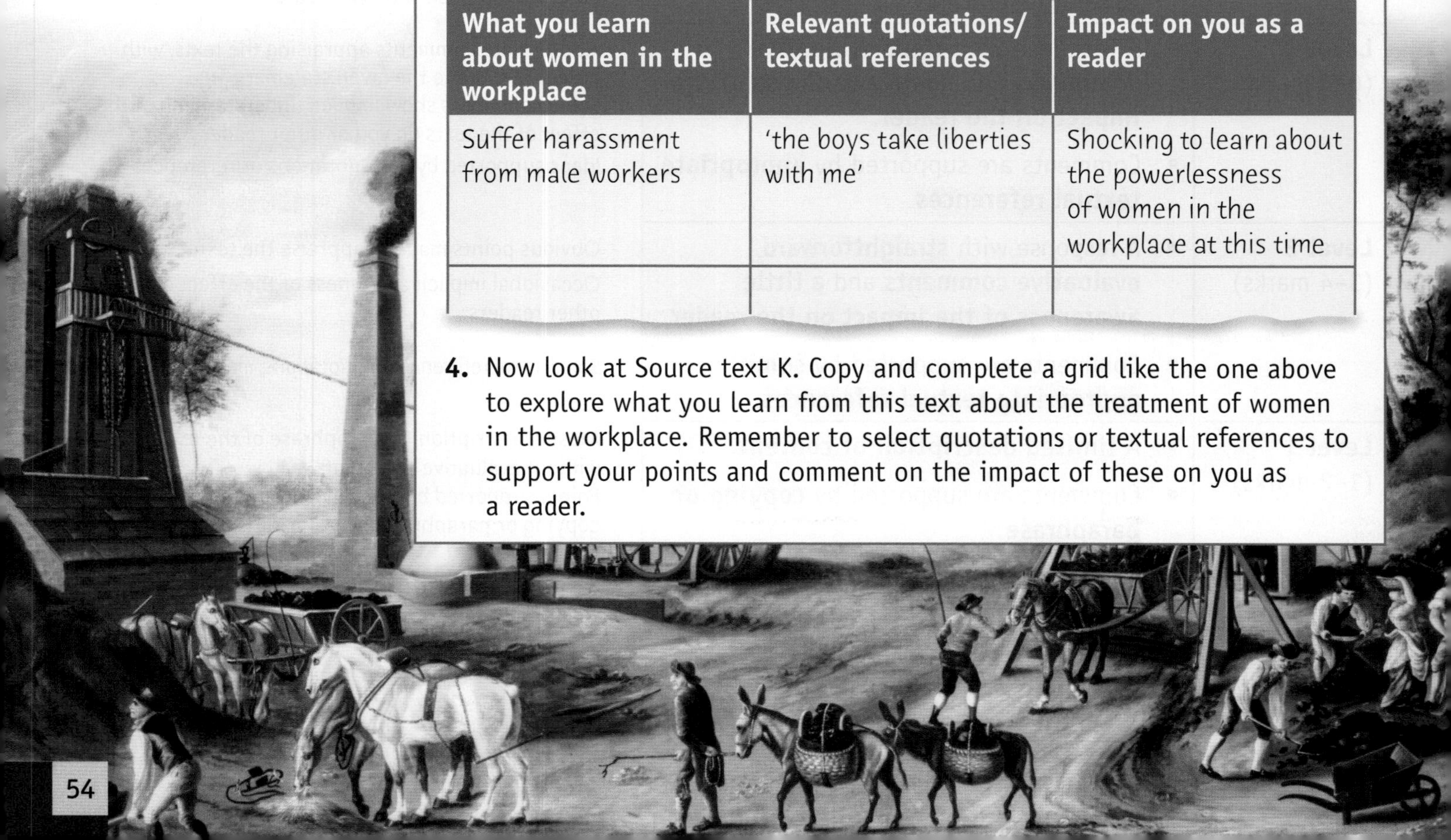

Source text J

Between 1841 and 1842, The Ashley Mines Commission interviewed mine employers and workers, which resulted in the Mines Act of 1842, which sought to reduce immoral behaviour and bullying by prohibiting underground work for all women and for boys younger than ten. The first text is evidence presented to the commission by a young woman, Patience Kershaw.

This is the evidence given by Patience Kershaw, aged 17

My father has been dead about a year; my mother is living and has ten children, five lads and five lasses; the oldest is about thirty, the youngest is four; three lasses go to mill; all the lads are colliers, two **getters** and three **hurriers**; one lives at home and does nothing; mother does nought but look after home.

All my sisters have been hurriers, but three went to the mill. Alice went because her legs swelled from hurrying in cold water when she was hot. I never went to day-school; I go to Sunday-school, but I cannot read or write; I go to pit at five o'clock in the morning and come out at five in the evening; I get my breakfast of porridge and milk first; I take my dinner with me, a cake, and eat it as I go; I do not stop or rest any time for the purpose; I get nothing else until I get home, and then have potatoes and meat, not every day meat. I hurry in the clothes I have now got on, trousers and ragged jacket; the bald place upon my head is made by thrusting the **corves**; my legs have never swelled, but sisters' did when they went to mill; I hurry the corves a mile and more underground and back; they weigh 300 hundredweight. I hurry 11 a-day; I wear a belt and chain at the workings, to get the corves out; the getters that I work for are naked except their caps; they pull off all their clothes; I see them at work when I go up; sometimes they beat me, if I am not quick enough, with their hands; they strike me upon my back; the boys take liberties with me sometimes they pull me about; I am the only girl in the pit; there are about 20 boys and 15 men; all the men are naked; I would rather work in mill than in coal-pit.

Comment: This girl is an ignorant, filthy, ragged, and deplorable-looking object, and such an one as the uncivilized natives of the prairies would be shocked to look upon.

Glossary

getters the people who mined the clay at the coalface

hurriers the people who transported coal in a mine

corves the trucks which carried the coal

Source text K

This text is written by Laura Bates, the founder of the Everyday Sexism Project, a website collecting examples of women's daily experiences of sexism and gender inequality. Here she writes about women and work.

So I started asking around – among friends and family, at parties, or even in the supermarket. The more stories I heard, the more I tried to talk about the problem. And yet time and time I found myself coming up against the same response: sexism doesn't exist anymore. Women are equal now, more or less. You career girls can have your cake and eat it – what more do you want?

Why do we continue to insist, even in the twenty-first century, on asking the **archaic** question: 'Can women really have it all?', instead of unpicking the bias that allows such rhetoric to exist in the first place? Why don't we stop to question the sexist idea in which women are the primary carers of children and the elderly and the part-time work they frequently must take on in order to maintain these responsibilities is paid less by the hour than full-time jobs and has few prospects for career advancement? Why do we keep asking why girls aren't as 'interested' in business or engineering or as 'driven' and 'ambitious' as boys, instead of stopping to consider the impact of the repeated background nonsense that tells them science isn't feminine, strong women are 'shrill' or 'bossy' and that their natural role – as the thousands of dollies and cookers and playhouses in the girls' section in the toy store will confirm – is to care and clean and cook and keep house?

From childhood onwards, both implicitly and explicitly, women are discouraged from certain careers or from having a career at all. They are subject to subconscious and overt bias at every stage of employment, starting with applications and interviews; they suffer verbal and sexual harassment in the work place then face being silenced or sacked when they complain about it; and they are written off and marginalized merely for approaching biological fertility.

Vital statistics

- Women working full time in the UK in 2012 earned 14.9 per cent less than men (Fawcett Society, 2013)
- 60% of women in the UK have had a male colleague behave inappropriately towards them (Slater and Gordon, 2012)
- 1 in 8 women have left a job because of sexual harassment (Slater and Gordon, 2013)

Glossary

archaic old-fashioned

Comparing texts

When answering Question 4, you need to focus your comparison on how effectively a specific topic, idea or perspective is presented in the two texts or how far a particular strength or feature is demonstrated by each text. The key skills you need for this are the ability to:

- identify similarities and differences between ways this theme, idea or perspective is presented in both texts
- compare the ways the texts are written, commenting on the use of language and structural features.

Look at the following statement about Source text J on page 55 and Source text K on page 56, then complete the activity below.

'These texts show that it is difficult for women to achieve equality in the workplace.'

Activity 2

1. Re-read the statement above about Source text J and Source text K. Copy and complete the Venn diagram below to identify similarities and differences in the way this idea is presented in the two texts.

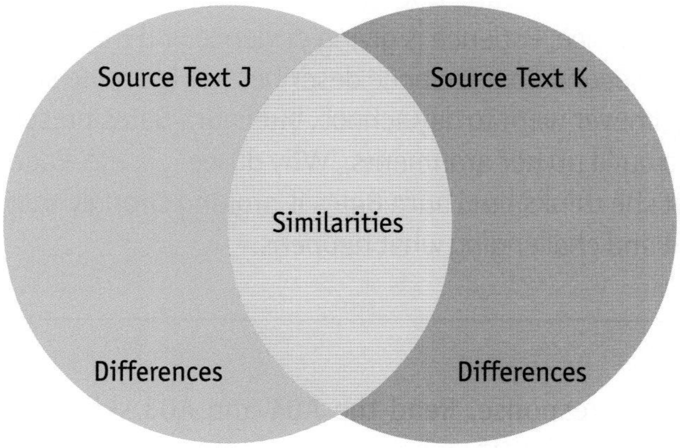

2. Think about the contexts in which Source text J and Source text K were written. Discuss how this helps you to understand the form, purpose and viewpoint of each text.
3. What contrasts can you identify in the viewpoints presented in Source text J and Source text K?
4. Using the notes you have made for Questions 1–3, compare the ways ideas about women's role in the workplace are presented in Source text J and Source text K.

Tip

It is important when you are comparing the two texts to make sure you focus on points of similarity and contrast, and don't write about each text individually.

Improving your answer

Look at Student A's response below to Question 4 on page 51.

Student A

In the first text Patience is describing her experience of working down a mine in the 19th century, while in the second text Laura Bates is describing women's experience of work in the 21st century. Both are about some of the difficulties of being a woman at work, especially in relation to men. Patience is the only girl down the mine and, in the second text, it's about the way people assume that women are only interested in certain jobs or are going to have children so won't be as good as men.

When Patience describes her experiences, it makes you realize how difficult life was for women like her then – either doing a really hard job – or just as hard having lots of children and looking after them. Then in the second text, the reader might feel surprised that so much sexism still takes place at work but I know from my mum and my own experience that although not everyone is like this, these views are still part of our society. So I think the second text shows more about the difficulties because they are relevant to me and my life.

Both texts explore the difficulties women have when they are at work – but the first is in the 19th century when people weren't very aware of sexism; the second is in the 21st century when people are. Both are first person and involve people giving their personal experience; Patience is giving evidence and there are also personal experiences in the second text. Patience describes her life quite simply, often in short sentences, 'I never went to day school', but Laura Bates presents her ideas in long sentences to build up her arguments, 'Why do we . . .', etc. Patience doesn't say much about what she thinks but Laura Bates is arguing strongly that we should be fighting against it and challenging what happens.

Activity 3

1. This is a Level 4 response. Read the A04 and A03 skills descriptors for Level 4 below and identify where the different skills are shown in the response.

A04	• A response with developed evaluative comments addressing the statement and some comments about the impact on the reader. • Comments are supported by well-chosen textual references.

A03	• A developed comparison of writers' ideas and perspectives and how they are conveyed.

2. Discuss whether you think Student A's response should be given 7 or 8 marks for A04.

To improve this response, Student A would need to:

- sharpen the focus on critical evaluation in relation to the given statement, rather than describing what is in each text (AO4)
- include more succinct, but deliberately selected, quotations to support the points made (A04)
- sustain the comparison throughout the response, ensuring all comments relate to setting the texts alongside each other and drawing out similarities and differences (A03).

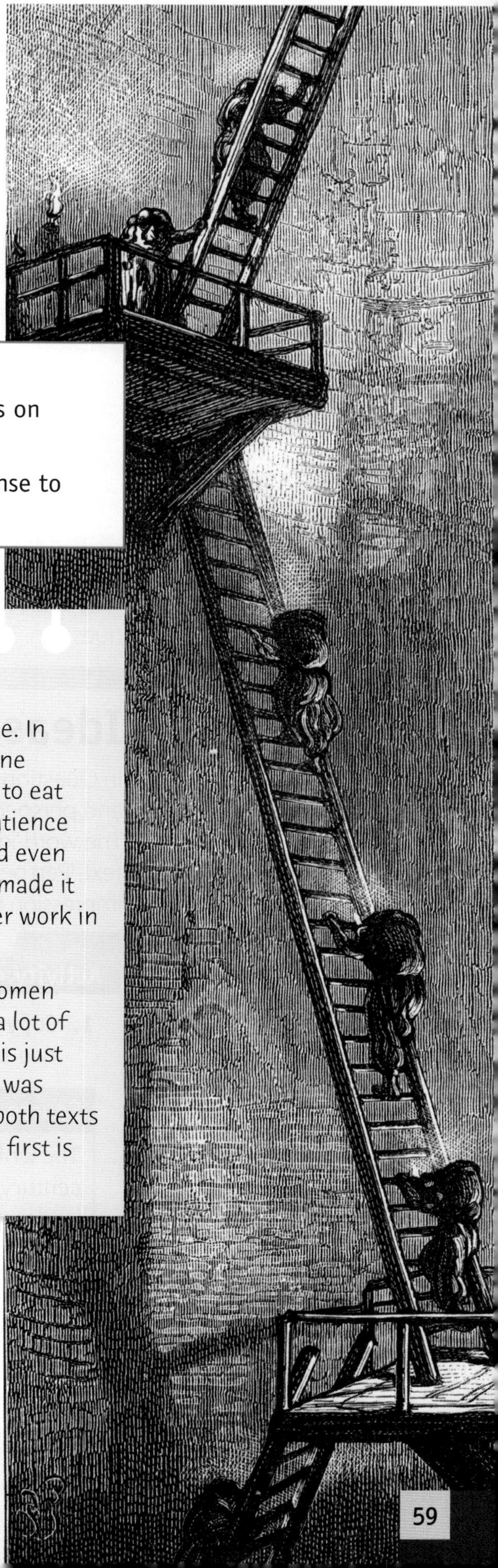

Activity 4

1. Now look at Student B's response and using the skills descriptors on pages 52–53, decide what marks to give for A04 and A03.
2. Discuss how this response could be improved. Rewrite the response to improve the marks you gave it.

Student B

These texts are both about the difficulties for women in the workplace. In the first text, it describes what is was like for girls working down a mine and Patience tells us about her life and how she doesn't have enough to eat and the work makes her lose her hair. This makes me feel sorry for Patience because it reminds you of how hard it was then for people at work and even children had to work in horrible jobs. She was the only girl too which made it harder for her because the boys and men bullied her. She would rather work in the mill than in the pit.

In the second text it's about nowadays and how it's still difficult for women at work and how they don't earn as much as men and sometimes get a lot of hassle at work. It includes facts which make it seem real and the first is just Patience telling her story but I still feel more sorry for Patience as life was much harder then. Women now often complain too much. So I agree both texts are about the difficulties women face in the workplace but I think the first is worse than the second.

Tip

In an exam question, the word 'views' encompasses 'ideas' and 'perspectives'. Remember to read the introductions to both texts carefully to help you to think about the perspective presented in each one.

Try it yourself WITH SUPPORT

Now you are going to practise using all the skills you have developed to answer the following Question 4. You'll be given some support to help you to do this.

This question is about Source Text L and Source Text M.

4 'These texts show how views on travel to wild places have changed.'

How far do you agree with this statement?

In your answer you should:

- discuss what you learn about different views on travel to wild places
- explain the impact of these ideas on you as a reader
- compare the ways views on travel to wild places are presented.

Support your response with quotations from both texts.

First of all, look back over pages 50–51 to remind yourself of how to approach the question. Then read Source text L and Source text M on pages 61–63.

Ideas and perspectives

In Question 4, the first bullet point is asking you to discuss or explore the ideas and perspectives in the two texts in relation to the statement you have been given. The word 'ideas' refers to the information, experiences, opinions or arguments in a text. 'Perspectives' refers to the viewpoint of the writer. You may be able to form an impression of the writer's viewpoint from the context in which the piece was written.

Activity 4

1. Copy and complete the grid below to note down what you learn from the two texts about different views of travel to wild places.

Source Text L	Source Text M
The writer, an explorer in the 19th century, is in awe at the beauty of the landscape and excited at the prospect of finding land for the first time.	

2. Look back at your completed grid and identify any similarities and differences between the views presented.

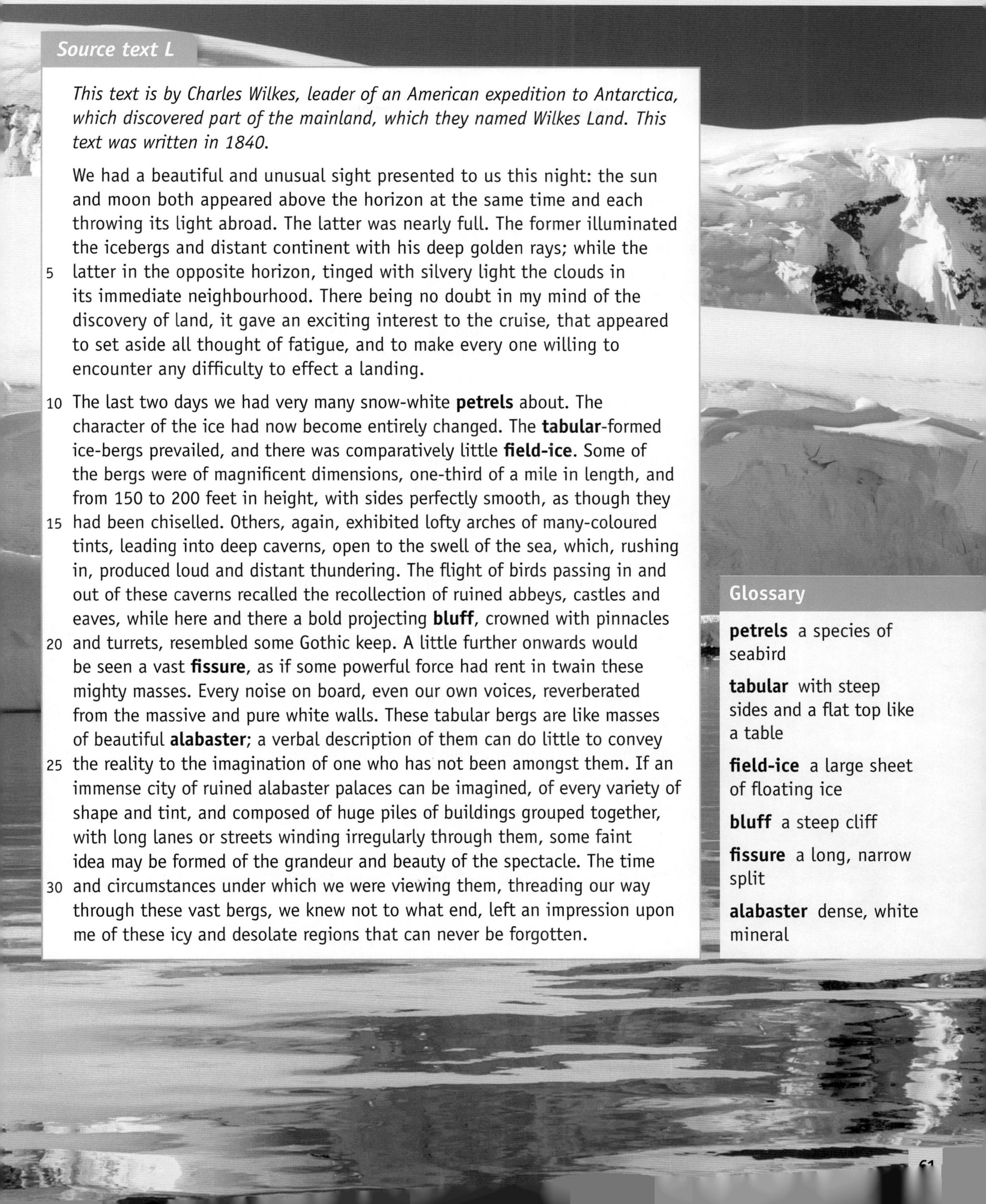

Source text L

This text is by Charles Wilkes, leader of an American expedition to Antarctica, which discovered part of the mainland, which they named Wilkes Land. This text was written in 1840.

We had a beautiful and unusual sight presented to us this night: the sun and moon both appeared above the horizon at the same time and each throwing its light abroad. The latter was nearly full. The former illuminated the icebergs and distant continent with his deep golden rays; while the latter in the opposite horizon, tinged with silvery light the clouds in its immediate neighbourhood. There being no doubt in my mind of the discovery of land, it gave an exciting interest to the cruise, that appeared to set aside all thought of fatigue, and to make every one willing to encounter any difficulty to effect a landing.

The last two days we had very many snow-white **petrels** about. The character of the ice had now become entirely changed. The **tabular**-formed ice-bergs prevailed, and there was comparatively little **field-ice**. Some of the bergs were of magnificent dimensions, one-third of a mile in length, and from 150 to 200 feet in height, with sides perfectly smooth, as though they had been chiselled. Others, again, exhibited lofty arches of many-coloured tints, leading into deep caverns, open to the swell of the sea, which, rushing in, produced loud and distant thundering. The flight of birds passing in and out of these caverns recalled the recollection of ruined abbeys, castles and eaves, while here and there a bold projecting **bluff**, crowned with pinnacles and turrets, resembled some Gothic keep. A little further onwards would be seen a vast **fissure**, as if some powerful force had rent in twain these mighty masses. Every noise on board, even our own voices, reverberated from the massive and pure white walls. These tabular bergs are like masses of beautiful **alabaster**; a verbal description of them can do little to convey the reality to the imagination of one who has not been amongst them. If an immense city of ruined alabaster palaces can be imagined, of every variety of shape and tint, and composed of huge piles of buildings grouped together, with long lanes or streets winding irregularly through them, some faint idea may be formed of the grandeur and beauty of the spectacle. The time and circumstances under which we were viewing them, threading our way through these vast bergs, we knew not to what end, left an impression upon me of these icy and desolate regions that can never be forgotten.

Glossary

petrels a species of seabird

tabular with steep sides and a flat top like a table

field-ice a large sheet of floating ice

bluff a steep cliff

fissure a long, narrow split

alabaster dense, white mineral

Source text M

This text is an article by the American writer, comic book creator, traveller and blogger, Marie Javins, about her experience of visiting Antarctica in 2008.

Black ocean waves crash onto rocky grey shores, or lap up against blindingly white icebergs, their shadowy pocket–caves reflecting blue light. Only a few hints of colour interrupt the stark landscape of contrasting black and white. No human walks here, aside from at a few scientific outposts. Antarctica is a lonely place. Lonely, that is, unless you are a krill, a penguin, a whale, or a seal. Or one of 37,500 tourists who cruised the Antarctic Peninsula this past year.

Ten thousand fewer people went two years ago, during the season that I visited Antarctica on the first 'budget' cruise. I stood on deck, near dozens of other passengers, on an ice-strengthened Russian-made expedition ship, gazing at sheer walls of ice from under my hat and parka. I daydreamed of Shackleton's *Endurance* expedition, anticipation sizzling in my gut.

I'd been giddy with excitement ever since I'd left home, bubbling over into the taxi from my home to the airport.

"Where are you going?" The driver was being polite.

"Antarctica," I'd blurted out.

"Oh." He looked puzzled at my excitement. "Are you from there?"

And here I was, lucky enough to be steaming past glaciers at the end of the world, in a wilderness too dangerous for mass tourism. An area so remote that my taxi driver had no idea what I was talking about.

I waited for awe to set in. Awe-on-demand. Pay one price, get all the awe you can handle.

Another tourist sidled up next to me on deck, interrupting my concentrated awe-expectation.

"How many countries have you been to?"

"What? I don't know. A lot."

"Whaddaya mean you don't know? C'mon. Everybody knows. Don't pretend you haven't counted."

I stared at him, aghast. Was that why he was here in Antarctica, to tick it off his list because he'd already been everywhere else? Was he no more than a country-counter?

And why exactly was I here? I shifted uncomfortably, as if I could physically subdue the dawning obvious. How many countries had I been to? Was contempt for the scorecard somehow as disdainful as actually keeping one?

Source text M (continued)

Later, in my cabin, I mused quietly to the enduring murmur of the ship's engine. I was disappointed, but how could this be? I was somewhere special, in the world's last pristine frontier: traipsing across its glaciers in the footsteps of Scott, Mawson, Amundsen, and Shackleton had long been a dream of mine.

And it would remain that way.

You know that dream of exploration, excitement, and a unique individualized adventure? The one where you are reverently stepping onto untouched ground in a part of the world where it's just you and the penguins?

That is just a dream.

Most cruise itineraries spend ten days cruising from Ushuaia to the Antarctic Peninsula. That's six days of travel, leaving four days for beautiful scenery, penguins, whales, and seals. And that's it.

Off-the-rack, mass tourism dampens our individual experiences. In Antarctica, shiploads of passengers act as a single managed unit, thousands of travellers having identical cookie-cutter adventures, communing with the wild a hundred people at a time. When you pay thousands of dollars to be shuffled around to look at penguins and barren landscape from a ship, you get exactly that. When you're travelling in a docile pack along a more-or-less set route, steered and directed by an expert crew used to managing a chatty crowd, you end up with canned awe.

I don't mean to imply that the Antarctic Peninsula has already turned into an icy theme park, complete with baristas hawking Frappucinos at the South Pole. The Antarctic continent, with its plateaus and ice shelves, pack ice, wildlife, and legends IS as awesome as it is desolate. Some visitors become enthralled with its stark beauty, returning again and again. My crankiness was related to my own excursion, and my own inflated expectations.

What I'd expected was isolation. The appeal of Antarctica is in its inaccessibility, its edgy sense of slight, managed danger. My disappointment stemmed from the crowds. No matter how empty the continent, I was never more than a few feet from a hundred other people as we travelled in a pack. My unique experience was rendered generic by the illusion that dozens of other tourists were traipsing nearby, conveying a sense more of high-season Cancun than of the world's last great wilderness.

If you crave the true beauty of Antarctica – the stark panoramas of a unique, natural continent at peace – avoid luxury cruises, generic itineraries, and unsafe ships. Try small expeditions, unique approaches, or scientific research.

Remind yourself of the question you are answering:

This question is about Source Text L and Source Text M.

4 'These texts show how views on travel to wild places have changed.'

How far do you agree with this statement?

In your answer you should:

- discuss what you learn about different views on travel to wild places
- explain the impact of these ideas on you as a reader
- compare the ways views on travel to wild places are presented.

Support your response with quotations from both texts.

Impact on the reader

In Question 4, the second bullet point is asking you to consider the impact on you as a reader of the views you have explored in relation to the first bullet point. In this, you can include a consideration of other reader's reactions to the texts.

Activity 5

Look again at the grid you completed in Activity 4 about the different views on travel to wild places. For each point, explain the impact of this idea on you and also how other readers might react to this. Two examples have been completed for you.

Text	View	Impact
Source Text L	The writer, an explorer in the 19th century, is in awe at the beauty of the landscape and excited at the prospect of finding land for the first time.	His descriptions of icebergs would have been fascinating and unforgettable to readers at the time, who would have been unfamiliar with the scenery. They are also impressive to the modern reader.
Source Text M	The writer, a modern-day tourist, expects to experience a feeling of awe when she visits Antarctica but is disappointed.	She makes you feel her frustration at the way adventures have now been packaged for mass tourism and how people have lost sight of the beauty and lost the ability to experience awe .

Tip

You have a good deal to cover in this question so it is particularly important to keep your quotations and references to the text brief and integrate them effectively into your answer.

Comparing texts

In Question 4, the third and final bullet point is asking you to compare the ways views on travel to wild places are presented. This means you have to compare the ways the texts are written, commenting on details from the texts.

In comparing the way ideas are presented in the two texts, make sure you don't simply repeat large chunks of your response to Question 3 in your answer to Question 4.

Tip

In order to achieve the highest levels in your answer to Question 4, focus on comparing the two texts throughout your answer.

Activity 5

1. Identify any similarities and differences between the ways views on travel to wild places are presented in the two texts. Copy and complete a grid like the one below to help you identify points of comparison.

	Source Text L	Source Text M
Genre		
Style		
Details of words and phrases		
Other points of comparison		

2. Now write your answer to Question 4. Remember to look back at the activities you have completed in this section as you write your response.

Try it yourself ON YOUR OWN

Read Source text N and Source text O. Then write your response to the Question 4 task below, applying all the skills you have learned.

This question is about Source text N and Source Text O.

4 'These texts show that people can have very different views on the importance of education.'

How far do you agree with this statement?

In your answer you should:

- discuss what you learn about different views on education
- explain the impact of these ideas on you as a reader
- compare the ways ideas about education are presented.

Support your response with quotations from both texts.

Progress check

1. Use the mark scheme on pages 52–53 to mark your response to this question.
2. Copy out and use the following checklist to reflect on the strengths of your response and areas where you need to improve.
   - ☐ I focused my answer on the statement given in the question.
   - ☐ I answered the question in detail.
   - ☐ I referred to both texts in my answer.
   - ☐ I covered all the bullet points in the question.
   - ☐ I included relevant quotations and textual references.
3. Now identify the areas where you think you still need to develop your skills further. Set yourself two targets to improve your answer to Question 4. The first target should be linked to evaluation skills (AO4) and the second target to comparison skills (AO3).

Source text N

This is an extract from Hansard June 1833 and is a record of Mr Roebuck's speech to the House of Commons about the importance of a national education system.

Sir, I would first solicit the attention of the House to the more prominent benefits to be obtained by a general education of the people.

At the outset, to prevent misconception, I may be permitted to describe what I mean by education. The narrow acceptation of this term so generally received, has done infinite harm. Education is usually supposed to signify merely learning to read and write, and sometimes, it is made to include arithmetic. But this is not education; it is simply some of the means of education. In ordinary conversation, when men say that education cannot relieve the **necessities**, or cure the **vices** of the people, they mean that learning to read and write cannot do this; and in so saying they are right.

Putting a hammer and saw into a man's hand does not make him a carpenter; putting a flute into his hands does not make him a musician; in both cases you give him certain instruments, which if he have the necessary knowledge, he may use to good purposes, but if he do not possess it, they will prove either useless or harmful. So may it happen with the instruments of knowledge. Unless the mind be trained to their exercise – unless they have the will and the determination to turn them to good purposes, be conferred, not only will they be useless, idle powers, but they may be made **eminently** harmful. But this narrow definition of the term education, is not the correct one.

Education means not merely the conferring these necessary means for the acquiring of knowledge, but it means also the training of the intellectual and moral qualities of the individual, that he may be able and willing to acquire knowledge, and to turn it to its right use. It means directing the mind of the individual, that he may become a useful and virtuous member of society. It means making him a good child, a good parent, a good neighbour, a good citizen, in short, a good man. All these he cannot be without knowledge, but neither will the mere acquisition of knowledge confer on him these qualities.

Glossary

necessities necessary or indispensable things in life, e.g. food, shelter, etc.

vices immoral or evil habits, e.g. gambling, etc.

eminently very

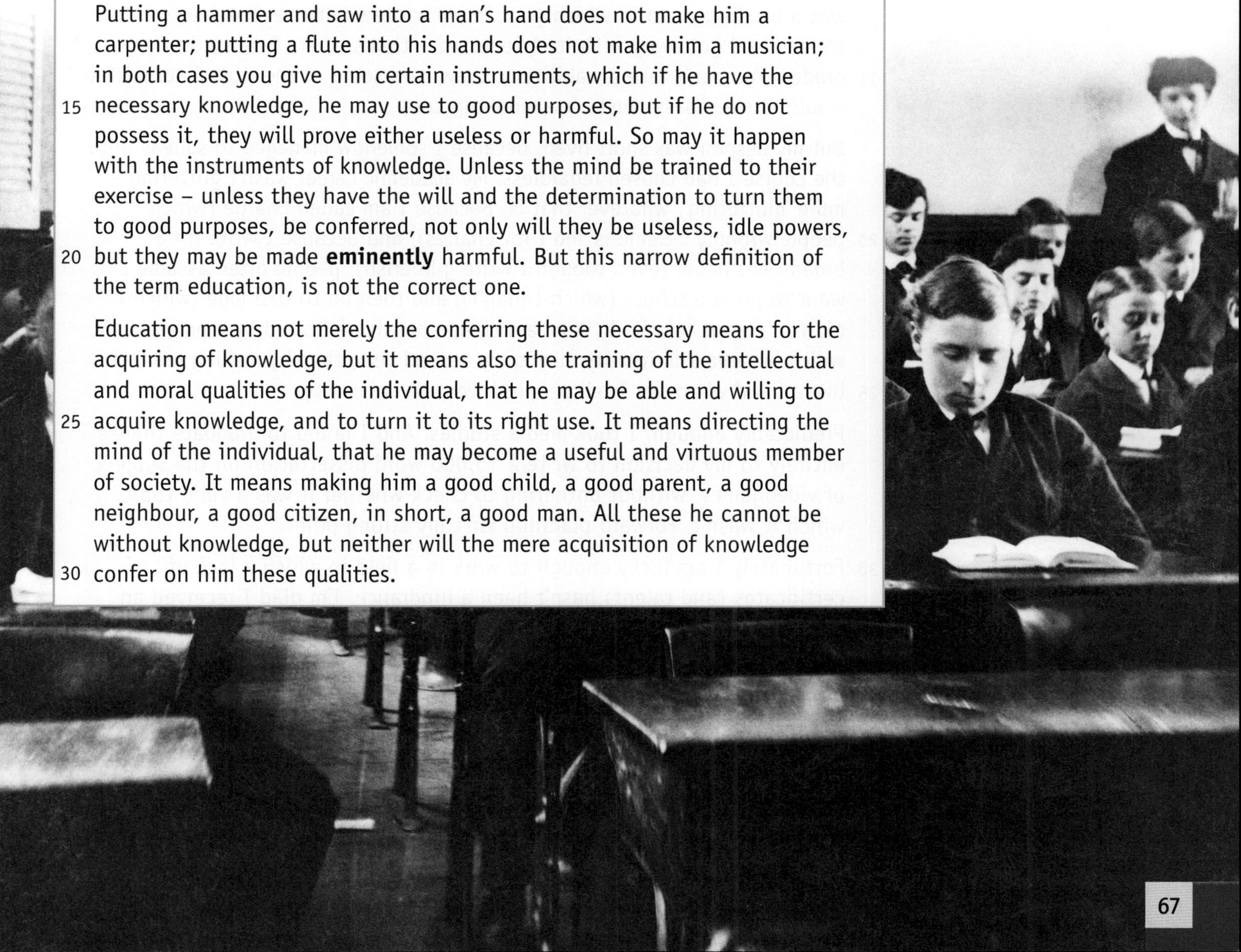

Source text 0

This text is an extract from an article by journalist Charlie Brooker about his experience of education and his view of its importance.

This one's for underperforming students, and anyone who got rubbish exam results. The rest of you can walk away. Go on. Shoo.

Gone? Right. Last week was A-level judgement week, which as per tradition, gave newspapers a brilliant excuse to run photos of attractive teenage girls leaping with delight as they receive their results, a phenomenon that has become such a cliché that pointing out its existence has become another cliché in its own right.

The day I got my own A level results, the only thing leaping was the pit of my gut, as I realised I hadn't got the grades I needed. No surprise: I was lazy and easily distracted in school. I didn't read half the books I was supposed to digest for my English literature course, for instance, and instead relied on Brodie's Notes. But then English lit. was easy to pass: it was a bluffing exam in which you simply wrote what the examiner wanted to read and got away with it. A-level art – that's where I messed up my grades. You can't fake an ability to draw, and some of the work I submitted wouldn't even pass muster on moonpig.com.

But my despair was short lived, because I somehow managed to squeak onto the course I had chosen regardless. My academic career wasn't glittering – more 'gluttering', whatever that is. Because I am called Charlie (which people wrongly assume is short for Charles), and because I write for a broadsheet paper (even though I write gibberish), people often assume I went to private school (which I didn't), and then on to Oxbridge (which I didn't). I went to a fairly standard comprehensive followed by a polytechnic, which became a university during my second year, thereby making me feel like a fraud whenever I tell people I went to university.

Predictably enough, I took media studies. And I failed to graduate thanks entirely to my decision to write a 15,000 word dissertation on the subject of videogames, without bothering to check whether it was a valid topic, which it wasn't. Forward planning isn't my strong point.

Fortunately I am lucky enough to work in a field in which a lack of certificates (and talent) hasn't been a hindrance. I'm glad I received an education, although beyond an ability to read and write I'm not quite sure what it gave me.

Source text 0 (continued)

The most valuable thing you get from education is a space in which you can make friends, gain experience, and figure a few things out. I spent the first half of my twenties deep in debt and working in a shop, with a vague idea what I wanted to do, but no idea how to go about doing it. At the time I thought I was incredibly lazy; looking back now I realise I kept trying my hand at different things: cartooning, writing, rudimentary web design and so on until eventually I started getting the kind of work I wanted.

Today it'd be harder for a younger me to get a break. For one thing the student debt would be so huge, I'd probably have to work at two jobs, thereby leaving little time or energy to dabble with articles or cartoons after hours. And although technology has made it possible to write, direct and edit a short film on a computer the size of a teaspoon, it's also flooded the internet with competition, making it harder to stand out.

Even so success is always possible if you forget about 'success' as a concept – it's hopelessly amorphous anyway – and focus instead on doing what satisfies you, as well as you can. Clichéd, bland advice, but true.

Your grades are not your destiny: they're just letters and numbers which rate how well you performed in one artificial arena – once.

Component 01 Communicating information and ideas

Section B: Writing for audience, impact and purpose

What is the content and focus of this section?

This section assesses your ability to write original non-fiction for different audiences and purposes. You will be given a choice of two writing tasks which will ask you to create an extended piece of non-fiction writing. You could be asked to write a speech, a letter or an article in which you describe, explain, inform, instruct, argue or persuade. Each writing task will make the audience you are writing for clear.

You will have a choice of two writing tasks (Question 5 and Question 6), but you do only **one**. There will be a thematic link between the writing tasks and the two texts you have read in Section A of Component 01. Both questions will include bullet points to indicate the content you should or could include in your response.

How to use your time in the exam

Section B of this exam is worth 40 marks and will form 25% of your total GCSE grade. You will have to choose one writing task to answer from a choice of two tasks. The exam paper will advise you to spend one hour on Section B. However, given what you have to do in the reading section, it is more likely that you will spend approximately 45 minutes on the writing task. Moreover, it is vital that you use this time wisely and fully. The grid below suggests how you might allocate your time.

Approach	Suggested timing
Choosing: Reading the writing tasks and selecting the one you will respond to	Approximately 2 minutes
Planning: Generating and structuring your ideas	Approximately 5 minutes
Drafting: Writing your response	Approximately 35 minutes
Proofreading: Checking your work and correcting mistakes	Approximately 3 minutes

How will my writing be assessed?

In Section B, your response to your chosen writing task will be assessed against the following Assessment Objectives:

Assessment Objective	
AO5	Communicate clearly, effectively and imaginatively, selecting and adapting tone, style and register for different forms, purposes and audiences. Organize information and ideas, using structural and grammatical features to support coherence and cohesion of texts.
AO6	Use a range of vocabulary and sentence structures for clarity, purpose and effect, with accurate spelling and punctuation.

The examiner will give you separate marks on each objective:

- 24 marks are available for content and organization (AO5)
- 16 marks are available for technical accuracy (AO6).

Your overall mark for the writing task will be a combination of the two marks. The maximum overall mark for this writing task is 40.This is 25% of your overall GCSE grade.

Mark scheme

The examiner will assess your work against a mark scheme. For AO5, there are six levels, with Level 1 being the lowest and Level 6 the highest. These levels are not related to the GCSE grades from 9 to 1. For each level, there are key words or descriptors which distinguish one level from the others. The key words for AO5 are shown in the grid below.

Level	Key words for content and organization
Level 6 (21–24 marks)	Form – deliberately adapted; sophisticated control of purpose and effect Tone, style and register – ambitiously selected Overall structure – skilfully controlled
Level 5 (17–20 marks)	Form – confidently adapted; secure understanding of purpose and audience Tone, style and register – sustained Overall structure – controlled
Level 4 (13–16 marks)	Form – confidently adapted; secure understanding of purpose and audience Tone, style and register – matched to task Overall structure – well-managed
Level 3 (9–12 marks)	Form – sustained; clear awareness of purpose and audience Tone, style and register – appropriate with some inconsistencies Overall structure – clear
Level 2 (5–8 marks)	Form – mostly appropriate; generally maintained Tone, style and register – attempted Overall structure – some evidence
Level 1 (1–4 marks)	Form – some attempt Tone, style and register – limited attempt Overall structure – some attempt

For AO6, there are four levels. Again, Level 1 is the lowest and Level 4 is now the highest. The key words or descriptors to distinguish between these levels are shown in the grid below.

Level	Key words for technical accuracy
Level 4 (13–16 marks)	Sentence structure – an ambitious range shapes meaning and creates impact Punctuation – accurate; makes writing clear and achieves specific effects Vocabulary – precise and subtle Spelling – accurate; very few mistakes
Level 3 (9–12 marks)	Sentence structure – a wide range used for deliberate purpose and effect Punctuation – consistently accurate Vocabulary – used convincingly; sometimes ambitious Spelling – accurate
Level 2 (5–8 marks)	Sentence structure – a range used and mostly secure Punctuation – generally accurate Vocabulary – appropriate Spelling – generally accurate
Level 1 (1–4 marks)	Sentence structure – simple mostly with some attempt at complex structures Punctuation – some Vocabulary – straightforward Spelling – simple spellings, mostly accurate

As you work through the chapters in this writing section, you will have opportunities to practise and improve your writing skills. You will also learn how to assess your own work against the mark scheme and how to gain the highest level mark that you can in the exam.

Choosing a writing task

Identifying purpose, form and audience

Tip

If you are asked to write a newspaper or magazine article, you do not need to write in columns or include pictures. The focus is on what you write and how your write it for your intended audience.

Section B includes two writing tasks, Question 5 and Question 6, but you should only write a response to **one** of these tasks. In order to decide which task to choose, you need to read each question carefully to identify:

- the **purpose** of the writing (e.g. to explain, to argue, to persuade, etc.)
- what **form** you need to write in (e.g. an article, a letter, a blog, a speech, etc.)
- who the **audience** will be (e.g. local residents, readers of the school magazine, parents, etc.).

Look at the example writing task below. The annotations give you further guidance on how to approach the question.

This indicates the form you should be writing, i.e. a magazine article.

This indicates the audience you are writing for, i.e. teenagers.

Write an article for a teenage magazine in which you describe your favourite holiday destination. This could be a place you have visited or would like to visit.

In your article you should:

- say where the place is and what it is like
- explain why it is your favourite holiday destination
- explain why you think teenagers should visit this destination.

This is the topic you will be writing about.

This indicates the purpose of your writing, i.e. to describe.

A secondary purpose is also indicated, i.e. to explain.

The bullet points give you guidance about the content you should include in your response.

It is important to pay particular attention to the audience you are asked to write for. This will have a huge influence on the language you use and how formal or informal your writing is. For example, if you are asked to write a letter to your local newspaper or MP, this would require a formal opening and ending and formal use of language. On the other hand, an article for a teenage magazine would require less formal content and use of language.

Activity 1

Read the two writing tasks below and for each one:

- identify the purpose, form and audience
- identify if it requires a formal or informal use of language.

5 Write a letter, to be placed in a time capsule and read by teenagers in the future, in which you describe the most important possession that you own and explain why it is so important to you.

In your letter you should:

- describe your most treasured possession
- explain why it is the most important possession that you own
- engage and entertain your future readers.

OR

6 Write the words of a speech to your class in which you argue that the Internet is a good OR a bad influence on young people.

In your speech you should:

- explain why you believe the Internet is a good or bad influence
- give some examples to support your argument
- convince your audience to agree with your point of view.

Once you have read each question and identified the purpose, form and audience for the writing, you need to decide which task you want to complete. Think about the ideas you have for each task and how confident you are in writing for the specific purpose it gives.

Planning your response

When you have chosen your writing task, you need to plan what you are going to write. Your plan should help you to think about:

- the content of what you are writing, i.e. what you are going to say
- the organization of your writing, i.e. how you are going to say it.

Remember to keep in mind the purpose, form and audience required by the task as you plan your writing.

Generating and organizing ideas

Look at the writing task below.

Tip

The bullet points are only a guide to support you. They do not have to be followed in strict order and you can include your own ideas too, as long as these are relevant.

> Write an article for a teenage magazine in which you describe your favourite holiday destination. This could be a place you have visited or would like to visit.
>
> In your article you should:
>
> - say where the place is and what it is like
> - explain why it is your favourite holiday destination
> - explain why you think teenagers should visit this destination.

You can use a variety of planning techniques to help you jot down any ideas you have which you think are relevant to this writing task, such as spider diagrams, mind-maps, flow-charts, etc.

If you get stuck, using questions beginning 'Who', 'What', 'Where', 'When' and 'Why' can help you to generate ideas for your writing. Each question prompt can become a section or paragraph in your response. Look at how the student on the facing page has used the 'five Ws' to begin to plan the content of a magazine article describing a favourite holiday destination as well as some of the techniques they could use in their response to make it successful.

Who – Who did I go with? Who did I meet while I was there?

Went with family to celebrate parents' wedding anniversary. Met friendly and interesting locals such as the fishermen who took us fishing with them for the day. Street artists and street sellers. Tour guide who was informative and very funny.

Use of personification to create images – *The bright colours of the street traders' stalls mesmerized our eyes and strange and unfamiliar smells intoxicated us.*

What – What did I do there? What attractions were there? What makes it special? What is my happiest memory of this place?

Use of simile – *The little whitewashed houses of the locals were cut into the mountainside as if sculpted by the hand of some giant master craftsman.* Use of **metaphor** – *The sea was a writhing snake of sapphire and emerald.*

When – When did I go there? When do I plan to go back?

Where – Where is it? Where did I stay?

Crete. Use of adjectives to be descriptive – Crete is a picturesque, quaint but vibrant and welcoming place.

Why – Why did I enjoy it so much? Why did I find it special? Why do I think other people should go there?

Use of alliteration – most of all I loved the soft shimmer of the sea as I surfed in the early morning sunshine.

Key term

metaphor the use of a word or phrase in a special meaning that provides an image

Tip

You should refer to your plan as you write your response, but you do not have to stick rigidly to this. If you think of a new point to include or a better way to sequence your ideas, don't be afraid to make changes to your plan.

Activity 1

1. Write your own 'five W' questions to help you plan your ideas for the following writing task.

> Write a letter, to be placed in a time capsule and read by teenagers in the future, in which you describe the most important possession that you own and explain why it is so important to you.
>
> - In your letter you should:
> - describe your most treasured possession
> - explain why it is the most important possession that you own
> - engage and entertain your future readers.

2. Look back at the bullet points in the writing task. Number your ideas in the sequence you will include them in your letter.

If a writing task asks you to argue a specific point of view, using a grid can help you to plan your response. Look again at the writing task below.

Write the words of a speech to your class in which you argue that the Internet is a good OR a bad influence on young people.

In your speech you should:

- explain why you believe the Internet is a good or bad thing
- give some examples to support your argument
- convince your audience to agree with your point of view.

The following student has begun to use a grid to identify the arguments they could make for and against the idea that the Internet is a good influence.

Good influence	Bad influence
Educational value – research...	Crime – online fraud...
Facilitates communication – Facebook, Twitter...	Impacts negatively on education – aids plagiarism...
Improved forms of entertainment – streaming music, online gaming...	Young people are vulnerable because of the Internet – online bullying...
Important for business – online banking, world trading...	

This planning approach can help you to identify:

- which point of view you have the most arguments in favour of – this will probably be the point of view you will be able to argue most effectively
- the arguments and counter-arguments you could include in your response – think of how you can disprove or challenge the counter-arguments you identify
- which arguments are the most effective – these are the ones you should definitely include in your response, including information and evidence to support these.

When you have identified the ideas you will include in your writing, you need to decide how to structure them. Look at the guidance on the next page to help you.

Introduction

The opening paragraph of your response needs to introduce the point of view you are arguing in a way that hooks the reader's interest. You could use:

- an anecdote that brings your argument to life for the reader
- quotations from experts or well-known people that support the point of view you are presenting
- surprising or thought-provoking statistics that help readers understand the point of view you will be arguing

Development

Think about the order you will present your arguments in. Look back at your grid and number the points in order of importance, making sure you can refer to ideas and evidence to support these points. You might be able to link arguments and counter-arguments in order to disprove the opposing point of view.

Conclusion

The final paragraph of your response should sum up your point of view. You could use a rhetorical question or other rhetorical device to ensure you communicate this powerfully to your readers.

Activity 2

Look at the writing task below.

> Write a letter to your headteacher in which you argue for OR against keeping the school uniform.
>
> In your letter you should:
>
> - explain why you believe school uniform should or should not be kept
> - give some examples to support your argument
> - convince your audience to agree with your point of view.

1. Use a grid like the one on the facing page to plan your initial ideas for and against keeping the school uniform.
2. Decide on the point of view you will argue and select the five key points you want to include in your response. Remember to think about the ideas and evidence you can use to develop and support these points and counter-arguments you can try to disprove.
3. Plan the introduction and conclusion to your letter.

Tip

Look at how the following examples hook the reader's interest and draw on these techniques in your own writing:

- 'I believe the Internet is a good thing and to prove this I'm presenting this speech to you via Skype.'
- 'Steve Jobs once said, "Creativity is just connecting things," and in this speech I'm going to explain how the Internet has helped us all to be more creative.'
- 'There are over two and a half billion Internet users in the world today and in this speech I'll help you to understand how the Internet is helping them to make the world a better place.'

Tip

An effective way to end your writing is to link back to the opening in some way. This might be reintroducing an idea or argument you made in the beginning and reminding the reader how you have now proved this.

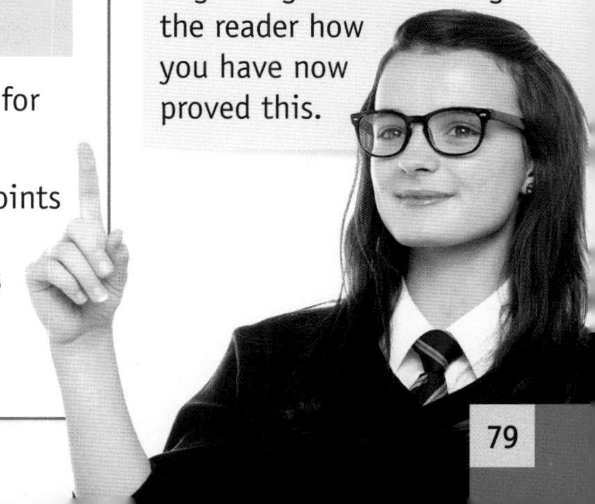

Practising key skills for AO5

When you have completed your planning, you will need to focus on writing your response. This will be assessed on two objectives, AO5 and AO6. In this section you will work on the skills you need to do well in AO5, which is divided into two sections.

AO5	• Communicate clearly, effectively and imaginatively, selecting and adapting tone, style and register for different forms, purposes and audiences. • Organize information and ideas, using structural and grammatical features to support coherence and cohesion of texts.

This is about the content of what write.

This is about how you organize tha content.

What are content and organization?

In order to gain high marks for content and organization you need to communicate your ideas clearly to the reader and match your writing to whatever purpose, audience and form you have been asked to write in.

This means making conscious choices about the language and structural features you use, so that your writing has the intended impact on readers. To assess this, the examiner will look at the way you use individual words and phrases, as well as the way you sequence, link and present your ideas. The organization of your whole piece of writing, and of paragraphs and sections within it, will be taken into account.

Writing conventions

Each specific purpose for writing has its own set of conventions. These are language and structural features that readers expect to find in writing of that kind.

Activity 1

1. Look at the writing purpose checklists on the facing page. For each purpose, find an example of that type of writing and identify the conventions it uses.
2. Discuss the pieces of writing you have explored. Did any of them use different conventions? Why do you think that might be?

It is important to remember that most writing has more than one purpose. For example, Question 5 on page 75 requires you to describe and explain as well as entertain your reader. Similarly, many of the features identified in the table on the next page overlap with each other, appearing in more than one form of writing.

Writing to describe	Writing to explain	Writing to inform
• Paragraphs of different lengths for effect • Appeal to the reader's senses through figurative language, **alliteration** and onomatopoeia • Use adjectives, verbs, adverbs • Varied sentence length for effect • Sense of mood and atmosphere created	• New paragraph for each main point with a **topic sentence** • **Present tense** verbs • **Time connectives** to show a sequence of events and ideas • Language of cause and effect • Technical language if necessary • Examples given to illustrate points made • Confident tone	• New paragraph for each key point with topic sentences • Present tense • Third person used • Time connectives to sequence points • Clear, easy-to-follow sentences • Technical language if necessary • Factual content • Direct address: 'you' • Authoritative tone
Writing to instruct	**Writing to argue**	**Writing to persuade**
• Clear, concise vocabulary • Present tense • Imperative verbs • Descriptive language used for clarity, not vividness or effect • Adverbs used for clarification • Numbers and/or time connectives • Clear, easy-to-follow sentence structures • Authoritative tone	• Recognize the other side of the argument while arguing specific viewpoint • New paragraphs for each main point, with topic sentences for clarity • Additional connectives and connectives of contrast to direct the reader • Examples used to illustrate points • Uses a wide range of rhetorical devices • Present tense	• Argues one point of view only • New paragraph for each main point • Uses additional connectives and topic sentences to direct reader • Examples used to illustrate points • Uses a wide range of rhetorical devices • Passionate tone

Tip

In the exam you could be asked to write in a variety of forms, such as a letter, an article for a newspaper or magazine, a blog, the words of a speech, a report or simply an essay. Read examples of these different forms of writing to familiarize yourself with the conventions they include and think about how you can draw on these in your own writing.

Key terms

alliteration the occurrence of the same letter or sound at the beginning of a group of words for special effect

topic sentence the sentence that introduces or summarizes the main idea in a paragraph

present tense verb forms used to describe something that is happening now, e.g. I drive the car; he climbs the mountain

time connective word or phrase used to indicate when something is happening, e.g. firstly, then, afterwards, instantly, meanwhile, next, shortly, later on, that night, the next day, etc.

Key terms

tone the writer's attitude towards their subject and audience, which is implied through their language choices, e.g. sarcastic, angry, apologetic, etc.

style the way in which the writer uses language

register the formality of the writing (e.g. vocabulary use, grammatical choices, etc.) which can vary according to the context and audience

Tone, style and register

Just as your voice has a **tone**, **style** and **register**, so does your writing. If someone is angry, they will raise their voice, use a harsher vocabulary and speak more quickly and forcefully. All of this contributes to the tone, style and register. In the exam, you need to create and convey an appropriate tone, style and register to maximize the impact and effect of your writing on your audience.

Activity 2

1. The extracts on the facing page have been taken from two students' speeches to their class arguing that the Internet is a good OR a bad influence on young people. As you read each extract, decide:
   a) What is the tone of the extract?
   b) How would you describe the style?
   c) How formal is the register?
2. Which extract do you think is most effective in arguing its point of view and why? Share your reasons with a partner.

Tip

Keeping the audience for your writing in mind can help you to make the right choices in terms of the tone, style and register you use.

Student A

People who say the Internet is a bad thing are IDIOTS! How can it be? Think about all the great stuff it does for us! Where would we be without it? We wouldn't be able to talk to friends or family in Australia or do our shopping from the comfort of our own sofa or look up friends we haven't seen in ages. That's where! If you don't like it, then I say you should clear off and leave it for the rest of us who love it!

Student B

Previously I really loved the Internet and could not imagine life without it until the day my grandfather logged on to find out, to his horror, that £5,000 had been stolen from his online account. This was money he had been saving in order to take my grandmother on a once in a lifetime cruise. They are both in their 60s and were distraught. My grandmother in particular was devastated. She could not believe that someone whom she had never met and who might be sitting on the other side of the world, could be so cruel. They have not used it since and probably never will again. It has changed my attitude towards it too.

Activity 3

1. Now look at the extract from the mark scheme below. What level would you give to each student based on this extract from their responses?

Level	Key words for tone, style and register
6	Tone, style and register are ambitiously selected and deployed to enhance the purpose of the task.
5	There is a sustained use of tone, style and register to fulfil the purpose of the task.
4	Tone, style and register are chosen to match the task.
3	Tone, style and register are appropriate for the task, with some inconsistencies.
2	There is some attempt to use a tone, style and register appropriate to the task.
1	There is a limited attempt to use a tone, style and register appropriate to the task.

Writing in role

You may be asked to write in role in your exam. This will require you to not only think carefully about the purpose, form and audience of your writing but to also consider a tone, style and register which is appropriate for the role you must write in.

Look at the writing task below. The annotations give you further guidance on how to approach the question.

> You are an angry resident, opposing plans for a new shopping centre in your neighbourhood. Write a letter to your local newspaper in which you argue why it should not be built.
>
> In your writing you should:
>
> - Make sure you write in role
> - Use a suitable language and tone of voice
> - Argue your point of view but show that you are aware of the other side of the argument

This instructs you to assume a role

Further guidance about what you are strongly against – a new shopping centre

This indicates the purpose for your writing – to argue

This makes clear that you must write as 'an angry resident'

This indicates the form for your writing – a letter

This indicates the audience – those who read the local newspaper so it must be quite formal

The bullet points give you further guidance about the task including what writing to argue involves

Level	Key words for tone, style and register
6	Tone, style and register are ambitiously selected and deployed to enhance the purpose of the task.
5	There is a sustained use of tone, style and register to fulfil the purpose of the task.
4	Tone, style and register are chosen to match the task.
3	Tone, style and register are appropriate for the task, with some inconsistencies.
2	There is some attempt to use a tone, style and register appropriate to the task.
1	There is a limited attempt to use a tone, style and register appropriate to the task.

Activity 4

Read Student A's response below.

1. Use the extract from the mark scheme on page 84 to give it a mark for the quality of its tone, style and register.
2. Explain why you have chosen this level.

Student A

Some foolishly argue that the new shopping centre will be economically good for the area. Wrong! It will be a complete disaster. Only an idiot can actually believe that jobs and prosperity will follow. Zero hour contracts in my opinion are nothing more than modern day slavery and exploitation – not proper employment. If this monstrosity is built, then local shopkeepers, many of whom have been trading in this area for several generations, will go out of business as the large multi nationals drive them out. It disgusts me! This shopping centre will drive a dagger through the heart of this community. Quicker than you can imagine, the town centre will be a wasteland, crime will be rampant and the perpetrators will be lining their filthy pockets while the rest of us suffer.

Activity 5

1. Write another paragraph as the 'angry resident' in which you argue that the building of the new shopping centre will have a negative impact on the local wildlife. Make sure that the language you use creates the appropriate tone.
2. Imagine you are a local politician in favour of the new shopping centre. Write a paragraph from a letter to the local newspaper persuading the readers that the shopping centre will be a positive thing for the local community.

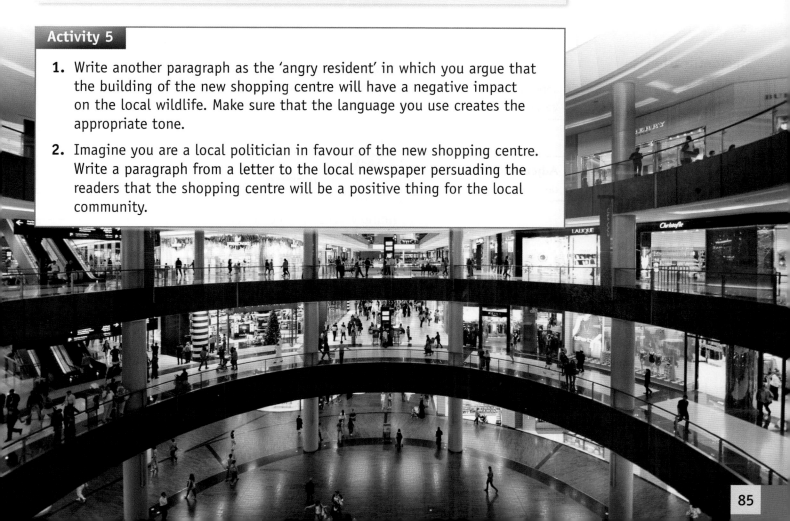

Tip

Be adventurous in your language choices, but avoid long words simply for the sake of it. Keep the form, purpose and audience in mind and tailor your choices to achieve deliberate effects.

Key terms

adjective a word added to a noun to describe it or change its meaning

simile a figure of speech in which one thing is compared to another using 'like' or 'as'

personification to present an idea in human form or a thing as having human characteristics

Communication

In order to communicate effectively you need to think carefully about the words that you use, making sure that your vocabulary achieves specific effects or has the intended impact on the reader. Think about how you can use rhetorical techniques, and stylistic and linguistic features to enhance the purpose of your writing.

The extract below is taken from Student A's response to the writing task below. Read the response, then look at the annotations, which explain how it uses vocabulary and linguistic devices to communicate successfully.

Write an article for a teenage magazine in which you describe your favourite holiday destination. This could be a place you have visited or would like to visit.

In your article you should:

- say where the place is and what it is like
- explain why it is your favourite holiday destination
- explain why you think teenagers should visit this destination.

Student A

Long and elongated, the beach at Fahan is a pleasure paradise for the sun worshippers and water sporting thrill seekers who populate it. Lying on the soft, silky sand are the sun bathers whose bronzed bodies glisten in the blazing sun. The foaming waves are like white stallions racing to shore against an azure sky, unblemished by clouds of any kind.

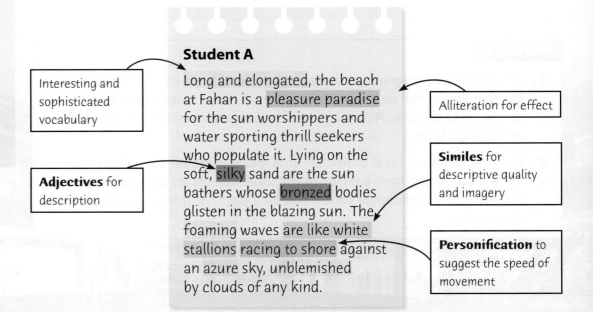

Interesting and sophisticated vocabulary

Adjectives for description

Alliteration for effect

Similes for descriptive quality and imagery

Personification to suggest the speed of movement

Now read the extract below, which is taken from Student B's draft response to the following writing task.

Write a letter to your headteacher in which you inform him or her about how the school could be improved further.

In your letter you should:

- explain what things about school life are of most concern to students
- inform him or her about how these things can be improved
- suggest why you think it is important that these improvements are made.

Student B

Students are so sad about the poor state of the boys' toilets. The cubicle doors are covered in graffiti and many of the locks are broken. Worse still is the bad smell that seems to be coming from the sewer. As a result, students do not want to use them, making life very hard for students. We want this to be dealt with soon because if this issue carries on, students will keep going off site rather than sit in classrooms unable to think because they are being refused basic rights.

Activity 6

1. In this response Student B has used some rather basic vocabulary. For this reason, the response may not receive a mark higher than a Level 3 for AO5.
   a) Look at the underlined words and phrases and discuss the alternative vocabulary you could use to make the writer's anger about this situation more obvious.
   b) For each choice recommend the replacement word or phrase you think Student B should choose in order to improve their response by at least one level.
2. Look again at the plan you wrote for Activity 2 on page 82 and write a draft paragraph of the letter to your headteacher in which you argue for OR against keeping the school uniform. Remember to think carefully about your vocabulary choices and the language features you use in order to create deliberate effects and influence the reader's response.

Organization

Remind yourself of the second part of AO5:

- Organize information and ideas, using structural and grammatical features to support coherence and cohesion of texts.

You are now going to focus on the skills required to organize your writing successfully. This is important so that the reader can easily follow what you have to say and you maximize the impact of the ideas you are trying to communicate.

Tip

Make sure that you are always consistent in the way that you show a new paragraph on the page. Do not mix both approaches to starting a new paragraph in the same piece of writing.

Paragraphs and topic sentences

When writing in the exam, it is essential that you use paragraphs to organize the information and ideas you present to the reader. Remember to:

- start a new paragraph when you start writing about a new argument, topic or idea
- show that you are starting a new paragraph by leaving a blank line between paragraphs or by indenting the first line of the new paragraph.

Topic sentences can also help you to structure your response, signalling to readers the key idea that will be covered in a paragraph. In non-fiction writing, the topic sentence is often the first sentence of a paragraph.

Tip

In the exam, your topic sentences should link to the purpose and focus of the writing task you are responding to. For example, if you are writing to argue a specific point of view, your topic sentences should help to signpost the main points of your argument.

Activity 7

1. Look at the three topic sentences below and identify the main argument presented in each one.

> Most importantly, the internet enables families and friends to communicate in a fast, reliable and inexpensive way which is vital for life in today's global village.

> Secondly, those less fortunate than us, who have disabilities which mean they cannot leave their homes, are offered a lifeline through the internet which improves their quality of life significantly.

> Furthermore, how would the world of business survive without the instant nature of the internet which allows billions of pounds to be spent and transferred from one account to another at the mere click of a mouse?

You can also use topic sentences to help link your ending to your opening, e.g. by reintroducing the idea you began with and showing how you have proved this in your writing.

Activity 8

Look again at the plan you wrote for the following writing task in Activity 2 on page 82.

> Write a letter to your headteacher in which you argue for OR against keeping the school uniform.
>
> In your letter you should:
>
> - explain why you believe school uniform should or should not be kept
> - give some examples to support your argument
> - convince your audience to agree with your point of view.

1. Write a topic sentence for each of the key points you plan to include in the letter.
2. Decide how you will organize your paragraphs. Number your topic sentences in the order you will present them in your writing.
3. Write a topic sentence for the opening and closing paragraphs of your response.

Tip

Think about how you could link different points in your argument. One idea might naturally follow on from or build on another. You can also use topic sentences to help counter opposing arguments, e.g. Some people say the Internet helps students to cheat, but the Internet actually helps teachers to uncover any students who try to cheat with tools to identify plagiarized work.

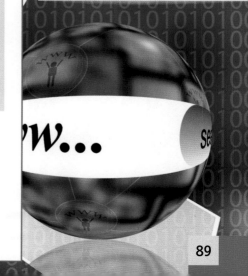

Structural features

Key term

cohesive device a word or phrase which links paragraphs together and links points within paragraphs

When assessing your writing, an examiner will be looking at the coherence and cohesion of your response.

- Coherence is the way you have organized your ideas across the text as a whole, e.g. how you have developed an argument or presented your point of view.
- Cohesion is how you have used words and phrases to make links between and within paragraphs.

These linking words and phrases are known as **cohesive devices**.

Activity 9

Read the following opening sentences, from five different paragraphs taken from a speech arguing that the Internet is a good influence.

1. a) Based on these opening sentences, what order do you think the paragraphs would appear in?

b) Which words and phrases helped you to identify the order? Discuss your choices with a partner.

A Secondly, those less fortunate than us, who have disabilities which mean they cannot leave their homes, are offered a lifeline through the Internet which improves their quality of life significantly.

B Radical, revolutionary and remarkable. Could you live without the Internet? I know I couldn't even contemplate life without it.

C Furthermore, how would the world of business survive without the instant nature of the Internet, which allows billions of pounds to be spent and transferred from one account to another at the mere click of a mouse?

D In conclusion, the Internet is now so much a part of our everyday lives that it is impossible to think about how we would live without. The 3,035,749,340 people across the world who use it daily would definitely agree!

E Most importantly, the Internet enables families and friends to communicate in a fast, reliable and inexpensive way which is vital for life in today's global village.

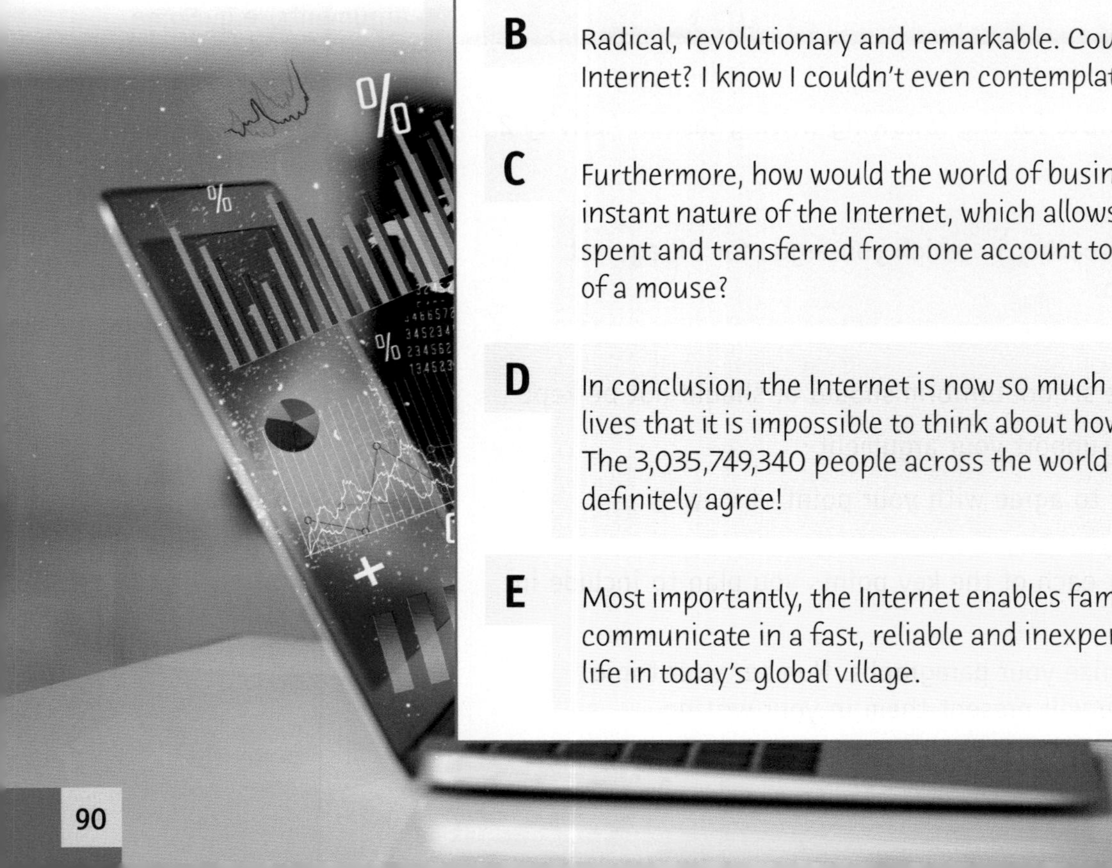

Now look at the cohesive devices Student A has used in the following paragraph from her speech arguing that the Internet is a bad thing.

Adverbials used as **discourse markers** help to navigate the reader through the text.

Use of synonyms, with repetition of students at beginning and end of paragraph to reinforce argument

Use of **pronoun** to refer back to 'students'

Student A

Finally, it's clear that the Internet holds real dangers for students, no matter what claims are made for the educational benefits of the web. It is my opinion that there are real risks to teachers encouraging children online. The Internet provides a haven for criminals and fraudsters, whilst bullies and trolls wait in the dark shadows of the web to intimidate and exploit vulnerable young people. Furthermore, why waste valuable curriculum time asking students to cut-and-paste the information they find online when they could spend their time developing the face-to-face skills they need to communicate effectively.

Introducing a new idea and stating opinion as fact

Use of **synonyms** to avoid repetition

Contrasts drawn

Emphasizing inclusion of a range of views

Two different references to time – wasting it and spending it valuably (a **reference chain**)

Key terms

adverbial a word or phrase that is used as an adverb and helps to link ideas together. A fronted adverbial is used at the start of a sentence and followed by a comma

discourse marker words and phrases used in written or spoken communication to connect or signpost information and ideas

synonym a word or phrase that means the same or almost the same as another word or phrase

pronoun a word used instead of a noun or noun phrase

reference chain different words or phrases used for the same idea, person or thing many times in a piece of writing, like links in a chain

Activity 10

Look back at the topic sentences you wrote for your letter to the headteacher arguing for or against school uniform in Activity 6 on page 87. Draft each paragraph of this response, using some of the cohesive devices in the grid below.

To make comparisons	To provide examples	To add more information	To draw conclusions	To draw contrasts
similarly in the same way likewise by the same token	for example to illustrate thus for instance take the case of	and also and then besides equally furthermore in addition next	to summarize in conclusion finally on the whole in summary	alternatively yet whereas although but however instead although

Practising key skills for AO6

In this section you will work on the skills you need to do well in AO6.

AO6	• Use a range of vocabulary and sentence structures for clarity, purpose and effect, with accurate spelling and punctuation.

The focus here is on the technical accuracy of your writing.

What is technical accuracy?

Technical accuracy is using words, punctuation and grammar correctly. Your writing needs to show that you can use a range of vocabulary in correctly punctuated sentences, written in Standard English. Accuracy in spelling and punctuation will be taken into account, as well as your control over sentence structure. This doesn't just mean forming sentences correctly, but also means using a variety of sentence structures for different purposes and effects in a controlled way.

Remind yourself of the key words or descriptors that the examiner will be looking for when they assess the technical accuracy of your work.

Level	Key words for technical accuracy
Level 4 (13–16 marks)	Sentence structure – an ambitious range shapes meaning and creates impact Punctuation – accurate; makes writing clear and achieves specific effects Vocabulary – precise and subtle Spelling – accurate; very few mistakes in complex, ambitious words
Level 3 (9–12 marks)	Sentence structure – a wide range used for deliberate purpose and effect Punctuation – consistently accurate Vocabulary – used convincingly; sometimes ambitious Spelling – accurate
Level 2 (5–8 marks)	Sentence structure – a range used and mostly secure Punctuation – generally accurate Vocabulary – appropriate Spelling – generally accurate
Level 1 (1–4 marks)	Sentence structure – simple mostly with some attempt at complex structures Punctuation – some Vocabulary – straightforward Spelling – simple spellings, mostly accurate

To achieve the highest marks for AO6 you need to demonstrate ambition, precision and accuracy. The activities in this chapter will help you to revise and practise the key skills you need to improve the technical accuracy of your writing.

Sentence structure

Using a range of sentence structures to create specific effects will improve your writing by adding variety to it and demonstrating your craft and control as a writer. Remind yourself of the three main types of sentences.

Simple sentences

A simple sentence or single-clause sentence contains a subject (which does the action) and a verb (the action) and expresses a complete thought. For example:

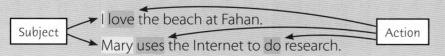

Subject → I love the beach at Fahan. ← Action

Subject → Mary uses the Internet to do research. ← Action

Compound sentences

Compound sentences or multi-clause sentences are formed when two simple sentences are joined together by a **coordinating conjunction**. For example:

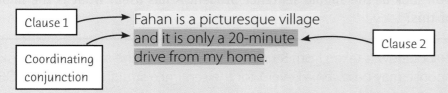

Clause 1 → Fahan is a picturesque village

Coordinating conjunction → and it is only a 20-minute drive from my home. ← Clause 2

Complex sentences

Complex sentences use a **subordinating conjunction** to join together a main clause (which can stand as a sentence on its own) and a subordinating clause (which cannot stand as a sentence on its own). For example:

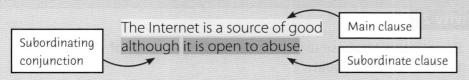

The Internet is a source of good ← Main clause

Subordinating conjunction → although it is open to abuse. ← Subordinate clause

This could also be expressed, 'Although it is open to abuse, the Internet is a source of good.' Think about the way you order the clauses in the complex sentences you use in your writing. Choosing a different order can help to emphasise a particular point or idea.

Tip

Remember, to achieve the highest levels for A06 you need to use an ambitious range of sentence structures, so employ simple sentences sparingly in your writing, e.g. to emphasize a particular point or to create a dramatic impact.

Key terms

coordinating conjunction a word used to join two single clauses of equal importance together, e.g. and, but, because, so, for, or, nor, yet

subordinating conjunction a word used to join two clauses which are not equal, e.g. although, as, before, once, though, until

The extract below is taken from Student A's response to the writing task below. As you read the response, think about the sentence structures used.

Write an article for a teenage magazine in which you describe your favourite holiday destination. This could be a place you have visited or would like to visit.

Student A

Even in the winter, Fahan beach is a beautiful place to visit. Lying in the distance are the steep, rocky mountains which protect you from the icy winds pouring in from the wild Atlantic. Although deserted, I love to walk here, taking in the cold, clean air while I think about the day just gone and the days to come, mentally recharging before heading back to the helter-skelter life of the city. Whether the skies above are bright blue or ashen grey, it does not bother me. This is home.

Activity 1 SPAG

1. Identify the types of sentences and the coordinating and subordinating conjunctions used in the extract.
2. Look at the complex sentences you have identified. What effects do these create?
3. Now look at the simple sentence Student A has used. What is the impact of this?

The extract below is taken from Student B's response to the same writing task. This response may be given a Level 1 for the sentence structure strand of AO6 as the student has used only simple sentences.

Student B

I love London. It is so cool. There is so much to do there. The sights are amazing. The Tower of London is great. Madame Tussaud's is fascinating too. Don't miss out on the London Eye as well! My friends and I just love the shops. We spend a fortune.

Activity 2 SPAG

1. Rewrite this response using a more ambitious range of sentence structures. Think about:
   - how you can use coordinating conjunctions to link simple sentences
   - how you can use subordinating conjunctions to link main and subordinating clauses.
2. Swap your rewritten response with a partner and look back at the extract from the mark scheme on page 92 to award this a level. Give feedback and discuss the changes made.

You can use different sentence structures to help you to achieve your purpose in writing.

For example, complex sentences with subordinating conjunctions can be useful when writing to argue as they allow to you to craft sentences which recognize the other side of the argument and then attack and undermine it.

Look at the examples below.

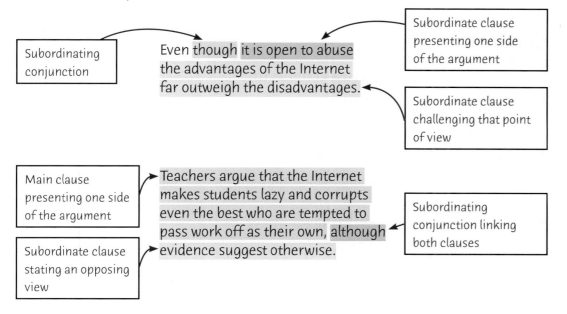

Even though it is open to abuse the advantages of the Internet far outweigh the disadvantages.

- Subordinating conjunction: though
- Subordinate clause presenting one side of the argument: it is open to abuse
- Subordinate clause challenging that point of view: the advantages of the Internet far outweigh the disadvantages.

Teachers argue that the Internet makes students lazy and corrupts even the best who are tempted to pass work off as their own, although evidence suggest otherwise.

- Main clause presenting one side of the argument: Teachers argue that the Internet makes students lazy and corrupts even the best who are tempted to pass work off as their own,
- Subordinating conjunction linking both clauses: although
- Subordinate clause stating an opposing view: evidence suggest otherwise.

Activity 3

SPAG

Look back at the draft letter to the headteacher arguing for or against school uniform that you wrote in Activity 8 on page 89. Check that you have:

- used a range of sentence structures
- thought about the effects the different sentence structures you have used create
- included complex sentences using a range of subordinating conjunctions to link and refute opposing points of view.

Redraft the letter to make improvements to the sentence structures used in your response.

Punctuation

You need to use punctuation to help you present your ideas clearly and craft sentences which achieve deliberate effects. Remind yourself of the different types of punctuation you can use and how you can employ these punctuation marks accurately to enhance the effectiveness of your writing.

Commas

In non-fiction writing, you can use commas to:

- separate items in a simple list, e.g.

  The Internet is fun, educational, entertaining and easy to use.

- separate main and subordinate clauses in a sentence, e.g.

  Despite apparently hating the Internet, my mother shops for bargains on it weekly.

- separate an adverbial word or phrase, e.g.

  Today's teens, more media savvy than their parents ever will be, live their lives online.

- to introduce direct speech, e.g.

  Bill Gates argues, "The Internet is becoming the town square of the global village of tomorrow."

Colons

You can use colons to introduce information or lists, including bullet point lists, e.g.

Online you can do many things: shop, chat, find love, buy a car or sell your house.

The Internet has introduced:

- new forms of communication
- on-demand entertainment
- online shopping and trading.

Semi-colons

You can use semi-colons to separate items in a complicated list, especially when the items within list already include commas, e.g.

The advantages include: improved family communication, especially between relatives who live at opposite ends of the world; better quality of life, in particular for those with certain disabilities; greater trading opportunities for small and large businesses alike.

You can also use semi-colons within a sentence to link clauses that are closely related, e.g.

Online games encourage violence and bad behaviour; they promote negative stereotypes and sexism too.

Tip

Using semi-colons can help you to encourage your readers to make connections between the ideas you present in your writing. However, you should only use a semi-colon to link two clauses if each clause can stand alone and make complete sense independent of the other.

Activity 4 SPAG

Read the sentences below. How does the use of punctuation create different effects on the reader and which have the most impact in your opinion?

1. a) Paul considers his constant playing of online games a hobby. His parents feel it is an addiction.

   b) Paul considers his constant playing of online games a hobby; his parents feel it is an addiction.

2. a) Online you can do many things: shop, chat, find love, buy a car or sell your house.

   b) Online you can do many things. You can shop, chat, find love, buy a car or sell your house.

3. a) The Internet is fun, educational and entertaining.

   b) The Internet is fun. It is also educational and entertaining.

Apostrophes

The apostrophe has two main functions. It can be used to show that letters are missed out of a word. This is called a contraction, e.g. didn't, don't, won't, etc.

The apostrophe can also be used to show ownership or possession. This means that something belongs to someone or something.

Brackets

Brackets can be used to provide extra information or provide an afterthought, e.g.

> The playing of games online (much criticized by teachers and parents alike) has many benefits for young people.

Note that if the brackets and information within them is removed, the sentence should still make sense.

Dashes

Dashes are used to include additional information in a sentence or to separate clauses, e.g.

> Mary loves the Internet – she's never off it!

In a sentence, a dash fulfils a similar role to a semi-colon or colon. They are usually found in more informal writing, so you should think about the audience, purpose and form for your writing before you use them in the exam.

Activity 5 SPAG

Look back at the draft letter to the headteacher arguing for or against school uniform that you wrote in Activity 8 on page 89. Check that you have used a range of punctuation accurately and for deliberate effect in this and make any corrections that you need to.

Tip

Follow these rules to use apostrophes of possession correctly.

- If a singular word doesn't end in -s, add 's: It was Paul's homework.
- If a singular word ends in -s, add either 's or just ': It was James's homework. No, it was Nicholas' homework.
- If a singular word ends is -ss, still add 's: It was Ross's homework.
- If a plural ends in -s, just add ': It was the girls' homework.
- If a plural doesn't end in -s, add 's: It was the children's homework.

Vocabulary

In order to achieve the highest levels for technical accuracy, you need to choose vocabulary that will help you to express complex ideas clearly. The more sophisticated and precise your vocabulary, the higher your mark will be, as long as it is used in the right context.

Look at the paragraph below in which Student A has described the appearance of a treasured possession, in this case a bracelet. Note how she has improved her use of vocabulary and her writing, by replacing her initial choices.

Student A

My bracelet is a series of smaller, ~~thinner~~ finer chains all ~~twisted together~~ entwined, ~~adding~~ combining to make one larger one. In ~~fancy~~ beautiful ~~writing~~ calligraphy is an inscription with a personal message from my nan.

Tip

Reading a wide range of novels, plays and non-fiction is a good way to develop and expand your vocabulary. Keep a log of new and interesting words that you come across for use in your own writing.

Activity 6

1. Write a paragraph describing a treasured possession that you own. Think about the vocabulary you choose in order to express why this possession is so important to you.
2. Re-read your paragraph. Are you happy with the vocabulary choices you have made? Use a thesaurus to help you to consider any alternative words you could use to express your meaning more precisely.

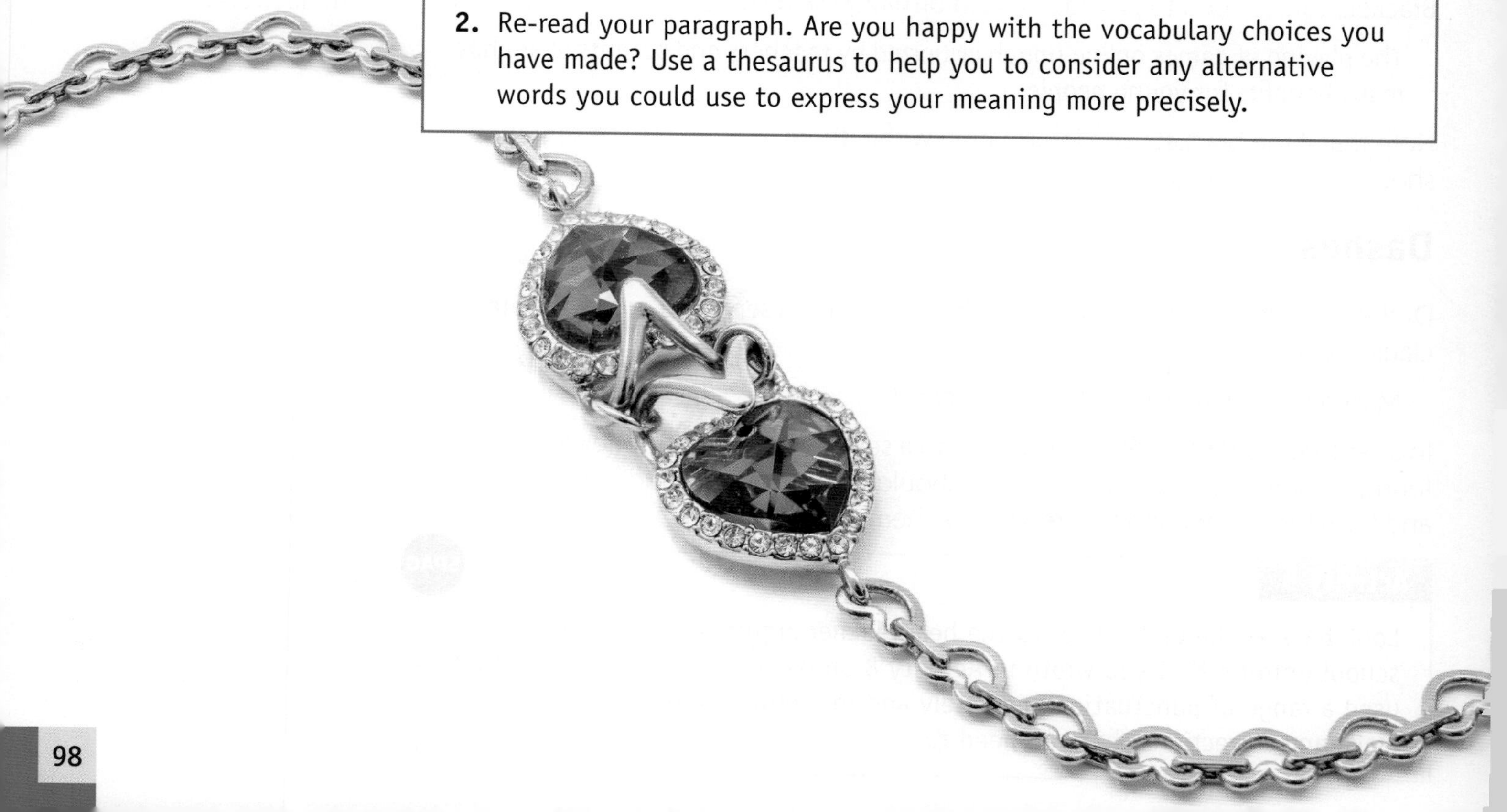

Spelling

Spelling words as accurately as you can is very important. You will lose marks for incorrect spelling in your writing response. Below are some of the most commonly misspelt words.

interesting beginning government argument accommodation

sincerely definitely commitment knowledge unfortunately

environment humorous independent occasion possession

privilege receive recommend separate vulnerable embarrass

Activity 7

1. Work with a partner to test yourself on how many of these words you can spell correctly.
2. Use some of the strategies below to learn any spellings you got wrong.

Strategies for learning spellings

There are a number of ways to learn spellings. Some of these include:

- The 'Look. Say. Cover. Spell. Check.' method.
- Writing out the correct spelling 10, 15 or 20 times.
- Writing out particularly important but tricky words in large letters and sticking them up around the house where you will see them frequently.
- Keeping a spelling log of words you spell incorrectly and learning two or three of these every evening, with a test on them all at the end of the week. Remember to reward yourself if you get them right!
- Making up sentences such as 'Big Elephants Can Always Understand Small Elephants' to help spell 'because'. Think also of catchy little tips in order to help you remember how to spell words you find difficult, like 'A shirt has one collar and two sleeves' to help remember that 'necessary' has one 'C' and two 'S's.

Activity 8 SPAG

Proofread the draft letter to the headteacher arguing for or against school uniform that you wrote in Activity 6 on page 87. Check that your spelling is accurate, especially the spelling of any ambitious vocabulary or words that you sometimes spell incorrectly.

Try it yourself WITH SUPPORT

Look at Student A's complete response to the following writing task. Pay particular attention to the examiner's notes in the margin and the comments which follow.

Write an article for a teenage magazine in which you describe your favourite holiday destination. This could be a place you have visited or would like to visit.

In your article you should:

- say where the place is and what it is like
- explain why it is your favourite holiday destination
- explain why you think teenagers should visit this destination.

Student A

Brilliant and breathtakingly beautiful! These are the only words to describe my favourite holiday destination. Situated on the north coast of Northern Ireland, it is a small, strip of land about six miles long, nestled at the foot of a magnificent mountain range. It has been a friend since childhood and always played an important part in the life of my family, which has holidayed there for generations. This place, which is so special to me for many reasons, is Benone Beach.

Benone is an awarding winning beach about 30 minutes' drive from where I live. In the summer it is a great place to spend a week or two. I love to feel the soft sand between my toes as I take a relaxing walk. Swimming in the crystal blue sea is another delight. Some complain the water is too cold but I simply love the refreshing and revitalising effect it always has on me. On hot days, the heat creates a haze in the distance and the mountains in the background look like a sleeping giant who might wake up at any moment.

My first memory of Benone Beach is when I was six. I remember digging a large hole with my bigger brother and sister, who then buried me in it! Crying to get out, my father came to the

Interesting opening (using alliteration for effect)

Varied sentence starters avoid repetition, although they are quite basic

Alliteration used to emphasize points

Destination deliberately not revealed until the very end of the last sentence in the paragraph to create a sense of suspense

Simile used to be descriptive

Paragraphs used, some of which use topic sentences to direct the reader

rescue. It was a glorious day with a big, summer sun smiling down on us as we played. Candyfloss clouds sat in the sky. I can still see the shimmering sea, feel the silky, soft sand and hear the seagulls squawking overhead. My mother always did her best to make sure there was no sand in the sandwiches but there always was. Happy childhood memories!

I suppose you think I only go there in the summer. Well, you'd be wrong! Benone welcomes its guests at any time, even in the winter. Every Christmas Day, my father and I join a local charity and go there and swim to raise money. He's always saying, "Never again!" but each year he returns to torture himself for another worthy cause. The mince pies and hot chocolate always taste incredible afterwards, as you can imagine.

Benone is my special holiday destination for a number of reasons. It obviously holds many special memories from my childhood – of happy days spent at play and of the family being together. This place seems to have a bewitching effect on the people who go there. Suddenly, people become happy, their frowns and worries melt away. Recently though, Benone has become an escape from city life, a refuge and place of calm where I can escape for some peace and quiet. A walk along that beach always helps to me to think straight and recharge the batteries.

Why not treat yourself and pay Benone a visit?

Tone and style are matched to task. The colloquial language, direct address and abbreviation create an informality which suit the teenage audience

A range of punctuation employed accurately

Topic sentence to direct the reader

An attempt to end in an interesting way (using a rhetorical question)

Personification used to make the **setting** seem alive

A range of sentence structures used securely – simple, compound and complex

Spelling consistently accurate

Vocabulary is appropriate, despite only limited evidence of more adventurous word choices

Key term

setting the place and time where the story occurs

This would be a Level 4 response for AO5 and be placed at the bottom of Level 3 for AO6. The student could improve this response by:

- using more ambitious vocabulary
- varying the range of sentence types to include more complex (multi-clause) sentences
- improving the range of cohesive devices within paragraphs.

Activity 1

Look back at your letter to your head teacher about school uniform, from page 89.

1. Use the mark schemes below to give your response a level for A05 and A06.
2. Set yourself three targets (two for A05 and one for A06), which you think would improve this response.

Level	Key words for content and organization (A05)
Level 6 (21–24 marks)	Form – deliberately adapted; sophisticated control of purpose and effect Tone, style and register – ambitiously selected Overall structure – skilfully controlled overall structure
Level 5 (17–20 marks)	Form – confidently adapted; secure understanding of purpose and audience Tone, style and register – sustained Overall structure – controlled overall structure
Level 4 (13–16 marks)	Form – confidently adapted; secure understanding of purpose and audience Tone, style and register – matched to task Overall structure – well-managed overall structure
Level 3 (9–12 marks)	Form – sustained; clear awareness of purpose and audience Tone, style and register – appropriate with some inconsistencies Overall structure – clear overall structure
Level 2 (5–8 marks	Form – mostly appropriate; generally maintained Tone, style and register – attempted Overall structure – some evidence
Level 1 (1–4 marks)	Form – some attempt Tone, style and register – limited attempt Overall structure – some attempt

Level	Key words for technical accuracy (A06)
Level 4 (13–16 marks)	Sentence structure – an ambitious range shapes meaning and creates impact Punctuation – accurate; makes writing clear and achieves specific effects Vocabulary – precise and subtle Spelling – accurate; very few mistakes
Level 3 (9–12 marks)	Sentence structure – a wide range used for deliberate purpose and effect Punctuation – consistently accurate Vocabulary – used convincingly; sometimes ambitious Spelling – accurate
Level 2 (5–8 marks)	Sentence structure – a range used and mostly secure Punctuation – generally accurate Vocabulary – appropriate Spelling – generally accurate
Level 1 (1–4 marks)	Sentence structure – simple mostly with some attempt at complex structures Punctuation – some Vocabulary – straightforward Spelling – simple spellings, mostly accurate

Try it yourself **ON YOUR OWN**

Read the questions below and write your response to **one** of these tasks, applying all the skills you have learned.

5 Write an article for your local newspaper which regularly invites local people to describe what they like about the area where they live and explain why it is special to them.

In your article you should:

- describe where you live
- describe what you like about living there
- explain why the area is special to you.

OR 6 Write a letter to your MP arguing that more money needs to be spent on facilities for teenagers in your local area.

In your letter you should:

- make clear your opinion
- give reasons to support it
- explain why you think the MP should agree with your point of view.

Progress check

1. Use the mark scheme on the facing page to give yourself a mark for AO5 and AO6.
2. Use the grid below to help you assess whether you have met the targets you set yourself in Activity 1 on the facing page.

Focus	Not met	Partly met	Fully met
The response is paragraphed.			
Paragraphs use topic sentences.			
The opening is attention-grabbing.			
The last sentence is impactful and leaves the reader thinking.			
Cohesive devices are used between paragraphs.			
Cohesive devices are used within paragraphs.			
Sentence structures are varied for effect.			
A wide range of punctuation is used accurately and for effect.			
Vocabulary is ambitious and interesting.			
Spelling is consistently accurate.			
The tone is appropriate for the task.			
The language is appropriate for the audience.			
Ideas are communicated clearly.			
The form is appropriate.			
Rhetorical devices have been used effectively.			

Component 02 Exploring effects and impact

Section A: Reading meaning and effects

What is the content and focus of this section?

Key term

theme a key idea or issue that the text is concerned with

In Component 02, Section A: Reading meaning and effects assesses your ability to read and respond to prose fiction. In this section you will have to answer four questions based on two unseen prose texts from the 20th and/or 21st centuries, such as extracts from novels and short stories. The texts will be linked by **theme** and one text may be an extract from a literary non-fiction text such as an autobiography.

How to use your time in the exam

Section A of this exam is worth 40 marks and will form 25% of your total GCSE grade. The four reading questions will increase in challenge, moving from short- to medium-length response questions on either Text 1 or Text 2 to a final more detailed task which asks you to evaluate and compare the two texts you have read. You are advised to spend an hour on this section, although you might choose to spend longer on it. The grid below suggests how you might allocate your time.

Question and approach	Marks available	Suggested timing
Initial read of the texts and questions		Approximately 5–10 minutes
Question 1: Re-read the part of the text indicated in the question before answering.	4 marks	Approximately 5 minutes
Question 2: Re-read the part of the text indicated in the question before answering.	6 marks	Approximately 10 minutes
Question 3: Re-read the part of the text indicated in the question before answering.	12 marks	Approximately 15 minutes
Question 4: Skim and scan both texts before answering.	18 marks	Approximately 20–25 minutes

How will my reading be assessed?

The grid below sets out the Assessment Objectives (AOs) that you will be assessed on in Section A of Component 02. An initial explanation of each Assessment Objective is provided as well as an indication of which question(s) will assess it, but a more detailed explanation is provided in the chapters that follow.

Assessment Objective		What does this mean?	Where you will apply this skill
A01 (i)	Identify and interpret explicit and implicit information and ideas	Find specific information or ideas in the text. This information may be explicit or implicit. Where the information is implicit, you will have to infer and interpret this to show your understanding.	Question 1: you will be asked to identify specific words, phrases, quotations or examples from Text 1 and explain what is suggested by them.
A02	Explain, comment on and analyse how writers use language and structure to achieve effects and influence readers, using relevant subject terminology to support their views	Analyse how a writer uses language (i.e. words, phrases, language features and techniques) and structure (i.e. sentences, punctuation, paragraphs and structural features) to achieve specific effects and influence the reader. Use the correct terminology (e.g. metaphor, verb, etc.) when explaining how a writer uses these techniques.	Questions 2 and 3: you will be asked to explore how language and structure are used to produce a particular effect such as conveying a mood or influencing how the reader feels about a character. Note that Question 2 will be about a specific section of Text 1 and Question 3 will be about a specific section of Text 2.
A03	Compare writers' ideas and perspectives, as well as how these are conveyed, across two or more texts	Compare different writers' thoughts and feelings and the ways in which they put these across.	Question 4: you will be asked to compare how Texts 1 and 2 present a particular idea or theme.
A04	Evaluate texts critically and support this with appropriate textual references	Appraise texts in a considered and analytical way, quoting or referring closely to the texts to justify your ideas.	Question 4: you will be asked to evaluate Texts 1 and 2 in relation to a statement, discussing your impressions in relation to this and explaining the impact of the texts on a reader.

Mark scheme

For Question 1, which is worth 4 marks, the examiner will award marks for specific points or quotations which will be listed in the mark scheme. However, for Questions 2, 3 and 4 your answers will be awarded a level from 1 to 6, with Level 1 being the lowest and Level 6 the highest. Each level is summed up by key phrases which helps explain what a typical answer at this level looks like.

Level 6: Skilled analysis, sophisticated appreciation

Level 5: Analysis, perceptive understanding

Level 4: Developed explanation, secure understanding

Level 3: Clear explanation, general understanding

Level 2: Straightforward commentary, some understanding

Level 1: Descriptive response, limited awareness

As you work through this chapter, you will learn how to assess your own work and how to improve it to gain the highest mark that you can in the exam.

Reading an unseen prose text

Tip

Reading is a skill which you can develop in preparation for an exam. The more you read, the more fluent and adept you will become and this will save you time and increase your ability to respond effectively to texts in exam situations.

In the exam you will be given a Reading Insert Booklet that will contain two source texts. These will be referred to as Text 1 and Text 2 and might be extracts from a novel, a short story or literary non-fiction such as an autobiography or memoir. Each text will have a brief introduction explaining where it comes from, when it was written and by whom, and definitions for any difficult vocabulary may be provided at the end of each text. You cannot predict what these prose texts will be and it is unlikely you will have read them before.

Reading a wide range of fiction and literary non-fiction will help you to develop the skills you need to read and respond to the unseen prose texts you will encounter in the exam. Try to make time to reflect on your reading and think analytically about the novels, short stories, autobiographies and memoirs you have read. You could use some of the following ideas to extend your reading experience.

- Read different genres and authors.
- Ask friends, teachers, librarians and booksellers for recommendations.
- Read reviews of books in newspapers and magazines.
- Use online book review sites to find recommendations.

At the start of each text there will be an introduction (usually in italics) explaining where the text is taken from and what the text is about. Always read this introduction as it will help you to understand what you are about to read.

Key term

setting the place and time where the story occurs

Activity 1

1. **Read the introduction to Source text A on the facing page. Before you read the rest of Source text A, write down and discuss your ideas about what might happen in the text.**
2. **Read Source text A, then copy and complete a reading log like the one below to record your ideas about the extract. You could create a similar reading log to record your responses to your own wider reading.**

Reading log	
Author and title	Michael Parkinson
Genre, e.g. fiction, autobiography, etc.	
Narrative viewpoint (e.g. first or third person)	
Content, e.g. events and characters	
Setting	
Themes	'Growing up, childhood'
What I noticed about the language	
What I noticed about the structure	
Personal response	I thought it was amusing when he describes the lift being dropped quickly to scare him.

Source text A

The following extract is taken from Michael Parkinson's autobiography. Michael Parkinson was a sports journalist and, later in his career, a famous talk show host. Here, he describes how his father took him to see the coal mine where he worked.

Every morning, when I woke, I could see the pit from my bedroom window. When you couldn't see it you could smell it, an invisible sulphurous presence. It was where my dad worked, where my granddad worked and his dad before him. It was where I expected to end up. I remember thinking it wouldn't bother me, providing I could marry **Ingrid Bergman** and get a house much nearer the pit gates. Shortly after **Vesting Day**, when **Attlee**'s government nationalised the mines, we were taken from Barnsley Grammar School to visit a Colliery. When I arrived home my father asked me where I had been. I told him. He said, "That's not a pit, it's a holiday camp."

He told me to be ready, 4 a.m. the following Sunday, and he would show me what a real coal mine was like. He took me down Grimethorpe Colliery and tipped the wink to his mate on the winding gear that there was a tourist on board. We dropped like a man without a parachute. Big laugh. The rest wasn't so funny. He took me where men worked on their knees getting coal, showed me the lamp he used to test for methane gas, explained how dangerous it was. He showed me the pit ponies. The only time I had seen them before was when they had their annual holiday from their work underground and emerged from the dark, their eyes bandaged against the light.

We stood in front of a seam of coal, black and shiny. "Let's see if you'd make a miner," he said. He gave me a pick and nodded at the seam. The harder I hit the coal, the more the pick bounced off the surface. "Find the fault," he said, running his fingers across the coal face. He tapped it and a chunk fell out, glittering in his lamplight. We walked back and he said nothing until we reached the pit gates.

"What do you reckon?" he said.

"You won't get me down there for a hundred quid a shift," I said.

Glossary

Ingrid Bergman a famous film star

Vesting Day the day government took ownership of the coal mines

Attlee Clement Attlee, the Prime Minister from 1945 to 1951

Reading: Question 1

AO1 Identify and interpret explicit and implicit information and ideas

Key term

ideas the information, experiences, opinions or arguments in a text

Tip

Make sure you only look at the lines you have been directed towards. If your evidence is taken from elsewhere in the text, you will not be awarded any marks. If you are asked to explain what the phrase or quotation suggests to you, you should use your own words to show that you understand and can interpret what you have read.

An overview of the question

Question 1 refers to the first text you will have read in your exam (Text 1) and is worth 4 marks. It assesses AO1 and is designed to test that you can select particular **ideas** or information from a specific section of the text. The question could be divided into two or more parts, e.g. 1a), 1b) and 1c).

In the question:

- You will be told to look again at a specific section of the text with line numbers given to guide you.
- You will be asked to identify key information, phrases, quotations or examples from this section of text which convey a certain idea or information.
- You may also be asked to explain, in your own words, how these phrases convey this idea or information.

Don't over-complicate your answer to Question 1. Examiners understand that, at the start of an exam, you may need to build your confidence and familiarity with the text by answering a relatively straightforward question.

How will my answer be assessed?

There are no levels for answers to Question 1 in the mark scheme. You will be allocated up to a maximum of 4 marks for the correct information you identify and interpret.

Look at the example Question 1 below. The annotations give you further guidance on how to approach each part of the question.

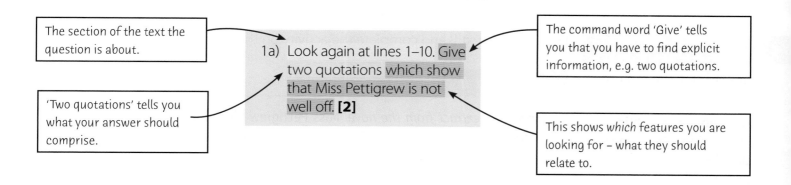

The section of the text the question is about.

'Two quotations' tells you what your answer should comprise.

1a) Look again at lines 1–10. Give two quotations which show that Miss Pettigrew is not well off. **[2]**

The command word 'Give' tells you that you have to find explicit information, e.g. two quotations.

This shows *which* features you are looking for – what they should relate to.

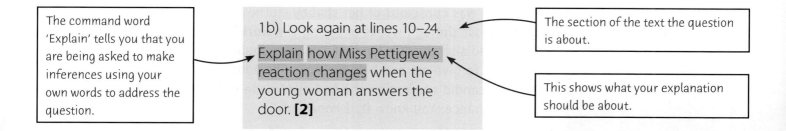

The command word 'Explain' tells you that you are being asked to make inferences using your own words to address the question.

1b) Look again at lines 10–24.

Explain how Miss Pettigrew's reaction changes when the young woman answers the door. **[2]**

The section of the text the question is about.

This shows what your explanation should be about.

Identifying explicit and implicit information

Glossary

gentility belonging to the upper classes

workhouse a public institution where poor people could live and work

benevolence kindness

Read Source text B and complete the activity on the facing page.

Source text B

This is an extract from the novel Miss Pettigrew Lives for a Day *by Winifred Watson, first published in 1938. Here, Miss Pettigrew, a middle-aged governess in need of work, is sent by her employment agency to the home of Miss LaFosse in the hope of securing a job with her.*

Miss Pettigrew went to the bus-stop to await a bus. She could not afford the fare, but she could still less afford to lose a possible situation by being late. The bus deposited her about five minutes' walk from Onslow Mansions, and at seven minutes to ten precisely she was outside her destination.

It was a very exclusive, very opulent, very intimidating block of flats. Miss Pettigrew was conscious of her shabby clothes, her faded **gentility**, her courage lost through weeks of facing the **workhouse**. She stood a moment. She prayed silently. "Oh Lord! If I've ever doubted your **benevolence** in the past, forgive me and help me now. She added a rider to her prayer, with the first candid confession she had ever made to her conscious mind. "It's my last chance. You know it. I know it."

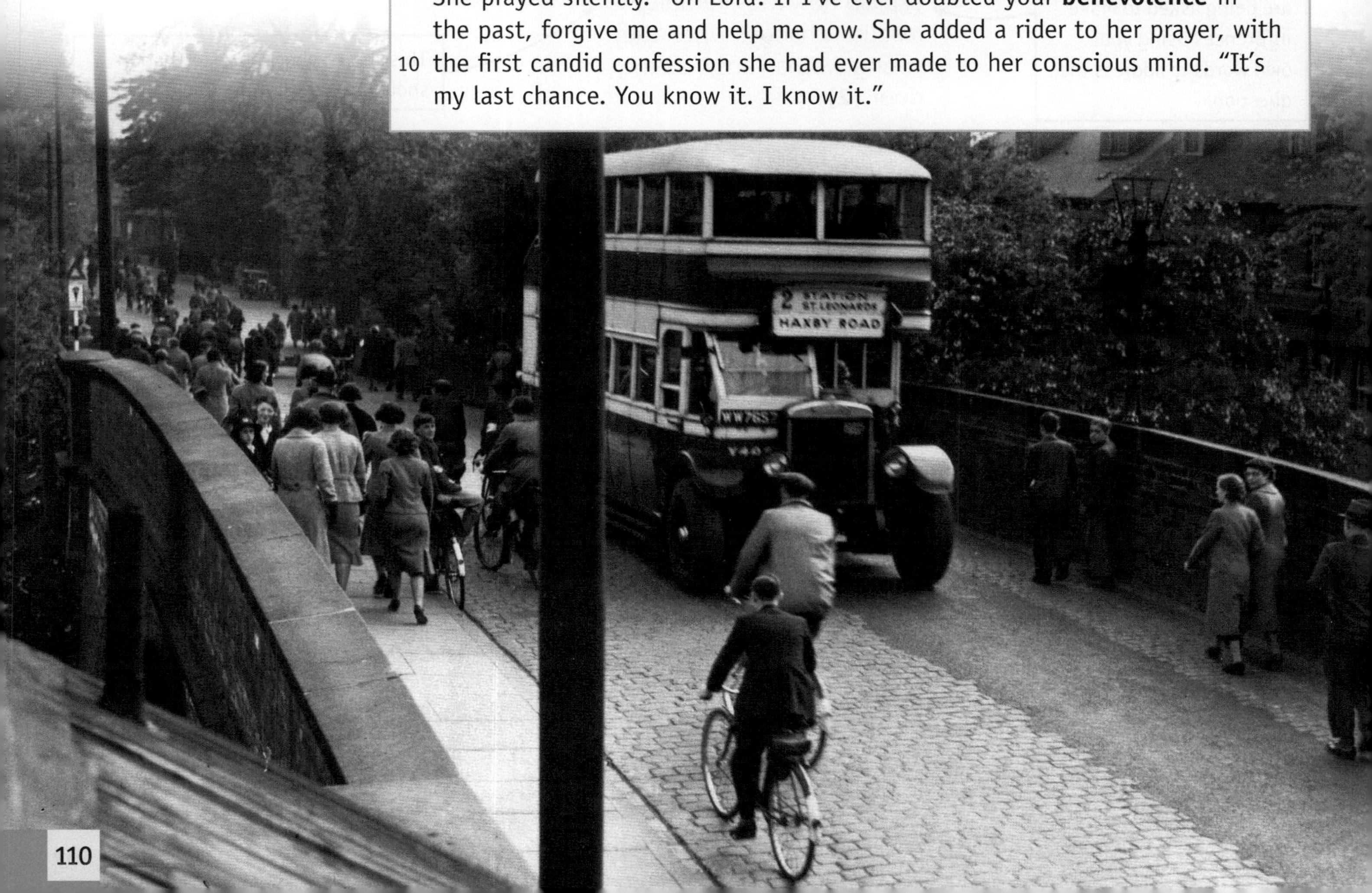

Some information in a text is **explicit** which means that it is obvious or clear to the reader. Other information and ideas are **implicit** which means you need to 'read between the lines' to **interpret** what is implied by the writer's words. For example:

Explicit information: Miss LaFosse lives in a flat, 'very intimidating block of flats.'

Implicit information: Miss Pettigrew is not well-off, 'She could not afford the fare.'

Key terms

explicit stating something openly and exactly

implicit implied but not stated openly

interpret to explain the meaning of something said or written

Activity 1

Look again at lines 1–7. Identify one other phrase which shows that Miss Pettigrew is not well off.

Try it yourself WITH SUPPORT

Now you are going to practise using your skills in response to Question 1. You will be given some support to help you do this.

Read the next section from Winifred Watson's novel *Miss Pettigrew Lives for a Day* on the facing page and then look at the example Question 1 below.

1 Look again at lines 10–24.

a) Identify one phrase from these lines which shows how Miss Pettigrew is impressed by Miss LaFosse. **[1]**

b) Explain what this shows about Miss Pettigrew's life. **[1]**

c) Give two examples of how Miss LaFosse reminds Miss Pettigrew of a film star. **[2]**

Activity 2

1. Look at the following quotation used in a student's answer to Question 1a). Discuss how effective you think the phrase selected is.

   'To see one of these lovely visions in the flesh was almost more than she could believe.'

2. Identify a shorter phrase you think the student could have selected from lines 10–24 in order to answer the question.
3. Now look at the same student's answer to Question 1b). Explain in your own words what you think the shorter phrase you have selected shows about Mrs Pettigrew's life.

   This shows that Miss Pettigrew is amazed at Miss LaFosse's appearance and that as a rule she does not meet very many glamorous people.

4. Here is the same student's answer to Question 1c). Give another example of how Miss LaFosse reminds Miss Pettigrew of a film star.

   Miss LaFosse is very beautiful and wears the kind of clothes Miss Pettigrew expects a film star to wear.

Tip

Try to avoid copying out long quotations unless the correct phrase is clearly indicated, i.e. by underlining it.

Source text C

She went in. A porter in the hall eyed her questioningly. Her courage failed at ringing for the lift so she mounted the main stairway and looked around until she discovered No. 5. A little plate on the door said Miss LaFosse. She looked at her watch, inherited from her mother, waited until it said precisely ten, then rang.

There was no answer. She rang again. She waited and rang again. She was not normally so assertive, but fear gave her the courage of desperation. She rang, on and off, for five minutes. Suddenly the door flew open and a young woman stood in the entry.

Miss Pettigrew gasped. The creature was so lovely she called to mind immediately beauties of the screen. Her golden, curly hair tumbled untidily about her face. Sleep was still heavy in her eyes, blue as **gentians**. The lovely rose of youth flushed her cheeks. She wore that kind of foamy robe, no mere dressing-gown, worn by the most famous of stars in seduction scenes in the films. Miss Pettigrew was well versed in the etiquette of dress and behaviour of young women on the screen.

In a dull, miserable existence her one wild extravagance was her weekly **orgy** at the cinema, where for over two hours she lived in an enchanted world peopled by beautiful women, handsome heroes, fascinating villains, charming employers, and there were no bullying parents, no appalling offspring, to tease, torment, terrify, harry her every waking hour. In real life she had never seen any woman arrive to breakfast in a silk, satin and lace **negligé**. *Everyone* did on the films. To see one of these lovely visions in the flesh was almost more than she could believe.

But Miss Pettigrew knew fright when she saw it. The young woman's face, when she opened the door, had been rigid with apprehension. At the sight of Miss Pettigrew it grew radiant with relief.

Glossary

gentians deep blue flowers

orgy unlimited indulgence

negligé a lightweight robe made of very fine fabric

Try it yourself **ON YOUR OWN**

Look again at Source text C on page 113. Write your response to the Question 1 task below, applying all the skills you have learned.

1 Look again at lines 1–5.

a) Identify two quotations which show how Miss Pettigrew behaves when she arrives at Onslow Mansions. **[2]**

b) What do these suggest about her character? **[2]**

Progress check

Read Source text D, another extract from *Miss Pettigrew Lives for a Day*, which directly follows on from Source text C.

1. Create your own Question 1 to assess AO1: Identify and interpret explicit and implicit information and ideas. This question should be divided into two parts, 1a) and 1b).
2. Create a mark scheme for your own Question 1 by listing the points that would be given a mark.
3. Swap questions with a partner and answer their Question 1.
4. Using the mark schemes, mark each other's answers. Give feedback on how your partner could improve their answer.
5. Copy and complete the following grid to assess how confident you are in using the skills required to answer Question 1. Reflect on the activities you have completed in this section and, for each skill, give yourself a confidence rating from one to five, with five being very confident.

Skill	Confidence rating (1–5)
Selecting phrases and quotations to identify explicit information and ideas	
Interpreting implicit information and ideas and explaining these in your own words	

Source text D

"I have come..." began Miss Pettigrew nervously.

"What time is it?"

"It was prompt ten when I first rang. The hour you named, Miss... Miss LaFosse? I have been ringing for about five minutes. It is now five-past ten."

"My God!"

Miss Pettigrew's surprising interrogator swung round and disappeared back into the room. She did not say come in, but for a gentlewoman to face destitution was a very serious crisis: Miss Pettigrew found courage, walked in and shut the door behind her.

"At least I shall ask for an interview," thought Miss Pettigrew.

She saw the whisk of draperies disappear through another door and heard a voice saying urgently,

"Phil. Phil. You lazy hound. Get up. It's half-past ten."

"Prone to exaggerate," thought Miss Pettigrew. "Not a good influence for children at all."

She now had time to take in her surroundings. Brilliant cushions ornamented more brilliant chairs and chesterfield. A deep, velvety carpet of strange, futuristic design, decorated the floor. Gorgeous, breathtaking curtains draped the windows. On the walls hung pictures not... not quite decent, decided Miss Pettigrew. Ornaments of every colour and shape adorned mantelpiece, table and stands. Nothing matched anything else. Everything was an exotic brilliance that took away the breath.

"Not the room of a lady," thought Miss Pettigrew. "*Not* the kind of room my dear mother would have chosen."

Reading: Question 2

AO2 Explain, comment on and analyse how writers use language and structure to achieve effects and influence readers, using relevant subject terminology to support their views

Tip

As with Question 1, only look at the lines you have been directed towards. If your evidence is taken from elsewhere in the text, you will not be awarded any marks. Remember to include relevant quotations and textual references in your answer.

An overview of the question

Question 2 refers to the first text you will have read in your exam (Text 1) and is worth 6 marks. It assesses AO2 and is designed to test that you can analyse how writers use language and structure to achieve specific effects and influence the reader in a certain way.

In the question:

- You will told to look again at a specific section of the text with line numbers given to guide you.
- You will need to find relevant examples of vocabulary, language techniques and structural features that help you to answer the question.
- You will need to analyse the examples you find, demonstrating your understanding of their effects and using relevant terminology.
- You will need to make sure you refer to both language and structure in your response, striking a reasonable balance in your analysis.

This question is worth 6 marks, but you should not spend too much time on it at the expense of Questions 3 and 4, which are worth many more marks. Whilst the question may not direct you to 'Support your response with quotations' or 'Support your ideas by referring to the language and structure of this section', you should still refer to the text and include relevant quotations in your response to help you to answer the question.

Look at the example Question 2 below. The annotations give you further guidance on how to approach the question.

The section of the text the question is about.

The question phrase 'How does' tells you that you have to analyse and explain.

This tells you that you need to use subject terminology in your response.

In the exam, you will be given ten blank lines to write your answer but this is just a guide. Depending on your handwriting style you could write more or less.

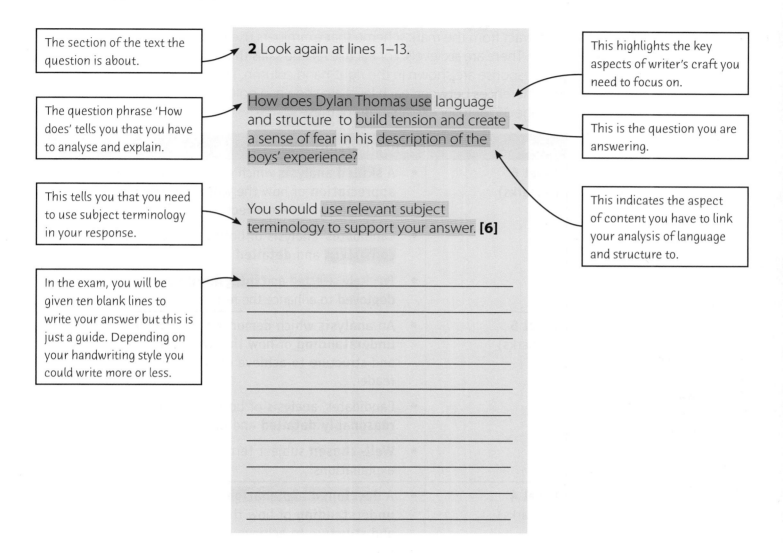

2 Look again at lines 1–13.

How does Dylan Thomas use language and structure to build tension and create a sense of fear in his description of the boys' experience?

You should use relevant subject terminology to support your answer. **[6]**

____

____

____

____

____

____

____

____

____

____

This highlights the key aspects of writer's craft you need to focus on.

This is the question you are answering.

This indicates the aspect of content you have to link your analysis of language and structure to.

How will my answer be assessed?

An extract from the mark scheme that examiners use to mark Question 2 is shown below. There are six levels. For each level, the skills that you have to demonstrate in your response are shown in the right-hand column. The key words which identify the differences between each level are shown in bold. Look back at the annotations on page 35 for fuller explanations of these.

Level	Skills descriptor
Level 6 (6 marks)	• A **skilled analysis** which demonstrates a **sophisticated appreciation** of how the writer has used language and structure to achieve effects and influence the reader. • Candidates' analysis of both language and structure is **consistent** and **detailed**. • Precisely selected and **integrated** subject terminology **deployed** to enhance the response.
Level 5 (5 marks)	• An **analysis** which demonstrates a **perceptive understanding** of how the writer has used language and structure to achieve effects and influence the reader. • Candidates' analysis of both language and structure is **reasonably detailed** and **balanced**. • **Well-chosen** subject terminology **integrated** into explanations.
Level 4 (4 marks)	• A **developed explanation** which shows a **secure understanding** of how the writer has used language and structure to achieve effects and influence the reader. • Candidates **comment** on the effects of both language and structure, but the **explanation may not be entirely balanced.** • **Relevant terminology** should be used to develop ideas.

Level 3 (3 marks)	• A **clear explanation** which shows a **general understanding** of how the writer has used language and structure to achieve effects and influence the reader. Candidates refer to language and structure but **may not give a full explanation of the effects of both.** • **Some use of relevant subject terminology** to support ideas.
Level 2 (2 marks)	• A **straightforward commentary** which shows **some understanding** of how the writer has used language and structure to achieve effects and influence the reader. • Candidates are likely to refer more fully to **either language or structure** and **note some features without explaining their effects.** • Some use of subject terminology, though it may not always be relevant.
Level 1 (1 mark)	• A **descriptive response** which shows **limited awareness** of how the writer has used language and structure to achieve effects and influence the reader. • Little or no use of subject terminology.

Language features

When you answer Question 2, you need to be identify different language features and use subject terminology to describe these accurately. This might mean identifying grammatical features or literary techniques used in words or phrases.

Look at the grid below to remind yourself of some of the most common grammatical features used at word and phrase level. Remember, simply identifying a word class or sentence type is not in itself worthy of credit.

Word class	Definition	Example
Noun	A word used to name a person, place or thing	**Lizzie** ate her **toast** in the **kitchen.** My **dream** caused great **sadness.**
Adjective	A word which describes a noun	Maths is **easy.** She is very **determined.**
Verb	A word used to describe an action, feeling or state.	Tom **finished** his homework. The students **enjoyed** the show. **Leave** him **be.**
Tense	The tense of the verb tells you when the action of the verb takes place (present, past or future)	I **am washing** the car now. I **washed** the car yesterday. I **will wash** the car tomorrow.
Adverb	A word used with a verb, adjective or other adverb to describe how, when or where something happened	It was **strangely** quiet. **Sometimes** we have pizza for tea. We looked **everywhere.**
Adverbial	A group of words that function as an adverb	He worked **very hard.** The dog slept **under the table.**

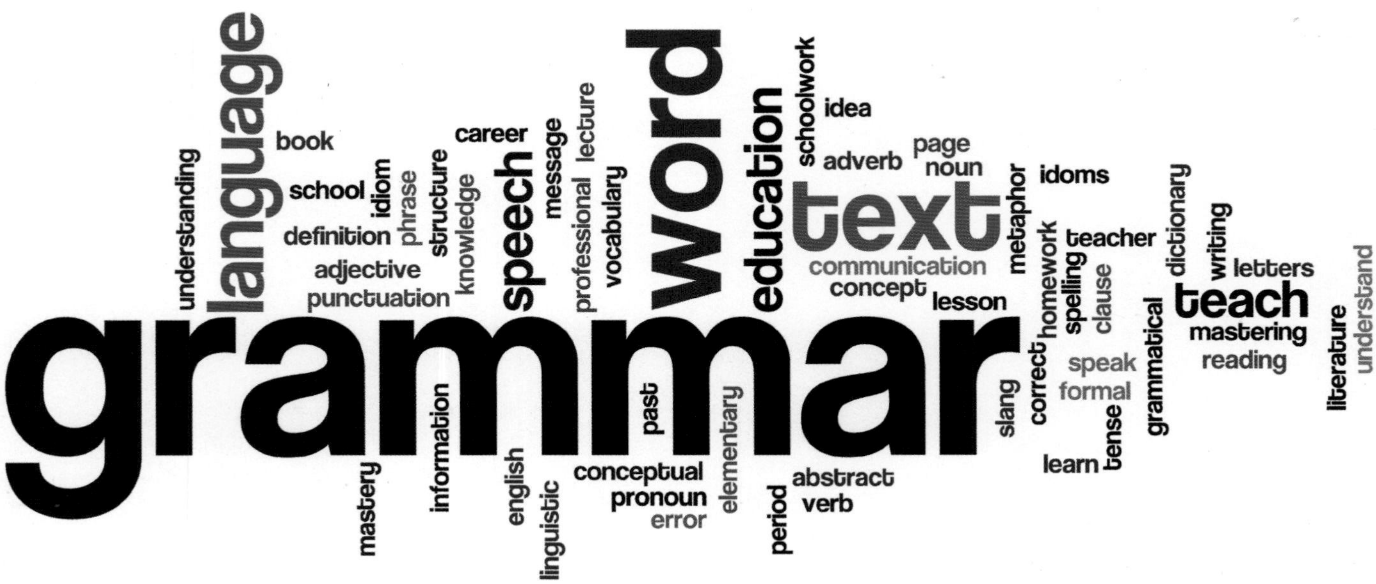

Activity 1

1. Look at the grid below to remind yourself of some of the most common literary techniques and add your own examples for each of these from your wider reading.
2. Try to add other literary techniques to this grid. Provide a definition and an example for any further techniques you can name.

Technique	Definition	Example
Alliteration	The repetition of the same letter or sound at the beginning of a group of words for special effect	Drab and depressing
Dialogue	Words spoken by characters in a play, film or story	"I can't work it out, can you?" "No, this kind of device was never my strong point," Jake replied.
Emotive language	Words and phrases that arouse emotion	This wasn't death; this was murder.
Hyperbole	Deliberately exaggerated statement	He was the size of an elephant.
Imagery/ descriptive detail	Writing which creates a picture or appeals to other senses, including simile, metaphor and personification, and the use of vivid verbs, nouns, adjectives and adverbs	We knew the house smelt fusty and dank but we didn't expect the lacy cobwebs and the oozing walls.
Irony	The use of words that mean the opposite of what is really intended, done for emphasis or humour.	The largest dog in the show was called Tiny.
Metaphor	A comparison where one thing is said to actually be another	He was a monkey in class.
Onomatopoeia	Words which imitate the sound they represent	Buzz, pop, crackle
Pathetic fallacy	When natural elements such as the weather or the landscape mirror the feelings of a character	The storm raged outside as she wept by the fire.
Personification	A form of metaphor whereby an inanimate object is given living qualities	The rocks reached for the sky.
Repetition	Words or phrases which are repeated for effect	She ran, ran for her life.
Rhetorical question	Question asked for dramatic effect and not intended to get an answer	Didn't I do the right thing?
Sibilance	The use of the 's' sound at the beginning or within neighbouring words	The geese seemed to whisper and snigger as he sidled past.
Simile	A comparison where one thing is compared to another, using the words 'like' or 'as ... as'	He was as quiet as a mouse.
Tricolon	Groups of three related words or phrases placed close together	The paint was peeling, the windows were cracked and the floorboards were rotting.

Structural features

When you answer Question 2, you also need to identify different structural features and use subject terminology to describe these accurately. Structural features can include the types of sentences, punctuation and paragraphs used.

When you look at the structure of a text, you should also explore the following aspects:

- the sequence through a text, i.e. how the narrative is organized
- the focus through a text, i.e. where the writer is directing the reader's attention
- the coherence of a text, i.e. the connections made between ideas, themes, characters, etc.

Use the questions in the grid below to help you to explore these aspects of structure in the texts you read.

Aspects of structure	Questions to ask yourself
Sequence	• Is the narrative told in chronological order or does it include flashback or non-chronological content? • How are characters, setting and events introduced? • Is there a key moment or climax which the author leads up to? • Are any elements of action, gesture, dialogue or description repeated within the text? • Can you spot any patterns or motifs?
Focus	• What narrative viewpoint is the story told from (i.e. first person, third person, etc.)? • How is the narrative spotlight placed on particular characters, events, places or feelings? • What is the balance between dialogue, action and description? • Can you identify any contrasts or opposites within the text? • Are there in shifts in mood, setting or perspective?
Coherence	• Are different parts of the text (such as the opening and ending) connected in any way? • Can you identify any links within or across paragraphs? • Are any paragraphs particularly long or short, or used to create a specific effect?

Activity 2

Look at a novel or short story you are reading. Re-read the opening two pages of it and use the questions in the table above to make notes about its structure.

Structure	Notes
Sequence	
Focus	
Coherence	

Activity 3

SPAG

1. Look at the grid below to remind yourself of some of the most common grammatical features at sentence level.

Structural features	Explanation	Example
Clause	Part of a sentence with its own verb	after she ran down the road
Simple sentence (single-clause sentence)	The most basic type of sentence consisting of a subject and a verb	The girl stood.
Compound sentence (a type of multi-clause sentence)	A sentence containing two independent clauses linked by a **conjunction**	The dog ate his dinner while I sat and watched.
Complex sentence (a type of multi-clause sentence)	A sentence containing a main clause and one or more subordinate clauses linked by a **subordinating conjunction** such as 'because', 'as', although' or a relative pronoun such as 'who', 'that' or 'which'.	The boy, who lived next door to me, was older than I was.

2. Look again at the opening two pages of the novel or short story you are reading. Find examples of any interesting structural features and explain the effects these create.

Key terms

conjunction word that links words, phrases and clauses

subordinating conjunction a word used to join two clauses which are not equal, e.g. although, as, before, once, though, until

Analysing language and structure

Read Source text E on the facing page and then look again at the example Question 2 below.

2 Look again at lines 1–13.

How does Dylan Thomas use language and structure to build tension and create a sense of fear in his description of the boys' experience?

You should use relevant subject terminology to support your answer.

Tip

Use some of the following words to link the quotation or language feature you have identified to your explanation of the effect it creates:

- adds
- creates
- suggests
- conveys
- evokes
- emphasizes

Tip

Make sure your explanation of the effects created is linked to the focus of the question. You could use some of the following synonyms for 'fear' and 'tension' in your explanation:

- suspense
- mystery
- threat
- anxiety
- unease
- dread
- terror

Activity 4

1. a) Which words and phrases do you think help to create a sense of fear in lines 1–13? Select three quotations that you think are the most effective.

b) Identify any language features that Thomas uses to build tension or add to the sense of fear in this section.

c) Using the examples you have found, copy and complete the grid below to explain the effects of the language features you have identified.

Quotation	Language feature	Effect

2. a) Read lines 1–13 again and pick out two sentences that you think help to build tension in this section.

b) Identify any other structural features that Thomas uses to build tension or add to the sense of fear in this section.

c) Using the examples you have found, copy and complete the grid below to explain the effects of the structural features you have identified.

Quotation	Structural feature	Effect

Source text E

This is an extract from A Child's Christmas in Wales *by Dylan Thomas, an autobiographical story first published in 1955. Here, a group of boys have decided to go carol-singing at a house they are afraid of.*

And I remember that we went singing carols once, a night or two before Christmas Eve, when there wasn't the shaving of a moon to light the secret, white-flying streets. At the end of a long road was a drive that led to a large house, and we stumbled up the darkness of the drive that night, each one of us afraid, each one holding a stone in his hand in case, and all of us too brave to say a word. The wind through the trees made noises as of old and unpleasant and maybe webfooted men wheezing in caves. We reached the black bulk of the house.

"What shall we give them? Hark the Herald?"

"No," Jack said, "Good King Wencelas. I'll count three."

One, two three, and we began to sing, our voices high and seemingly distant in the snow-felted darkness round the house that was occupied by nobody we knew. We stood close together, near the dark door.

Good King Wencelas looked out
On the Feast of Stephen ...

And then a small, dry voice, like the voice of someone who has not spoken for a long time, joined our singing: a small, dry, eggshell voice from the other side of the door: a small dry voice through the keyhole. And when we stopped running we were outside our house; the front room was lovely; balloons floated under the hot-water-bottle-gulping gas; everything was good again and shone over the town.

"Perhaps it was a ghost," Jim said.

"Perhaps it was trolls," Dan said, who was always reading.

"Let's go in and see if there's any jelly left," Jack said. And we did that.

Try it yourself WITH SUPPORT

Now you are going to practise using all your skills in a complete response to Question 2. Look back at your answers to Activity 4 on page 124 to help you do this.

Tip

Remember to link your analysis of specific aspects of language or structure to the question you have been asked. Try to give an equal focus to your analysis of language and structure in your answer to this question.

2 Look again at lines 1–13.

How does Dylan Thomas use language and structure to build tension and create a sense of fear in his description of the boys' experience?

You should use relevant subject terminology to support your answer.

Improving your answer

To achieve Level 4 in an AO2 question like this, your answer should provide a developed explanation which shows a secure understanding of how language and structure are used to achieve effects and influence the reader. Look at Student A's response below:

Student A

The writer uses **alliteration** to emphasize how threatening the house is; 'the black bulk' suggests that it is huge and dark. The **short sentence** at the end of the first paragraph shows that they have suddenly reached their destination. The use of 'we' and 'us' makes the writing seem personal and real. The **simile**, which compares the wind to 'old and unpleasant and maybe webfooted men wheezing in caves', makes us think that the weather adds to their fear. The writer **uses** the words 'each one' which shows that they are all as frightened as each other. The **metaphor** 'snow-felted darkness' creates an **image** of a blanket of snow.

This would be a Level 4 response because:

- the explanation is 'developed' and demonstrates a 'secure understanding' of how language and structure are used to achieve effects, as shown by the parts of the response that are underlined
- the student does comment on language and structure but the explanation is not 'entirely balanced' because features of language are referred to more than structural features
- the student uses 'relevant subject terminology', shown in **bold** in the response, to 'develop ideas'.

To improve this response the student needs to:

- develop their analysis in more detail
- demonstrate a more perceptive or sophisticated understanding of the effects achieved
- include more analysis of structural features
- use more precise and extended subject terminology which is better integrated into the response.

Activity 5

Rewrite Student A's response so that it achieves a Level 5 or Level 6. Think about:

- which points you could develop in more detail
- which additional structural features you could analyse
- the way you express ideas to demonstrate a more perceptive understanding of the effects achieved
- how you could integrate subject terminology more effectively.

Look back at the mark scheme on pages 118–119 to help you.

Tip

Make sure you focus on what the question is asking you to explore. For example in this question you are being asked about how tension and a sense of fear are created.

To achieve Level 6 in an AO2 question like this, your answer should provide a skilled analysis which shows a sophisticated appreciation of how language and structure are used to achieve effects and influence the reader. Look at another response.

Student B

The boys' approach to the house takes the form of a **long, rambling sentence** which could suggest that they felt it took ages to reach the house because they were frightened. The **very short sentence** at the end of the first paragraph reflects the way they are forced to come to a sudden halt when they reach the door. **Repetition** of 'each one' draws our attention to the fact that they are all as frightened as each other. The **narrative viewpoint** is **first person plural** which makes the extract feel personal as if we are on the journey with the boys. The **simile** which compares the wind to 'old and unpleasant and maybe webfooted men wheezing in caves' also **personifies** the wind and makes it seem ancient and threatening. The **phrase** 'all of us too brave to say a word' is **ironic** because the boys don't want to admit to being scared and are only pretending to be brave.

This would be a Level 6 response because:

- the analysis demonstrates a sophisticated appreciation of the effects achieved and how the reader is influenced by specific features of language and structure as shown by the parts of the response that are underlined
- the analysis of both language and structure is consistent and detailed
- the subject terminology used is deployed in a way that that enhances the analysis, demonstrating a precise understanding of the technique or feature and its effect in the text.

Activity 6

Student B's response analyses lines 1–13. Continue Student B's response, addressing the rest of the text (lines 14–24). Can you keep the response in Level 6?

Progress check

1. Swap your response to Question 2 with a partner. Use the mark scheme on pages 118–119 to award a level to their response.
2. Discuss the level awarded. What improvements could be made to the response?
3. How confident are you now in using the skills required by Question 2? Complete the self-assessment below to reflect on your progress.

Skill	I am confident that I can do this	I think I can do this but need a bit more practice	This is one of my weaker areas, so I need more practice
I can identify language features in a text.			
I can comment on and analyse how the writer has used language to achieve effects.			
I can identify structural features in a text.			
I can comment on and analyse how the writer has used structure to achieve effects.			
I can use precise subject terminology to develop and enhance the response.			

4. Pick out one skill that you would like to target for improvement. Plan how you will improve that skill and monitor your progress. For example:

Plan – practise analysing the structure of extracts from novels, short stories and autobiographies I read outside the classroom.

Monitor – keep a reading log to record the structural features I identify and my comments on the effects these create for me as a reader.

Try it yourself ON YOUR OWN

Read Source text F on the facing page and write your response to the Question 2 task below, applying all the skills you have learned.

2 Look again at lines 1–20.

How does Julie Walters use language and structure to make her description of Cissie's and Luke's experience suspenseful?

You should use relevant subject terminology to support your answer.

Source text F

This text is from Maggie's Tree, *a novel by Julie Walters published in 2006. Here, Cissie and Luke are searching for their friend, Maggie, who has gone missing during a trip to New York.*

Cissie and Luke are standing in silence, watching as the giant flakes swirl and dive to their extinction on the black, oily surface of the Hudson. It is uncertain which of them sees her first but neither speaks as the pale form floats into view: a strange shape, encrusted with snow and illuminated by the cold grey night lights of an empty pleasure-cruiser. It could be a bag of rubbish, it could be; but that is unmistakably a shoulder and that is unmistakably a neck, a jawline, an upper arm. They both step forward at the same time, their right feet in unison, and lean over the balustrade, destroying its snowy cover.

"What's...?"

"It looks..."

It is now bobbing and bumping against the pleasure-cruiser, nudging for attention, a helping hand, a drop of kindness. Cissie spots a set of steps leading down to a lower landing stage, but the way is barred by a thick chain fluffed with snow. She leaps it without disturbing a flake, leaving the thing hanging motionless like some bizarre Christmas decoration, then springs down the steps, landing perilously on the wharf. She is now only four or five feet above the water and, leaning as far forward as she safely can, she peers out into the darkness. The water is bringing it closer. She can see the long hair just below the surface. It is blond.

"Nooo!" Her voice is small and gruff.

"What? For God's sake be careful." Luke has stayed at the top. "Look, we can call the police."

The snow is now darting aggressively, hitting her eyes before she can blink; she doesn't hear Luke, she remains fixed, unable to avert her gaze from the body. It is now just ten or twelve feet from her and is moving from shadow into light; at last she can see it. It is floating rigidly on its front, the head is tilted round to the side but the face is obscured by snow, the right arm is partly raised as if she were doing the Australian crawl and has become frozen in midstroke.

"It's a bloody shop dummy."

There is no left arm. There are no legs. All at once a tiny avalanche and one side of its face is visible: the lips are a full cupid's bow, a perfect button nose, and the right eye partially closed, the lid trimmed by thick black lashes.

Reading: Question 3

AO2 Explain, comment on and analyse how writers use language and structure to achieve effects and influence readers, using relevant subject terminology to support their views

Tip

Think about what aspect of the text Question 3 is asking you to analyse. Mark the beginning and end of the section of text you have been asked to look at and then annotate this section as you are re-reading. This might involve underlining or highlighting relevant quotations and adding explanatory notes around the text.

An overview of the question

Question 3 refers to the second text you will have read in your exam (Text 2) and is worth 12 marks. It assesses AO2 and is designed to test that you can analyse how writers use language and structure to achieve specific effects and influence the reader in a certain way.

In the question:

- You will be told to look at a specific section of the text, with line numbers given to guide you. In Question 3, the section of text you will be asked to analyse will be longer than in Question 2.
- You will be asked to explore or analyse the way in which the writer presents a particular character, theme, setting or idea.
- You will need to find relevant examples of vocabulary, language techniques and structural features that help you to answer the question.
- You will need to analyse the examples you find, demonstrating your understanding of their effects and using relevant terminology.
- You will need to refer to both language and structure in your response, striking a reasonable balance in your analysis.

This question is worth 12 marks, twice as many marks as for Question 2, so you will be expected to write a longer and more detailed response. Typically the section of text you will asked be analyse will be about 20–30 lines long.

Look at the example Question 3 below. The annotations give you further guidance on how to approach the question.

The section of the text the question is about.

3 Look again at lines 1–26.

The command word 'Explore' tells you that you have to provide detailed analysis.

This indicates the aspect of content you have to link your analysis to.

Explore how the writer presents the build-up to the cycling accident in this extract.

Highlights the key aspects of writer's craft you need to focus on.

This tells you that you need to use subject terminology in your response.

Support your ideas by referring to the language and structure of this section, using relevant subject terminology. **[12]**

In the exam, you will be given 18 blank lines to write your answer but this is just a guide. Depending on your handwriting style you could write more or less.

How will my answer be assessed?

An extract from the mark scheme that examiners use to mark Question 3 is shown below. There are six levels. For each level, the skills that you have to demonstrate in your response are shown in the right-hand column. The key words that identify the differences between each level are shown in bold. Look back at the annotations on page 35 for fuller explanations of these. In each level you can be awarded a higher or lower mark; your answer will need to consistently meet the criteria set out in the skills descriptors to be awarded the higher mark.

Level	Skills descriptor
Level 6 (11–12 marks)	• A **skilled analysis** which demonstrates a **sophisticated appreciation** of how the writer has used language and structure to achieve effects and influence the reader. • Candidates' analysis of both language and structure is **consistent** and **detailed**. • **Precisely selected** and **integrated** subject terminology **deployed** to enhance the response.
Level 5 (9–10 marks)	• An **analysis** which demonstrates a **perceptive understanding** of how the writer has used language and structure to achieve effects and influence the reader. • Candidates' analysis of both language and structure is **reasonably detailed** and **balanced**. • **Well-chosen** subject terminology **integrated** into explanations.
Level 4 (7–8 marks)	• A **developed explanation** which shows a **secure understanding** of how the writer has used language and structure to achieve effects and influence the reader. • Candidates **comment** on the effects of both language and structure, but the **explanation may not be entirely balanced.** • **Relevant terminology** should be used to develop ideas.

Level 3 (5–6 marks)	• A **clear explanation** which shows a **general understanding** of how the writer has used language and structure to achieve effects and influence the reader. • Candidates refer to both language and structure but **may not give a full explanation** of the effects. • **Some use of relevant subject terminology** to support ideas.
Level 2 (3–4 marks)	• A **straightforward commentary** which shows some understanding of how the writer has used language and structure to achieve effects and influence the reader. • Candidates are likely to refer more fully to either language or structure and **note some features without explaining the effects.** • Some use of subject terminology, though it may not **always be relevant.**
Level 1 (1–2 marks)	• A **descriptive response** which shows **limited awareness** of how the writer has used language and structure to achieve effects and influence the reader. • **Little or no use** of subject terminology.

Exploring aspects of a text

In Question 3 you could be asked to analyse how a writer uses language and structure to present one or more of the following aspects of Text 2:

- Character
- Setting
- Relationships
- Mood
- Atmosphere
- Tone

Use the questions in the grid below to help you to explore some of these different aspects in the texts you read.

Character and relationships	• Which character or characters does the text focus on? Does this focus change at all within the text? • How is the character presented – through their actions, description and/or dialogue? • Do you as a reader have access to the character's thoughts and feelings? • What do the character's actions and/or dialogue reveal about their mood, attitudes or behaviour? • How does the character relate to others? Is there a contrast between specific characters? • How do you think the author wants you to feel towards this character? E.g. do you like or dislike them, sympathize with them or feel alienated from them?
Setting	• How is the setting described? • Is a sense of place and time clearly conveyed? • Does the setting change at all within the text? • How do characters respond to the setting? • How does the setting reflect the plot or characters? • How do you think the author wants you to feel about the setting? E.g. at ease, unsettled, threatened, etc.
Mood, atmosphere and tone	• What mood or atmosphere is created in the text? E.g. dark and threatening, bright and hopeful, etc. • How do the writer's language choices contribute to this? E.g. imagery, descriptive details, etc. • What emphasis is created by the sentence structures used? How do these reflect or contrast with the mood or atmosphere created? • Is the text full of action or do events unfold at a gentler pace? • Does the writer seem to be expressing a particular attitude or emotion in their writing? E.g. a sad tone, a disapproving tone, an optimistic tone, etc. • How does the text make you feel as a reader?

You will need to find examples of language techniques, grammatical features and structural devices which help to convey effectively the aspect of the text Question 3 asks you about. Remember that writers make decisions about the language they use and the way they choose to structure their writing in order to achieve specific effects and influence a reader's response to the text.

Activity 1

Look at a novel or short story you are reading. Choose two pages from this at random and re-read these. Then make notes about what you notice about:

- the way the main character is presented
- how the setting is conveyed
- the mood, atmosphere and **tone** created.

You could use the questions in the grid on the facing page to help you to make notes about these aspects of the text you have chosen. You could also look back at:

- the grids on pages 120–121 to remind yourself of some of the grammatical features and literary techniques you can comment on when analysing a writer's use of language
- the grids on pages 122–123 to remind yourself of some of the structural features you can comment on when analysing a writer's use of structure.

Key term

tone the writer's or narrator's attitude, which is implied through their language choices

Analysing structure

Remember that when you answer Question 3, you also need to identify different structural features and use subject terminology to describe these accurately. Structural features can include the types of sentences, punctuation and paragraphs used, and:

- the sequence through a text, i.e. how the narrative is organized
- the focus through a text, i.e. where the writer is directing the reader's attention
- the coherence of a text, i.e. the connections made between ideas, themes, characters, etc.

Look at Source text G, which begins on the facing page and continues on page 138. Then complete Activity 2 to explore how the structure of the text helps the writer to present the build-up to the narrator's cycling accident.

Activity 2

1. Look again at the first two sentences (lines 1–3).
   a) What do you think is the key word in each of these sentences? Think about what the writer wants you to focus on.
   b) How does this opening help to present the build-up to the narrator's cycling accident?
2. Now look again at the next three sentences (lines 3–7).
   a) What is the focus of these sentences?
   b) What links the sentence, 'Or, at least, without looking for a bike, because people don't look for bikes.' with the first sentence of the text?
   c) What do you now know about the narrator which you didn't know before and what do you think will happen next?
3. Now look again at the second paragraph (lines 8–16). This paragraph begins by describing accidents as 'tumbles' but then introduces an anecdote about a more serious accident. How does this change the mood of this paragraph?
4. Now look again at the third paragraph (lines 17–22). How is this paragraph structured to reflect the narrator's thoughts?
5. Now look again at the fourth paragraph (lines 23–30).
   a) How does this paragraph echo the first?
   b) Why do you think the writer refers to time and distance at this point in the story?
   c) How do the sentence structures used add to the impact of this paragraph?
6. Finally, look back at the whole text. Can you identify any patterns or **motifs**?

Key term

motif an element, idea or theme that is repeated throughout a text

Source text G

This text is taken from the novel, Until It's Over *by Nicci French, first published in 2007. Here, Astrid, a London cycle courier, is reflecting on the dangers of her job.*

I had cycled around London for week after week, month after month, and I knew that one day I would have an accident. The only question was, which kind? One of the other messengers had been heading along Regent Street at speed when a taxi had swung out to make a U-turn without looking. Or, at least, without looking for a bike, because people don't look for bikes. Don had hit the side of the taxi full on and woken up in hospital unable to recall his own name.

There's a pub, the Horse and Jockey, where a whole bunch of us despatch riders meet up on Friday evenings and drink and gossip and share stories and laugh about tumbles. But every few months or so there'd be worse news. The most recent was about the man who was cycling down near the Elephant and Castle. He was alongside a lorry that turned left without indicating and cut the corner. That's when the gap between the lorry and the kerb shrinks from about three feet to about three inches. All you can do is get off the road. But in that case there was an iron railing in the way. The next time I cycled past I saw that people had taped bunches of flowers to it.

When these accidents happen, sometimes it's the cyclist's fault and sometimes it isn't. I've heard stories of bus drivers deliberately ramming bikes. I've seen plenty of cyclists who think that traffic lights don't apply to them. But the person on the bike always comes off second best. Which is why you should wear a helmet and try to stay away from lorries and always assume that the driver is a blind, stupid psychopath.

Even so, I knew that one day I would have an accident. There were so many different kinds, and I thought the most likely was the one that was hardest to avoid or plan against. So it proved. But I never thought it would take place within thirty yards of my own house. As I turned into Maitland Road, I was about to swing my leg over the cross-bar. I was forty-five seconds from a hot shower and in my mind I was already off the bike and indoors, after six hours in the saddle, when a car door opened into the road in front of me, like the wing of a metal bird, and I hit it.

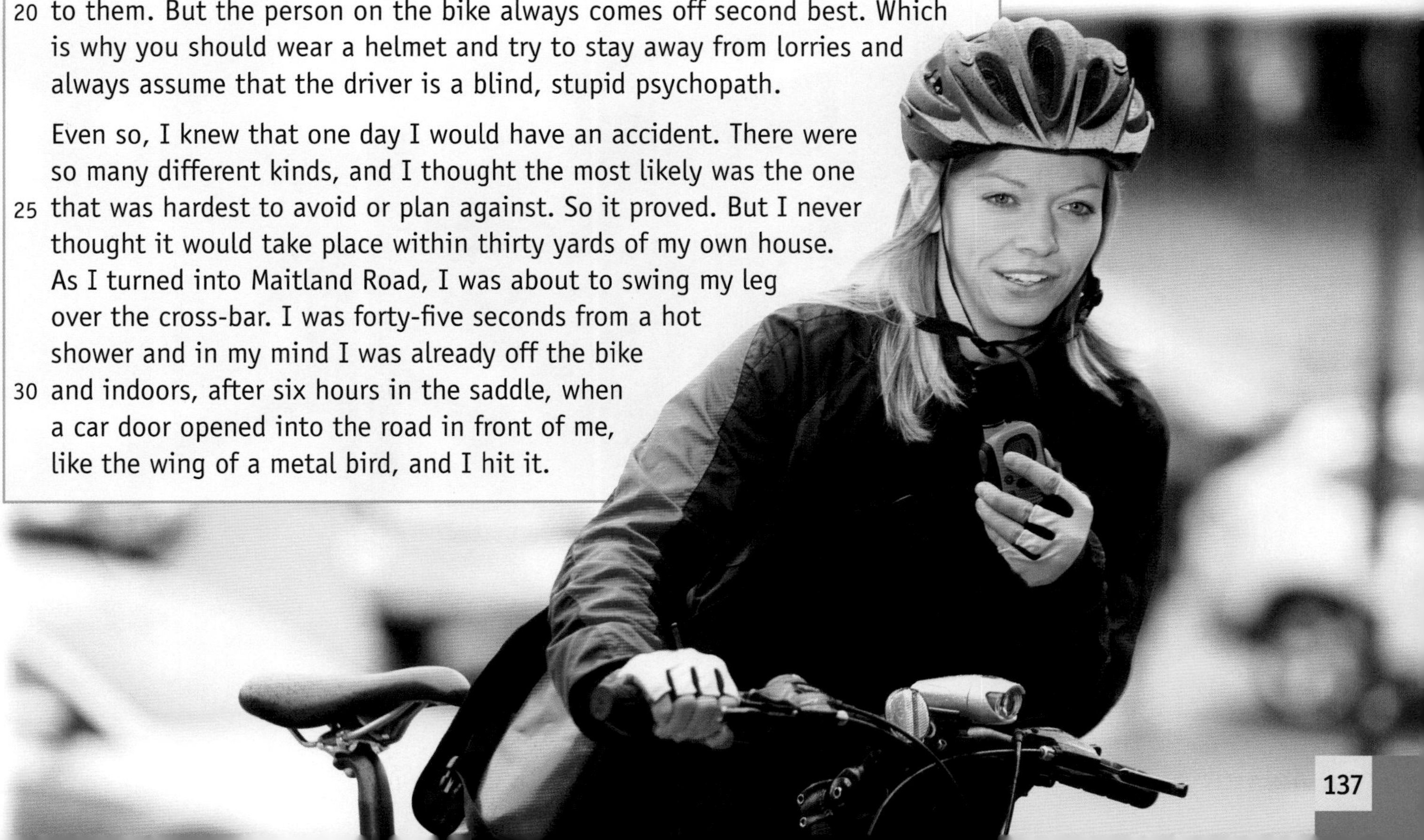

Source text G (continued)

There was no time for me to respond in any way, to swerve or to shield myself. And yet the events seemed to occur in slow motion. As my bike slammed against the door I was able to see that I was hitting it from the wrong direction: instead of pushing the door shut, I was pushing it further open. I felt it screech and bend but then stop as the momentum transferred itself from the door back to the bike and especially to the most mobile part of the bike, which was me. I remembered that my feet were in the stirrups and if they remained fastened, I would get tangled in the bike and might break both my legs. But then, as if in answer, my feet detached themselves, like two peas popped from a pod, and I flew over the door, leaving my bike behind.

Analysing language

In Question 3, you also need to be identify different language features and use subject terminology to describe these accurately. This might mean identifying grammatical features or literary techniques used in words or phrases.

Look back again at Source Text G on pages 137–138 and then complete Activity 3.

Tip

Look back again at the grids on pages 120–123 to remind yourself of some of the grammatical features and literary techniques you can comment on when analysing a writer's use of language.

Activity 3

For each paragraph, identify two language features used. Comment on how each one helps the writer to present the build-up to the narrator's cycling accident.

Copy and complete a grid like the one below and aim to develop your analysis in more detail as shown in the two examples from the first paragraph.

Quotation	Language feature	Comment	Further analysis
'week after week, month after month'	Repetition	Emphasizes how much cycling the narrator has been doing	Introduces the idea of the inevitability of the narrator's accident
'I knew that one day I would have an accident'	Verbs	The verb 'knew' suggests that the narrator thinks he will have an accident.	The modal verb 'would' emphasizes that the narrator believes this is certain.

Analysing language and structure

Remember that when you answer Question 3, you need to be able to develop your comments on language and structure into a balanced analysis. This means giving equal attention to language and structural features.

Activity 4

Using the notes you made in Activities 2 and 3, write a complete response to the following Question 3 on Source text G.

3 Look again at lines 1–26.

Explore how the writer presents the build-up to the narrator's accident.

Support your ideas by referring to the language and structure of this section, using relevant subject terminology. **[12]**

Improving your answer

To achieve Level 5 in an AO2 question like this, your answer should provide an analysis which shows a perceptive understanding of how language and structure are used to achieve effects and influence the reader. Look at Student A's response to this question.

Student A

The writer creates a sense of suspense when the narrator states 'I knew that one day I would have an accident'. The word 'knew' makes us feel that an accident is inevitable. This is followed by a rhetorical question, which makes us join the narrator in wondering how it will happen. The anecdotes about other serious cycling accidents then draw us into feeling the narrator must be about to get hurt – perhaps badly.

In the third paragraph, the writer uses some very powerful vocabulary to describe the drivers of vehicles – 'ramming bikes' and 'a blind stupid psychopath'. This makes us sympathize with cyclists and therefore with the narrator. She gives advice about staying safe on the road, 'you should wear a helmet' and this direct address draws us into feeling concerned for her safety.

At the beginning of the fourth paragraph, the clause 'I knew that one day I would have an accident' is repeated, echoing and reinforcing what was said in the first paragraph. The short sentence 'So it proved.' is very final and signals to the reader that the accident is about to happen. The writer mentions a very exact amount of time and distance – ' forty-five seconds from a hot shower' to show us how close the narrator was to home when the accident happened and this makes it seem all the more awful when it does happen. A simile is used to compare the car door, which opens to a bird's 'metal wing', and this seems to mirror the fact that the narrator then flies through the air. The final sentence of this section is a long, complex sentence made up of a series of details and ending with 'and I hit it'. Just like the accident, these final words seem very sudden.

Activity 5

1. This response is Level 5. Read the skills descriptor for this level and identify where the different skills are shown in the response.

Question 3	Skills descriptor
Level 5 (9–10 marks)	• An analysis which demonstrates a perceptive understanding of how the writer has used language and structure to achieve effects and influence the reader. • Candidates' analysis of both language and structure is reasonably detailed and balanced. • Well-chosen subject terminology integrated into explanations.

2. Discuss whether you think Student A's response should be given 9 or 10 marks. Give reasons for your decision. Remember, an answer has to consistently meet the criteria to be awarded the higher mark.

To improve this response, Student A would need to:

- further develop a sophisticated appreciation of how language and structure are used to create effects and influence the reader
- further develop the use of precisely selected and integrated subject terminology.

Activity 6

1. Rewrite Student A's response to improve it. Think about how you could incorporate some of the following points into the rewritten response:
   - When she says that 'people had taped bunches of flowers' to the railing where a man had an accident, alarm bells ring because flowers are symbolic of sympathy and we associate such scenes with death.
   - It is like we are bracing ourselves for the inevitable moment.
   - The placing of a full stop between 'second best' and 'Which' is grammatically incorrect, and so adds weight to the advice about wearing a helmet.
   - Writing from the first-person viewpoint makes us feel as if we are heading for the accident along with the narrator. It all feels very real.
   - Instead of saying that the cyclist died, we are told that 'there was an iron railing in the way' and this makes us imagine what happened to him in more detail.
   - We wonder if this advice could be ironic and if it will turn out that she is not wearing a helmet herself.
2. Look again at your answer to this question. Look back at the skills descriptors on pages 132–133 and decide what mark you would give the rewritten response.

Try it yourself WITH SUPPORT

Look at Source text H on pages 143–144. You are going to answer the following Question 3 about this text. You'll be given some support to help you do this.

3 Look again at lines 1–27.

Explore how the writer presents the narrator's attitude towards Manderley.

Support your ideas by referring to the language and structure of the text, using relevant subject terminology.

Source text H is taken from the opening of the novel *Rebecca* by Daphne Du Maurier. In the exam, the text you study could be taken from any part of a novel, short story or autobiography. Think about the focus of the question and how the structure of the text helps to present this.

Activity 7

1. **a)** Re-read each paragraph of the text and summarize in 10 words or fewer what the focus of this is.

b) Compare your paragraph summaries with a partner. What do these show you about the structure of the text?

2. Look again at the first sentence.

a) Do you think this is an effective opening? Give reasons for your answer.

b) What does this sentence suggest about the narrator's attitude to Manderley?

3. How do the sentence structures and punctuation used help structure the narrative so that we share the narrator's journey? You could also think about the references to direction and distance.

4. Copy and create an attitude graph like the one below to chart how the narrator's attitude towards Manderley is presented in the text. Identify a quotation from each paragraph and comment on what this suggests about the writer's attitude.

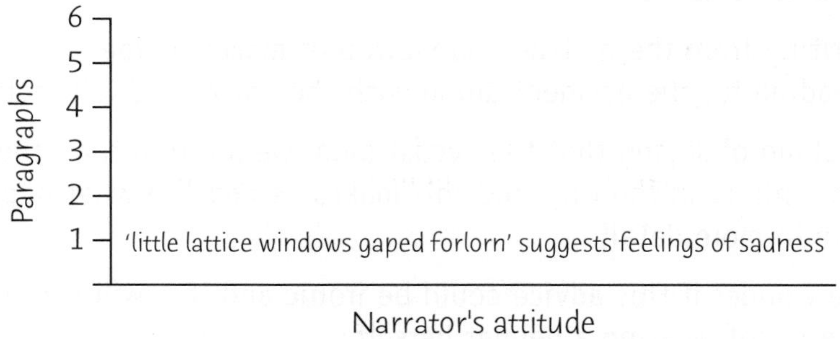

5. Identify any examples of repetition, patterns and contrasts in the text. Explain the effects these create.

Source text H

This text is taken from the opening of the novel Rebecca *by Daphne Du Maurier, first published in 1938. Here, the narrator, Mrs de Winter, describes a dream in which she returns to a grand house called Manderley.*

Last night I dreamt I went to Manderley again. It seemed to me I stood by the iron gate leading to the drive, and for a while I could not enter, for the way was barred to me. There was a padlock and a chain upon the gate. I called in my dream to the lodge-keeper, and had no answer, and peering closer through the rusted spokes of the gate I saw that the lodge was uninhabited. No smoke came from the chimney, and the little lattice windows gaped forlorn. Then, like all dreamers, I was possessed of a sudden with supernatural powers and passed like a spirit through the barrier before me.

The drive wound away in front of me, twisting and turning as it had always done, but as I advanced I was aware that a change had come upon it; it was narrow and unkept, not the drive that we had known. At first I was puzzled and did not understand, and it was only when I bent my head to avoid the low swinging branch of a tree that I realized what had happened. Nature had come into her own again and, little by little, in her stealthy, insidious way had encroached upon the drive with long, tenacious fingers.

The woods, always a menace even in the past, had triumphed in the end. They crowded, dark and uncontrolled, to the borders of the drive. The beeches with white, naked limbs leant close to one another, their branches intermingled in a strange embrace, making a vault above my head like the archway of a church. And there were other trees as well, trees that I did not recognize, squat oaks and tortured elms that straggled **cheek by jowl** with the beeches, and had thrust themselves out of the quiet earth, along with monster shrubs and plants, none of which I remembered.

The drive was a ribbon now, a thread of its former self, with gravel surface gone, and choked with grass and moss. The trees had thrown out low branches, making an impediment to progress; the gnarled roots looked like skeleton claws. Scattered here and again amongst this jungle growth I would recognize shrubs that had been landmarks in our time, things of culture and grace, hydrangeas whose blue heads had been famous.

No hand had checked their progress, and they had gone native now, rearing to monster height without a bloom, black and ugly as the nameless parasites that grew beside them. On and on, now east now west, wound the poor thread that once had been our drive. Sometimes I thought it

Glossary

cheek by jowl next to one another (jowl is the lower part of the cheek)

Source text H (continued)

lost, but it appeared again, beneath a fallen tree perhaps, or struggling on the other side of a muddied ditch created by the winter rains. I had not thought the way so long. Surely the miles had multiplied, even as the trees had done, and this path led but to a labyrinth, some choked wilderness, and not to the house at all. I came upon it suddenly; the approach masked by the unnatural growth of a vast shrub that spread in all directions, and I stood, my heart thumping in my breast, the strange prick of tears behind my eyes.

There was Manderley, our Manderley, secretive and silent as it had always been, the grey stone shining in the moonlight of my dream, the mullioned windows reflecting the green lawns and the terrace. Time could not wreck the perfect symmetry of those walls, nor the site itself, a jewel in the hollow of a hand.

Look again at Question 3 on page 142.

Complete the following activities to help you to analyse how the writer uses language to present the narrator's attitude towards Manderley.

Tip

Try to balance your analysis of language and structure, and keep this analysis focused on the question you have been asked. Do not retell the text as you won't be awarded any marks for doing this. In the exam, the number of blank lines provided beneath the question will show you how much you should write.

Activity 8

1. **a)** Look again at lines 1–27 and find examples of vocabulary associated with:
- threat
- beauty
- decay

b) Now find examples of the following language features:
- metaphor
- personification
- simile
- alliteration

c) Discuss what the examples you have found could suggest about the narrator's attitude towards Manderley.

2. Do you think the writer has used pathetic fallacy? Explain your answer.

3. In lines 21–24, the writer compares the branches overhead to 'the archway of a church'. Mind-map the associations a reader might have with churches and use these to develop a perceptive and original analysis of this comparison.

4. Copy and complete the grid below to explain what the different symbols included in the extract might represent in the context of this text.

Symbol	What it might represent
Gate	This could represent the threshold into a different world – in this case the world of her memories.
Padlock and chain	
Rusted spokes of the gate	
Nature	
The woods	

5. The sibilance in lines 7–9 could be said to sound like a whisper. Why do you think the writer chose to use this technique here?

Writing your response

Use the notes you have made to help you write your response to Question 3 on page 142.

Progress check

1. Read Student B's response to Question 3 on the facing page and then look at the mark scheme for Levels 5 and 6 below to decide which level you would award this response. Think about whether:
   - the points made show a clear understanding or a more sophisticated appreciation of how language and structure are used to present the narrator's attitude towards Manderley
   - the analysis of language and structure is consistent and detailed throughout the response
   - the subject terminology is integrated into the answer in a way that improves Student B's explanation of the effects achieved.

Level	Skills descriptors
Level 6 (11–12 marks)	• A skilled analysis which demonstrates a sophisticated appreciation of how the writer has used language and structure to achieve effects and influence the reader. • Candidates' analysis of both language and structure is consistent and detailed. • Precisely selected and integrated subject terminology deployed to enhance the response.
Level 5 (9–10 marks)	• An analysis which demonstrates a perceptive understanding of how the writer has used language and structure to achieve effects and influence the reader. • Candidates' analysis of both language and structure is reasonably detailed and balanced. • Well-chosen subject terminology integrated into explanations.

2. Write down three reasons to justify the level you have awarded Student B's response. Swap your reasons with a partner and discuss what the key differences between a Level 5 and Level 6 answer are.
3. Set yourself a target that would help you to aim for Level 6 when answering Question 3.

3 Look again at lines 1–27.

Explore how the writer presents the narrator's attitude towards Manderley.

Support your ideas by referring to the language and structure of the text, using relevant subject terminology.

Student B

The opening sentence is effective because it is short and direct whilst ensuring that an element of mystery is created for the reader. The reader wonders what 'Manderley' is and why the narrator says 'again'. Because the narrator tells us that she 'dreamt' of her return we also wonder if the place is real. The 'padlock and chain' in the opening paragraph may symbolise that she cannot ever return to this place. The narrator compares herself to a 'spirit' with 'supernatural powers'; this evokes feelings of unease and fear, increased by the use of sibilance at this point in the text.

By taking the reader through the gate and along the 'drive' we feel that we are on a journey with her and because the text is told from the first-person viewpoint, we are encouraged to see exactly what she sees, 'as I advanced', 'in front of me' and 'above my head'. In the third paragraph, the focus shifts from the drive to the woods, as if we too are exploring this 'menace' which has 'triumphed'. The long sentence with several commas adds layers of detail to the description of the trees and mirrors the abundance of growth.

Throughout this part of the text, the writer uses personification to show nature taking over in a sinister and threatening way: 'stealthy, insidious', 'encroached', 'long tenacious fingers'. The trees are described as 'tortured elms' and 'squat oaks', which the narrator doesn't 'recognise'. Personifying nature suggests that the narrator wants to blame someone for what has happened to the place she no longer seems to know. The reference to the trees merging above her head 'like the archway of a church' makes Manderley seem sacred to her, but this is contrasted with the 'monster shrubs and plants', emphasizing her confusion and sense of loss.

Try it yourself ON YOUR OWN

Tip

Re-read the full mark scheme on pages 132–133 before you complete this task. It will help you to remember what is being assessed.

Now read Source Text I and write your response to the Question 3 task below, applying all the skills you have learned.

3 Look again at lines 15–47.

Explore how the writer presents his experience of this particular mission.

Support your ideas by referring to the language and structure of this section, using relevant subject terminology.

Source text I

This text is taken from Roald Dahl's autobiography, Going Solo, *published in 1986, and describes his experiences as a fighter pilot in the Second World War. Here, Dahl has been sent on a mission to deliver an important package to Elevsis, a port in Greece, as the German forces invade the country.*

I went over to my Hurricane and got in and did up my straps. I put the mysterious package on my lap. On the floor of the cockpit under my legs I had the paper-bag with my belongings, as well as my Log Book. My camera, I remember clearly, was hanging by its strap from my neck. I taxied out and took off. I flew very low and fast, and in eight minutes I had reached Elevsis airfield. I circled the field once, looking for Germans or their planes. The place seemed totally deserted. I glanced at the windsock and banked straight in to land against the wind.

Just as I came to the end of my landing run, I heard the air-raid sirens wailing somewhere in the distance. I jumped out of my plane with my precious package and lay down in the ditch that surrounded the field. A great swarm of Stuka dive-bombers came over with their escort of fighters above them, and I watched as they flew on to Piraeus harbour. At Piraeus they began dive-bombing the ships.

I got back into my Hurricane and taxied up to the Operations Hut. The small buildings were splattered with bullet marks and the glass in all the windows was shattered. Several of the huts were smouldering.

I got out of my plane and walked towards the wreckage of huts. There was not a soul in sight. The entire aerodrome was deserted. In the distance I could hear the Stukas diving on to the shipping in Piraeus harbour and I could hear the bombs exploding.

"Is there anybody here?" I called out.

I felt very lonely. It was like being the only man on the moon. I stood between the Ops Hut and another small wooden hut alongside. The small hut had grey-blue smoke coming out of its shattered windows. I held the famous package tightly in my right hand.

Source text I (continued)

"Hello?" I called out. "Is there anybody here?"

Again the silence. Then a figure shimmered into sight beside one of the huts. He was a small middle-aged man wearing a pale-grey suit and he had a trilby hat on his head. He looked absurd standing there in his immaculate clothes amidst all that wreckage.

"I believe that parcel is for me," he said.

"What is your name?" I asked him.

"Carter," he said.

"Take it," I said. "By the way, what's in it?"

"Thank you for coming," he said, smiling slightly.

I took an instant liking to Mr Carter. I knew very well he was going to stay behind when the Germans took over. He was going underground. And then he would probably be caught and tortured and shot through the head.

"Will you be all right?" I said to him. I had to raise my voice to make it heard over the crash of bombs falling on Piraeus harbour.

He reached out and shook my hand. "Please leave at once," he said. "Your machine is rather conspicuous out there."

I returned to the Hurricane and started the engine. From my cockpit I glanced back to where Mr Carter had been standing. I wanted to wave him goodbye, but he had disappeared. I opened the throttle and took off straight from where I was parked.

Reading: Question 4

AO4 Evaluate texts critically and support this with appropriate textual references

AO3 Compare writers' ideas and perspectives, as well as how these are conveyed, across two or more texts

An overview of the question

Question 4 refers to both of the texts you will have read in your exam (Text 1 and Text 2) and is worth 18 marks. It assesses AO4 and AO3 and you will be expected to evaluate and compare the texts in response to a statement that links the two texts.

In the question:

- You will be given a statement that links the two texts, i.e. highlighting a common theme, idea or **perspective** presented in both texts. This statement will give you a focus for your evaluation and comparison of the texts.
- You will be asked how far you agree with this statement.
- You will be given three bullet points to help guide your response. The first two bullet points focus on evaluation of the texts (AO4) and the third bullet point focuses on comparison of the texts (AO3).
- You will be asked to use quotations from both texts to support your response.

Question 4 is worth 18 marks, more than for any of the other reading questions, so make sure you leave sufficient time to produce a substantial and detailed answer. In this question up to 12 marks will be awarded for AO4 (evaluation) and up to 6 marks for AO3 (comparison), so keep this in mind as you write your response.

Key term

perspective viewpoint, e.g. a narrator's viewpoint or the viewpoint of the writer

Look at the example Question 4 below. The annotations give you further guidance on how to approach the question.

4 'Both of these texts show how new and unfamiliar experiences can be very frightening.'

How far do you agree with this statement?

In your answer you should:

- discuss your impressions of the experiences presented
- explain what you find frightening about the environments described
- compare the ways the writers present the protagonists' experiences.

Support your response with quotations from both texts. **[18]**

This is the contextualizing statement, which gives you the starting point for your comments on the ideas in both texts.

'How far' allows you to decide the extent to which you agree with the statement and how you would relate it to the two texts.

This is the question you are answering, which asks you to evaluate the statement in relation to the two texts. Notice it is an open question.

This bullet point is also linked to AO4 and asks you to think about the impact of the text on you as the reader.

The first bullet point, linked to AO4, has a command word 'discuss', which means explore or examine in detail, considering different points of view.

This reminds you that you need to use quotations and textual references to support your ideas.

The final bullet point is linked to AO3 and asks you to compare the ideas and perspectives in the two texts and how they are conveyed.

In the exam, you will be given 40 blank lines to write your answer but this is just a guide. Depending on your handwriting style you could write more or less.

How will my answer be assessed?

An extract from the mark scheme that examiners use to mark Question 4 is shown below. The mark scheme is separated into the skills required for AO4 (evaluation) and the skills required for AO3 (comparison). For each Assessment Objective there are six levels and the key words that identify the differences between each level are shown in bold. Look back at the annotations on pages 52–53 for explanations of these.

AO3 Compare writer's ideas and perspectives, as well as how these are conveyed, across two or more texts	
Level	**Skills descriptor**
Level 6 (6 marks)	• A **detailed interwoven** comparison which explores writers' ideas and perspectives and how they are conveyed.
Level 5 (5 marks)	• A **sustained comparison** of writers' ideas and perspectives and how they are conveyed.
Level 4 (4 marks)	• A **developed comparison** of writers' ideas and perspectives and how they are conveyed.
Level 3 (3 marks)	• A **clear comparison** of writers' ideas and perspectives which **begins to consider** how they are conveyed.
Level 2 (2 marks)	• A response which **identifies main points of comparison** between writers' ideas and perspectives.
Level 1 (1 mark)	• A response which makes **simple points of comparison** between writers' ideas and perspectives.

A04: Evaluate texts critically and support this with appropriate textual references	
Level	**Skills descriptor**
Level 6 (11–12 marks)	• A **sustained critical evaluation** demonstrating a **perceptive and considered response to the statement** and a **full explanation of the impact of the texts on the reader.** • Comments are supported by **apt, skilfully selected and integrated textual references.**
Level 5 (9–10 marks)	• An **informed critical evaluation** showing a **thoughtful response to the statement** and a **clear consideration of the impact of the texts on the reader.** • Comments are supported by **persuasive textual references.**
Level 4 (7–8 marks)	• A response with **developed evaluative comments addressing the statement** and **some comments about the impact on the reader.** • Comments are supported by **well-chosen textual references.**
Level 3 (5–6 marks)	• A response with **clear evaluative comments** and **some awareness of the impact on the reader.** • Comments are supported by **appropriate textual references.**
Level 2 (3–4 marks)	• A response with **straightforward evaluative comments** and **a little awareness of the impact on the reader.** • Comments are supported by **some appropriate textual references.**
Level 1 (1–2 marks)	• A **limited description of content.** • Comments are supported by **copying or paraphrase.**

Tip

In the exam, you should take a positive view of the statement you are given and look for evidence of how the texts effectively present the specific theme, idea or perspective. In your answer aim to give an appreciation of the two texts you are evaluating and don't be too negative in the comments you make. If you consider one text is more successful than the other, make sure you support your view with evidence from the texts.

Key terms

theme a key idea or issue that the text is concerned with

Evaluating texts

When you evaluate a text you need to consider how effectively the writer has presented and explored a specific **theme**, idea or perspective, and also to explain the impact this has on you as a reader. The key skills you need for this are the ability to:

- identify how a theme, idea or perspective has been presented
- explain how effectively this has been achieved and the impact of this on you as a reader
- select relevant quotations and textual references to support your comments.

Read Source text J, which begins on the facing page, and then complete the activities below.

Activity 1

How does the writer give you the impression that falling from the cart was a frightening experience? Copy and complete the grid below to record your ideas.

How the experience is conveyed	Relevant quotations/ textual reference	Impact and effectiveness
First-person narrator	'It towered above me...'	Presents a child's view of the experience, helping the reader to share the narrator's fear
Imagery	'... each blade tattooed with tiger-skins of sunlight'	Threatening imagery conveys...

Source text J

This is an extract from Laurie Lee's memoir of his childhood, Cider With Rosie, *published in 1959. Here he describes being abandoned briefly when he accidentally slips from the cart in which he was travelling as a toddler.*

I was set down from the carrier's cart at the age of three; and there with a sense of bewilderment and terror my life in the village began.

The June grass, amongst which I stood, was taller than I was, and I wept. I had never been so close to grass before. It towered above me and all around me, each blade tattooed with tiger-skins of sunlight. It was knife-edged, dark, and a wicked green, thick as a forest and alive with grasshoppers that chirped and chattered and leapt through the air like monkeys.

I was lost and didn't know where to move. A tropic heat oozed up from the ground, rank with sharp odours of roots and nettles. Snow-clouds of elder-blossom banked in the sky, showering upon me the fumes and flakes of their sweet and giddy suffocation. High overhead ran frenzied larks, screaming, as though the sky were tearing apart.

For the first time in my life I was out of the sight of humans. For the first time in my life I was alone in a world whose behaviour I could neither predict nor fathom: a world of birds that squealed, of plants that stank, of insects that sprang about without warning. I was lost and did not expect to be found again. I put back my head and howled, and the sun hit me smartly on the face, like a bully.

From this daylight nightmare I was awakened, as from many another, by the appearance of my sisters. They came scrambling and calling up the steep rough bank, and parting the long grass found me. Faces of rose, familiar, living; huge shining faces hung up like shields between me and the sky; faces with grins and white teeth (some broken) to be conjured up like genii with a howl, bashing off terror with their broad scoldings and affection. They leaned over me – one, two, three – their mouths smeared with red currants and their hands dripping with juice.

"There, there, it's all right, don't you wail any more. Come down 'ome and we'll stuff you with currants."

And Marjorie, the eldest, lifted me into her long brown hair and ran me jogging down the path and through the steep rose-filled garden, and set me down on the cottage doorstep, which was our home, though I couldn't believe it.

That was the day we came to the village, in the summer of the last year of the First World War. To a cottage that stood in a half-acre of garden

Source text J (continued)

on a steep bank above a lake; a cottage with three floors and a cellar and a treasure in the walls, with a pump and apple trees, syringa and strawberries, rooks in the chimneys, frogs in the cellar, mushrooms on the ceiling, and all for three and sixpence a week.

I don't know where l lived before then. My life began on the carrier's cart which brought me up the long slow hills to the village, and dumped me in the high grass, and lost me. I had ridden wrapped up in a Union Jack to protect me from the sun, and when I rolled out of it, and stood piping loud among the buzzing jungle of that summer bank, then, I feel, was I born. And to all the rest of us, the whole family of eight, it was the beginning of a life.

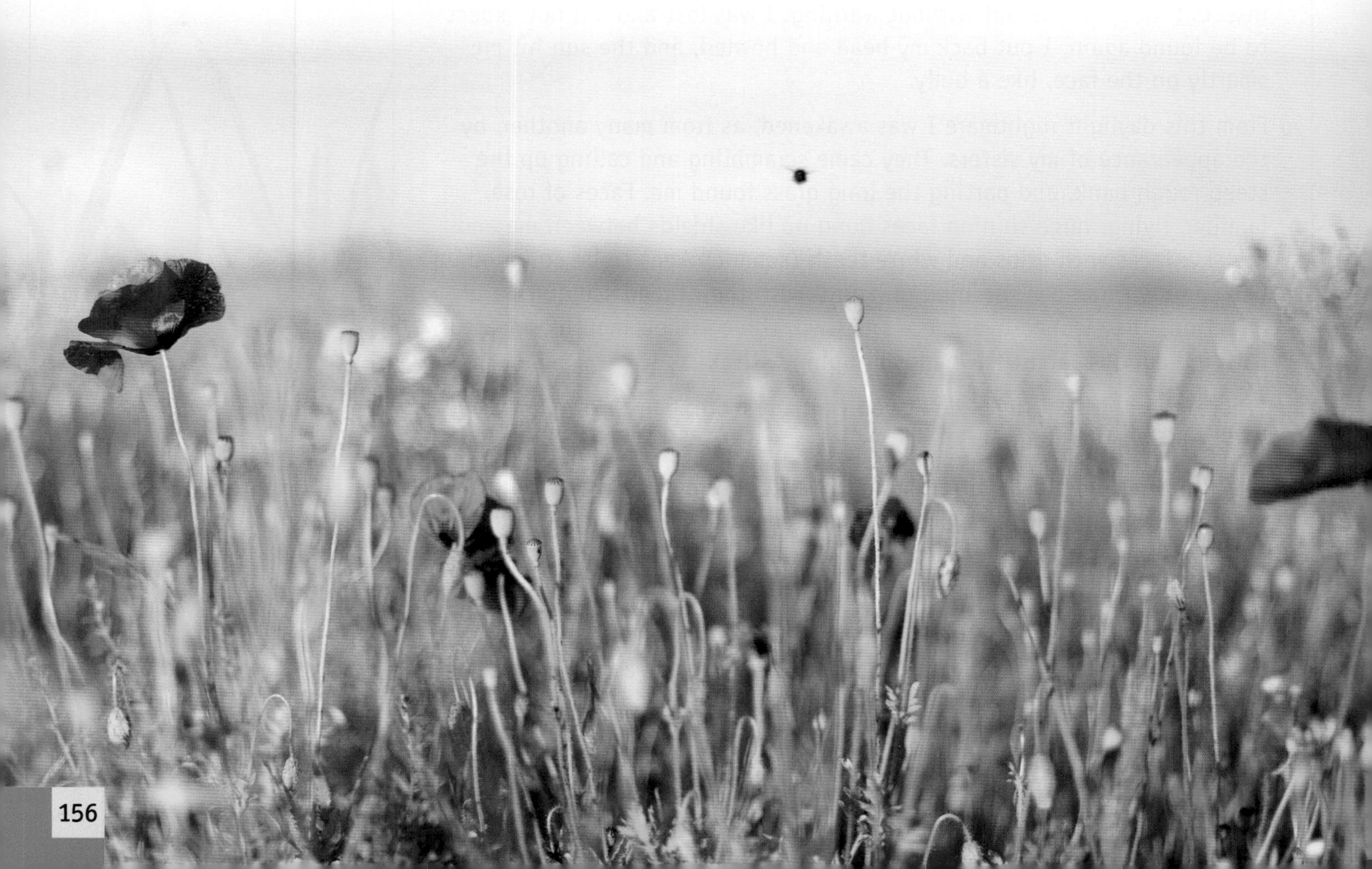

When you evaluate a text, you could use some of the following sentence prompts to help you to explore how effectively a theme, idea or perspective has been presented and the impact of this on you as a reader.

Effectiveness	Impact
The writer conveys a sense of... by...	The writer wants the reader to feel...
There is an element of... when the...	The impact of this vocabulary/ description is...
This part of the text is effective because...	As we read about... we feel...
As a result we expect...	We can identify with... when...

Activity 2

Look at Source text K and evaluate how the writer presents the underwater swim as a frightening experience. Use some of the sentence prompts above in your answer.

Source text K

This text is taken from a short story called 'Through the Tunnel' by Doris Lessing, which was first published in 1955. Here, a teenage boy called Jerry, who is on holiday with his mother, decides to copy some local boys who have swum through a tunnel of rock under the water.

If he did not do it now, he never would. He was trembling with fear that he would not go, and he was trembling with horror at that long, long tunnel under the rock, under the sea. Even in the open sunlight the barrier rock seemed very wide and very heavy; tons of rock pressed down on where he would go. If he died there he would lie until one day – perhaps not before next year – those big boys would swim and find it blocked.

He put on his goggles, fitted them tight, tested the vacuum. His hands were shaking. Then he chose the biggest stone he could carry and slipped over the edge of the rock until half of him was in the cool, enclosing water and half in the hot sun. He looked up once at the empty sky, filled his lungs once, twice, and then sank fast to the bottom with the stone. He let it go and began to count. He took the edges of the hole in his hands and drew himself into it, wriggling his shoulders in sideways as he remembered he must, kicking himself along with his feet.

Soon he was clear inside. He was in a small rock-bound hole filled with yellowish-grey water. The water was pushing him up against the roof. The roof was sharp and pained his back. He pulled himself along with his hands – fast,

Source text K (continued)

fast – used his legs as levers. His head knocked against something; a sharp pain dizzied him. Fifty, fifty-one, fifty-two... He was without light, and the water seemed to press upon him with the weight of rock. Seventy-one, seventy-two... There was no strain on his lungs. He felt like an inflated balloon, his lungs were so light and easy, but his head was pulsing.

He was being continually pressed against the sharp roof, which felt slimy as well as sharp. Again he thought of octopuses, and wondered if the tunnel might be filled with weed that could tangle him. He gave himself a panicky convulsive kick forward, ducked his head, and swam. His feet and hands moved freely, as if in open water. The hole must have widened out. He thought he must be swimming fast, and he was frightened of banging his head if the tunnel narrowed.

A hundred, a hundred and one... The water paled. Victory filled him. His lungs were beginning to hurt. A few more strokes and he would be out. He was counting wildly; he said a hundred and fifteen, and then, a long time later, a hundred and fifteen again. The water was a clear jewel-green all around him. Then he saw, above his head, a crack running up through the rock. Sunlight was falling through it, showing the clean dark rock of the tunnel, a single mussel shell and darkness ahead.

He was at the end of what he could do. He looked up at the crack as if it were filled with air and not water, as if he could put his mouth to it to draw in air. A hundred and fifteen he heard himself say inside his head – but he had said that long ago. He must go on into the blackness ahead, or he would drown. His head was swelling, his lungs cracking. A hundred and fifteen, a hundred and fifteen pounded through his head, and he feebly clutched at rocks in the dark, pulling himself forward, leaving the brief space of sunlit water behind. He felt he was dying. He was no longer quite conscious. He struggled on in the darkness between lapses into unconsciousness. An immense, swelling pain filled his head, and then the darkness cracked with an explosion of green light. His hands, groping forward, met nothing and his feet kicking back propelled him out into the open sea.

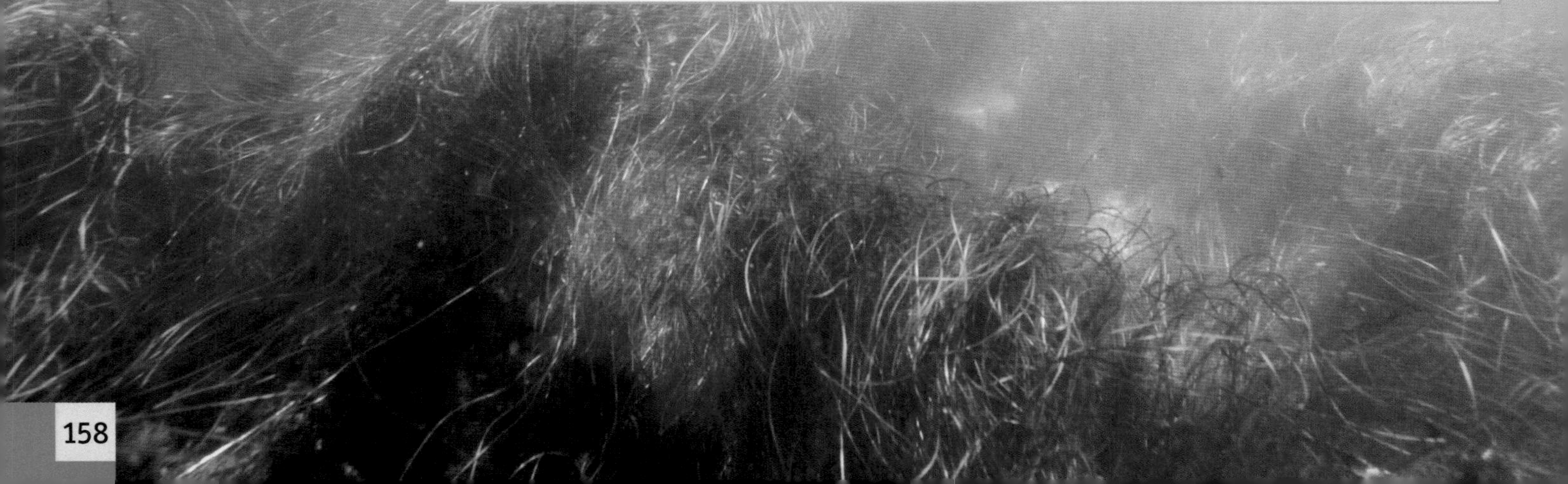

Comparing texts

When answering Question 4, you need to focus your comparison on the ways a specific theme, idea or perspective is presented in the two texts. The key skills you need for this are the ability to:

- identify similarities and differences between ways this theme, idea or perspective is presented in both texts
- compare the ways the ways the texts are written, commenting on the use of language and structural features.

Activity 3

Look again at Source text J and Source text K.

1. How are the experiences of the **protagonists** in the two texts similar?
2. What differences are there in the reactions of the two protagonists to their experiences?
3. Copy and complete a grid like the one below to compare the ways the two texts are written. You could look back at the grids on pages 120–123 to remind yourself of some of the language and structural features you could compare.

	Source Text L	Source Text M
Genre		
Style		
Structural features		
Language features		
Narrative view point		
Other points of comparison		

When you compare two texts, you could use some of the following words and phrases to help you to explore points of comparison and contrast:

Similarities	Differences
Both writers…	By contrast...
Like the first writer, the writer of... also…	However...
Similarly...	On the other hand...
Just as…, so too…	Whereas...

Tip

In the exam you will have already written about how language and structure are used in sections of Texts 1 and 2 in your answers to Questions 2 and 3. However in Question 4 you are focusing on **comparing** the ways language and structure are used and looking at both texts in full. Try to avoid simply repeating large chunks of your answers to Questions 2 and 3.

Key terms

protagonist the chief character, or one of the leading characters, in a drama or narrative

Activity 4

Using the notes you made for Activities 2 and 3, write a complete response to the following Question 4.

4 'Both of these texts show how new and unfamiliar experiences can be very frightening.'

How far do you agree with this statement?

In your answer you should:

- discuss your impressions of the experiences presented
- explain what you find frightening about the environments described
- compare the ways the writers present the protagonists' experiences.

Support your response with quotations from both texts.

Improving your answer

Read the following extract from Student A's answer. This is a Level 4 response for both AO3 and AO4, but the annotations show how it could move up to Level 5.

Textual references could be presented more persuasively by explaining why these details make the place sound more frightening and how they help to draw the reader into the child's experience.

Develops the evaluation of how the reader shares the child's viewpoint, but the comments could be expanded to explain how this makes the environment appear more frightening.

Evaluates each text in turn, but could compare the techniques used more effectively by interweaving the comparison of both texts.

Straightforward comments on the impact of the text on the reader, but the textual references chosen could be unpacked to explain more clearly how they evoke sympathy and convey danger.

Student A

Laurie Lee writes about a young child who is briefly lost in the countryside. He uses powerful imagery to convey the details around the child, which seem very threatening to him. Lee writes, 'grasshoppers... like monkeys' and 'tiger-skins of sunlight' which make the place sound more frightening than usual and draw the reader into the child's experience. He makes sure that we can hear and smell the things that the child experiences as well as picture the place. It is written in the first person, which makes us feel like we are actually there. When the child's sisters arrive suddenly, the reader sees them from the child's viewpoint too and this is amusing because he mentions 'broken teeth' and faces 'like shields'. It forms a contrast to the darker language Lee has used up to this point.

Lessing uses the third-person narrative viewpoint and this makes us feel we are watching the character. She uses the idea of Jerry counting so that we have a sense of time passing and feel his panic about whether he will get through the unfamiliar tunnel in time. Lessing chooses to use a range of vocabulary that suggests fear like 'shaking' and 'trembling'. She makes Jerry seem young because he talks about the 'big boys' and this evokes more sympathy for him because he is trying to do something that only older boys can do. The writer mentions 'octopuses', which we associate with danger and fear.

The writers use different viewpoints to tell a story. Lee uses more imagery whereas Lessing describes what happens in a more straightforward way.

Makes a straightforwa[rd] comment abo[ut] the impact o[n] the reader.

Comments o[n] how structur[e] and language used to conv[ey] a sense of ho[w] frightening t[he] experience is

Comparison could be developed further here explore how [the] writers' style[s] help to conv[ey] the experien[ce]

Now read the following extract from Student B's response to the question.

Student B

In Text 1 the reader sympathises with the narrator because he is clearly young, lost and upset. He says he was 'set down', which suggests he had no choice in the matter and we are told at the outset that he experiences a 'sense of bewilderment and terror'. In Text 2 Lessing also ensures that we sympathise with Jerry by encouraging us to admire his courage when he chooses to swim into the unknown, 'If he did not do it now, he never would.' She reiterates that he is 'trembling' and uses repetition to emphasize the length of the tunnel and the size of the rock it runs through. We follow each stage of the boy's journey down into the sea and through the tunnel. The use of counting followed by ellipsis throughout the text builds a sense of suspense about whether he will survive and this engages the reader, making it seem like the clock is ticking and time is running out. In Lee's text we also follow each detail of the child's experience from the grass, which 'towered' over him, to the 'insects which sprang about'.

Through the use of vivid imagery, including simile and personification, Lee intends the reader to sense the sights, sounds and smells, even the feel, of the child's environment. His use of threatening vocabulary such as 'dark... wicked... sharp... frenzied' ensures that we share the child's viewpoint of this unfamiliar place. Both texts use some child-like phrases, 'the sun hit me... like a bully' and 'those big boys', reminding us that these are vulnerable children. The personification of the sun as a 'bully' suggests a child's perspective as does the word 'big' rather than 'older' boys. There is some repetition in both texts which helps to convey the panic both boys feel. Lee and Lessing both refer to childhood symbols of fear: 'octopuses', 'darkness', 'tiger-skins' and 'knife-edged'. In each extract the end of the child's experience is marked using exaggerated language – 'like shields... like genii... bashing off terror' and 'an explosion of green light' – suggesting sudden relief.

This would be a Level 6 response for AO4 because:

- a critical evaluation of both texts is sustained throughout the response, with the student producing a detailed, perceptive and considered response to the statement presented in the question
- a full explanation of the impact of both texts on the reader is threaded through the response
- comments are supported by relevant and skilfully selected quotations and textual references which are skilfully integrated into the evaluation.

This would be a Level 6 response for AO3 because:

- it provides a detailed and interwoven comparison exploring the ways both writers present the protagonists' experiences as very frightening experiences, identifying similarities and differences in both the content of the two texts and techniques used.

Progress check

1. Look again at your own response. With a partner, decide which level it fits into for AO4 and AO3. Use the mark scheme on pages 152–153 to help you make your decision.
2. Discuss which parts of your response you could develop in order to improve it. Set yourself a target to improve your evaluation and comparison skills.

Try it yourself WITH SUPPORT

Now you are going to practise using all the skills in a complete response to Question 4. You'll be given some support to help you do this. First of all, look back over pages 150–151 to remind yourself of how to approach the question, then read Source Text L and Source Text M on pages 162–164.

This question is about Source text L and Source text M.

4 'These texts show that parents and their offspring can disappoint each other.'

How far do you agree with this statement?

In your answer, you should:

- discuss your impressions of the situations presented
- explain what you find interesting about the characters and the situations depicted
- compare the ways in which the writers present the disappointment experienced by the characters.

Support your response with quotations from both texts.

Tip

Keep the question in mind as you re-read both texts and think about the points you could include in your answer. You could use the bullet points to structure your evaluation and comparison of the two texts, but you can also combine the different bullet points to create a more integrated evaluative and comparative response to the question.

Activity 5

Use the following checklist to help you to write your response.

Remember to:

- write a detailed and sustained response
- select quotations and references thoughtfully and integrate these into your analysis
- give a full explanation of the impact the texts have on you as a reader
- explore the writers' ideas and perspectives and discuss how these are conveyed through the narrative
- try to interweave your comparison of the texts rather than writing about each text separately.

Source text L

This text is taken from the novel A Week in December *by Sebastian Faulks, which was first published in 2009. Here, a woman called Nasim is trying to understand her son, Hassan, who has grown up and away from her.*

By giving Hassan all the advantages that she and Knocker hadn't had, she believed she would remove him from friction, place him in a comfortable mainstream where he could use all his energies to flourish and waste none of them, as his parents had on the **attritional** business of surviving.

Glossary

attritional difficult and tiring

Source text L (continued)

She was cut to the heart to see it wasn't so. The boy didn't seem to rejoice in the place that had been carved out for him by the sweat and love of his parents. He became distrustful, separated from them and from their beliefs and alienated too, in some way Nasim couldn't start to understand, even from himself. She asked advice from friends and she consulted parenting manuals. They all stressed that children were their own creatures; that while genetically they were a half each of their parents, this input was of relatively little importance because what they chiefly were was something else: themselves. And there was almost nothing you could do to influence this hard, unknowable core. One of the self-help books compared the mother to a gardener who'd lost the labels on her seed packet. When the young plant grew up you didn't know if it would turn out nasturtium or broad bean; all you could do was encourage it to be as good a flower or pulse as it could be.

Whatever Hassan was, whatever the true nature that he was growing to fulfil, Nasim thought, he wasn't happy. She had to nerve herself for these conversations because she found his abruptness so upsetting and because she feared that by interfering she would make things worse. She approached his bedroom door, therefore, only when she was certain that not to do so risked causing greater damage.

"My love, if there's anything wrong, you would tell me, wouldn't you?"

"What sort of thing?"

"If you were unhappy? People get depressed. It's not a weakness. And boys of your age. Everyone knows that puberty is hard but in fact it was fine for you, wasn't it?"

"Yup."

"I mean, it's quite fun, growing up, going out and so on. But for young men I think your age is harder. The early twenties. I don't know why. Anyway, all I want to say is, you'd always come to Mummy, wouldn't you? If I could help."

"Aye. Thanks."

Nasim stood up. She felt saddened by her inability to reach the heart of Hassan's problems and bruised by his coldness. Her offer of help if he needed it, to be 'always there' for him... Pathetic, really, she thought, when once, when he was young, they had had this majestic intimacy.

But what more could you do?

Source text M

This text is taken from the novel Every Light in the House Burnin' *by Andrea Levy, which was first published in 1995. Here, the narrator, Angela, remembers an incident from her childhood.*

My dad once drank six cups of tea and ate six buttered rolls. Not in the course of a day, which would be nothing unusual. No, he drank six cups of tea and ate six buttered rolls one after the other to avoid them being wasted.

It happened in a motorway café where we had stopped on our coach journey down to Devon. It was the first holiday I had ever taken in my life. I was eleven. We all went, my mum and dad, my two sisters and my brother. Our destination was a Pontin's holiday camp in Brigham.

When we stopped at the motorway café we had all wanted various items from the display of food. "Fish and chips please, Dad," I said hopefully. "Cake and cola please," from my sister. We had never been out with our dad for a meal before so we had no idea what his response would be.

My dad sucked his teeth and jangled loose change around in his pocket as he looked at the prices on the menu. Then he ordered six cups of tea and six buttered rolls. We were all disappointed.

We sat watching my dad slurp at his tea with relish and shower his suit with crumbs from the roll. It was us and him. One by one, with our roll and tea in front of us we said we didn't feel hungry any more. My dad looked surprised at first. Eat up, he encouraged with a mouthful of bread. But then resigned himself as he made us all pass the items down to him. My mum was the last. She looked embarrassed, sitting at a table with a man who had five cups of tea and five plates of rolls around him, which he was systematically devouring. She said she had to go to the toilet and left to get back on the coach.

The humiliation did not stop there. Because my dad finished every last item, he was late getting back to the coach. The driver paced up to us to ask where he was. One of the other passengers said he was still eating in the café. We all waited with people tutting and staring at us. Then my dad emerged from the toilets at the side of the café. He was running. He smiled at everyone as he walked to his seat but nobody smiled back. He sat down and we were off.

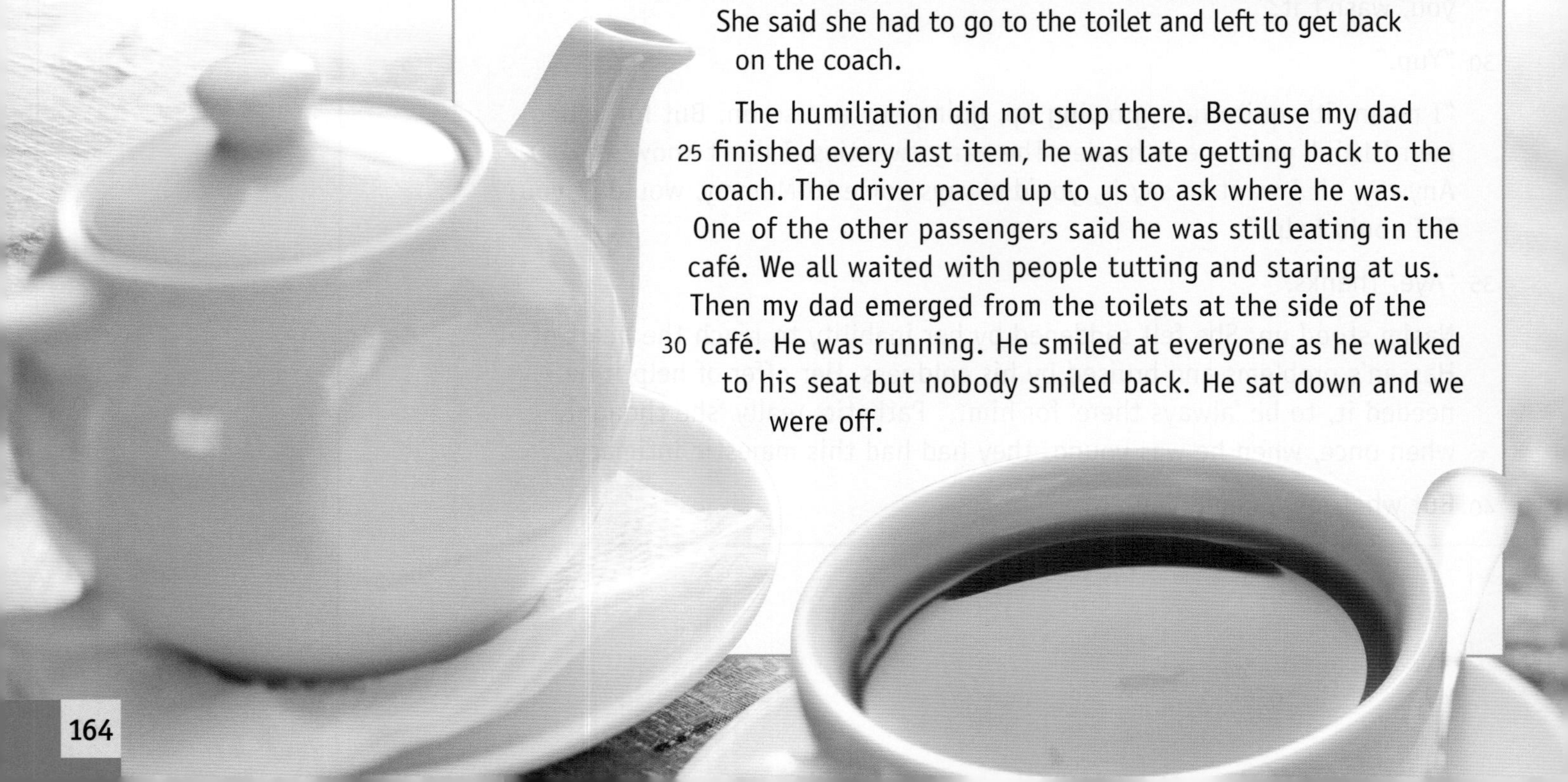

Try it yourself **ON YOUR OWN**

Read Source text N and Source text O. Then write your response to the Question 4 task on page 167, applying all the skills you have learned.

Source text N

This text is taken from the autobiography of John Cleese, an actor and comedian, published in 2014. Here he writes about his relationship with his mother.

In many ways she was a good mother; sometimes a very good mother. In all day-to-day matters she was extremely diligent: preparing good meals, making sure I was properly clothed and **shod** and warm and dry, keeping the house neat and clean, and fiercely protective of me. Under light hypnosis, I once recalled a German air raid, with the sound of the bombers not far away, and Mother throwing herself on top of me, under a big kitchen table. If it was a false memory, it's still what she would have done.

From a practical point of view, then, she was impeccable. But she was also self-obsessed and anxious, and that could make life with her very uncomfortable indeed.

A clue to her self-obsession, I always felt, was her extraordinary lack of general knowledge. On one of her visits to London in the late 80s, a salad was prepared for lunch which contained quails' eggs. She asked what kind of eggs they were and I explained that they were moles' eggs, and that when we wanted them, we would go up to Hampstead Heath very early in the morning, as moles laid them at the entrance to their burrows during the night, collect the eggs and make sure we ate them the same day before they had time to hatch. She listened with great attention, as my family's jaws sagged, and said she thought them delicious. Later that day she caught a mention of **Mary, Queen of Scots**. She recognised the name and asked me who this was. With my family listening, I **pushed the envelope** a little, telling her that Mary was a champion Glaswegian darts player who had been killed in the Blitz. What a shame, she said.

I was being a bit naughty, of course, but I also wanted to prove to my family the truth of a comment I had made earlier about Mother, which they had not accepted on first hearing. I had told them that *she had no information about anything that was not going to affect her life directly in the immediate future*; and that consequently she possessed no general knowledge – and when I said no general knowledge, I didn't mean very, very little. Naturally they had thought I was exaggerating.

Glossary

shod wearing shoes

Mary, Queen of Scots Queen of Scotland, 1542–1567

pushed the envelope went beyond accepted boundaries

Source text 0

This text is taken from a short story 'Rules of the Game' by Amy Tan, written in 1985. Here, Meimei, a talented young chess player, argues with her mother because she tends to boast about Meimei.

She grasped my hand even tighter as she glared at me.

I looked down. "It's not that, it's just so obvious. It's just so embarrassing."

"Embarrass you be my daughter?" Her voice was cracking with anger.

"That's not what I meant. That's not what I said."

"What you say?"

I knew it was a mistake to say anything more, but I heard my voice speaking, "Why do you have to use me to show off? If you want to show off, then why don't you learn to play chess?"

My mother's eyes turned into dangerous black slits. She had no words for me, just sharp silence. I felt the wind rushing around my hot ears. I jerked my hand out of my mother's tight grasp and spun around, knocking into an old woman. Her bag of groceries spilled to the ground.

"Aii-ya! Stupid girl!" my mother and the woman cried. Oranges and tin cans careened down the sidewalk. As my mother stooped to help the old woman pick up the escaping food, I took off. I raced down the street, dashing between people, not looking back as my mother screamed shrilly, "Meimei! Meimei!" I fled down an alley, past dark, curtained shops and merchants washing the grime off their windows. I sped into the sunlight, into a large street crowded with tourists examining trinkets and souvenirs. I ducked into another dark alley, down another street, up another alley. I ran until it hurt and I realized I had nowhere to go, that I was not running from anything. The alleys contained no escape routes.

My breath came out like angry smoke. It was cold. I sat down on an upturned plastic pail next to a stack of empty boxes, cupping my chin with my hands, thinking hard. I imagined my mother, first walking briskly down one street or another looking for me, then giving up and returning home to await my arrival. After two hours, I stood up on creaking legs and slowly walked home.The alley was quiet and I could see the yellow lights shining from our flat like two tigers eyes in the night. I climbed the sixteen steps to the door, advancing quietly up each so as not to make any warning sounds. I turned the knob: the door was locked. I heard a chair moving, quick steps, the locks turning – click! click! click! – and then the door opened.

"About time you got home," said Vincent. "Boy, are you in trouble."

He slid back to the dinner table. On a platter were the remains of a large fish, its fleshy head still connected to bones swimming upstream in vain

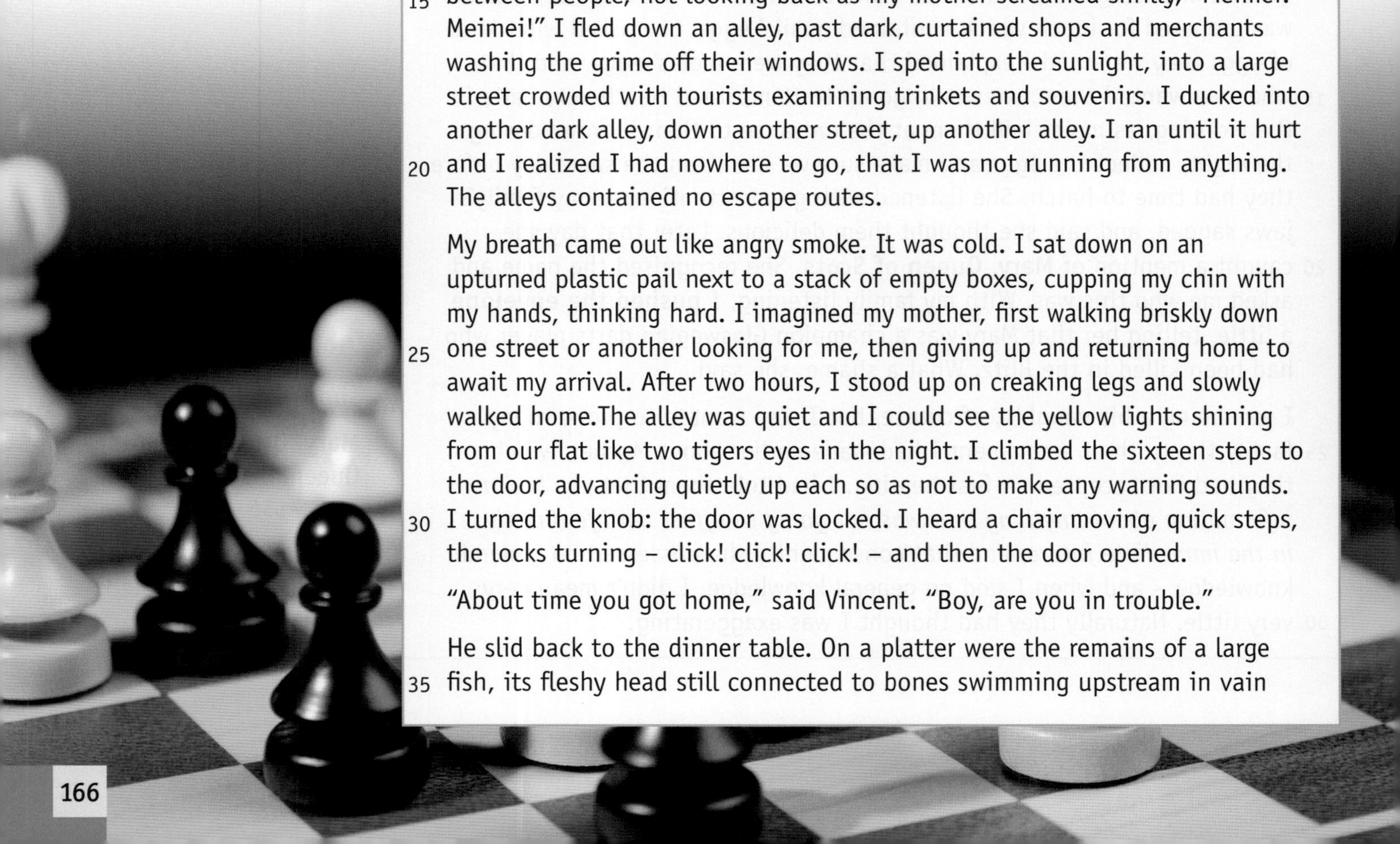

Source text O (continued)

escape. Standing there waiting for my punishment, I heard my mother speak in a dry voice.

"We not concerning this girl. This girl not have concerning for us."

Nobody looked at me. Bone chopsticks clinked against the inside of bowls being emptied into hungry mouths.

I walked into my room, closed the door, and lay down on my bed. The room was dark, the ceiling filled with shadows from the dinnertime lights of neighbouring flats.

In my head, I saw a chessboard with sixty-four black and white squares. Opposite me was my opponent, two angry black slits. She wore a triumphant smile. "Strongest wind cannot be seen," she said.

This question is about Source text N and Source text O.

4 'In these texts family relationships are presented as complex and difficult.'
How far do you agree with this statement?

In you answer, you should:

- discuss your impressions of the relationships presented
- explain what you find interesting about these relationships
- compare the way the writers present family relationships.

Support your response with quotations from both texts.

Progress check

Copy and complete the following grid to assess how confident you are in using the skills required to answer Question 4. Reflect on the activities you have completed in this section and for each skill award yourself a confidence rating from one to five, with five being very confident.

Skill	Confidence rating (1–5)
I can make critical judgements about how effectively each text explores a specific theme, idea or perspective.	
I can explain the impact this has on me as a reader.	
I support my ideas with relevant and appropriate textual references.	
I can compare writers' ideas and perspectives and how they are presented.	

Component 02 Exploring effects and impact

Section B: Writing imaginatively and creatively

What is the content and focus of this section?

This section assesses your ability to produce original creative writing. You will be given a choice of two writing tasks which will ask you to create an extended piece of creative writing in a range of forms such as a short story, autobiographical writing or personal writing.

You will have a choice of two writing tasks (Question 5 and Question 6) but you do only **one**. There will be a thematic link between one of the writing tasks and the two texts you have read in Section A of Component 02. Both questions will include bullet points to indicate the content you should include in your response.

How to use your time in the exam

Section B of this exam is worth 40 marks and will form 25% of your total GCSE grade. You will have to choose one writing task to answer from a choice of two tasks. The exam paper will advise you to spend one hour on Section B. However, given what you have to do in the reading section, you will likely spend around 45 minutes on the writing task. It is vital that you use this time wisely and fully. The grid below suggests how you might allocate your time.

Approach	Suggested timing
Choosing: Reading the writing tasks and selecting the one you will respond to	Approximately 2 minutes
Planning: Generating and structuring your ideas	Approximately 5 minutes
Drafting: Writing your response	Approximately 35 minutes
Proofreading: Checking your work and correcting mistakes	Approximately 3 minutes

How will my writing be assessed?

In Section B, your response to your chosen writing task will be assessed against the following Assessment Objectives:

Assessment Objective	
AO5	• Communicate clearly, effectively and imaginatively, selecting and adapting tone, style and register for different forms, purposes and audiences. • Organize information and ideas, using structural and grammatical features to support coherence and cohesion of texts.
AO6	• Use a range of vocabulary and sentence structures for clarity, purpose and effect, with accurate spelling and punctuation.

The examiner will give you separate marks on each objective:

- 24 marks are available for content and organization (AO5)
- 16 marks are available for technical accuracy (AO6).

Your overall mark for the writing task will be a combination of the two marks. The maximum overall mark for this writing task is 40. This is 25% of your overall GCSE grade.

Mark scheme

The examiner will assess your work against a mark scheme. For AO5, there are six levels, with Level 1 being the lowest and Level 6 the highest. For each level, there are key words or descriptors which distinguish one level from the others. The key words for AO5 are shown in the grid below.

Level	Key words for content and organization
Level 6 (21–24 marks)	Form – deliberately adapted; sophisticated control of purpose and effect Tone, style and register – ambitiously selected Overall structure – skilfully controlled overall structure
Level 5 (17–20 marks)	Form – confidently adapted; secure understanding of purpose and audience Tone, style and register – sustained Overall structure – controlled overall structure
Level 4 (13–16 marks)	Form – confidently adapted; secure understanding of purpose and audience Tone, style and register – matched to task Overall structure – well-managed overall structure
Level 3 (9–12 marks)	Form – sustained; clear awareness of purpose and audience Tone, style and register – appropriate with some inconsistencies Overall structure – clear overall structure
Level 2 (5–8 marks)	Form – mostly appropriate; generally maintained Tone, style and register – attempted Overall structure – some evidence
Level 1 (1–4 marks)	Form – some attempt Tone, style and register – limited attempt Overall structure – some attempt

For AO6, there are four levels. Again, Level 1 is the lowest and Level 4 is now the highest. The key words or descriptors to distinguish between these levels are shown in the grid below.

Level	Key words for technical accuracy
Level 4 (13–16 marks)	Sentence structure – an ambitious range shapes meaning and creates impact Punctuation – accurate; makes writing clear and achieves specific effects Vocabulary – precise and subtle Spelling – accurate; very few mistakes
Level 3 (9–12 marks)	Sentence structure – a wide range used for deliberate purpose and effect Punctuation – consistently accurate Vocabulary – used convincingly; sometimes ambitious Spelling – accurate
Level 2 (5–8 marks)	Sentence structure – a range used and mostly secure Punctuation – generally accurate Vocabulary – appropriate Spelling – generally accurate
Level 1 (1–4 marks)	Sentence structure – simple mostly with some attempt at complex structures Punctuation – some Vocabulary – straightforward Spelling – simple spellings, mostly accurate

As you work through the chapters in this writing section, you will have opportunities to practise and improve your writing skills. You will also learn how to assess your own work against the mark scheme and how to gain the highest level mark that you can in the exam.

Choosing a writing task

Writing imaginatively and creatively

Section B includes two writing tasks, Question 5 and Question 6, but you should only write a response to **one** of these tasks. You need to read each task carefully to identify what form of writing you are being asked to produce. This could be:

- autobiographical writing – a narrative recount of events or experiences from the writer's own life.
- narrative fiction – such as a short story or the opening to a longer story
- personal writing – narrative non-fiction which reads like a story but is rooted in the writer's own experiences.

All these forms of writing are types of narrative and share many of the same features and techniques.

Features of autobiographical writing	Features of narrative fiction	Features of personal writing
• Based on the writer's experiences • Uses **first-person narrator**, who is the writer • Events retold in chronological order • Uses the **past tense** • Uses **time connectives** or sequencing connectives	• Invented event • Can use **first-** or **third-person narrator** • Events do not have to be told in chronological order • Can use past or **present tense** • Uses time or sequencing connectives	• Based on the writer's experiences • Uses a **first-person narrator** • Events retold in chronological order • Uses the past tense • Uses time or sequencing connectives

Key terms

past tense verb forms used to describe something that happened earlier, e.g. I drove the car, He climbed the mountain

time connective word or phrase used to indicate when something is happening, e.g. firstly, then, afterwards, instantly, meanwhile, next, shortly, later on, that night, the next day, etc.

present tense verb forms used to describe something that is happening now, e.g. I drive the car, He climbs the mountain

Look at the example writing tasks below and on the facing page. The annotations give you further guidance on how to approach each task.

> Imagine you are writing your autobiography. Describe a special childhood occasion such as a birthday party or school trip.
>
> You could write about:
>
> - the things you did and who was involved
> - the way that you felt.
> - how you feel now, looking back.

This indicates the form, i.e. autobiographical writing.

This indicates the purpose of your writing, i.e. to describe.

This indicates the topic you should write about, i.e. a special childhood occasion. Focus on a very specific and important event, in this case a happy one

The bullet points offer some ideas about what you could include in your response.

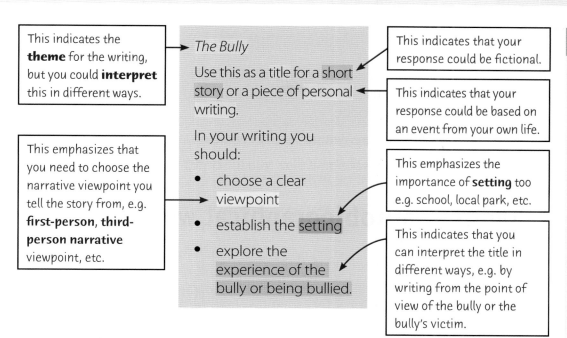

This indicates the **theme** for the writing, but you could **interpret** this in different ways.

The Bully

Use this as a title for a short story or a piece of personal writing.

In your writing you should:

- choose a clear viewpoint
- establish the setting
- explore the experience of the bully or being bullied.

This indicates that your response could be fictional.

This indicates that your response could be based on an event from your own life.

This emphasizes that you need to choose the narrative viewpoint you tell the story from, e.g. **first-person, third-person narrative** viewpoint, etc.

This emphasizes the importance of **setting** too e.g. school, local park, etc.

This indicates that you can interpret the title in different ways, e.g. by writing from the point of view of the bully or the bully's victim.

Activity 1

Look below at two more example writing tasks of the type that you could encounter in Section B of Component 02.

1. Copy out and annotate each task like the examples above.
2. Discuss your initial ideas about each task and decide which one you would choose to write.

5 Imagine you are writing your autobiography. Describe a time when you felt afraid.

You could write about:

- where you were and what you did
- how you felt about the experience.
- how you feel now, looking back.

OR

6 *The Dark*

Use this as a title for a story or piece of personal writing.

In your writing you should:

- think carefully about the form and structure of your writing
- create a suitable tone and atmosphere
- use language in an interesting and imaginative way.

Key terms

theme a key idea or issue that the text is concerned with

interpret to explain the meaning of something said or written

first-person narrative story or experience told by someone who is part of the story and action, using the words 'I' and 'we'

third-person narrative story or experience told by someone outside of the story, using the words 'he', 'she' or 'they'

setting the place and time where the story occurs

Tip

The texts you will have read in Section A of the exam can provide you with models of autobiographical writing and narrative fiction. You could draw on the techniques from these texts in your own writing.

Planning your response

Whichever writing task you choose, it is vital that you plan what you are going to write. This will help you to use the time that you have in the exam effectively. Your plan should help you think about:

- the content of what you are writing, i.e. the characters, setting, plot, etc.
- the organization of your writing, i.e. how you are going to write it, etc.

Planning autobiographical writing

Look again at the following writing task.

> Imagine you are writing your autobiography. Describe a special childhood occasion such as a birthday party or school trip.
>
> You could write about:
>
> - the things you did and who was involved
> - the way that you felt
> - how you feel now, looking back.

Student A has used a spider diagram to note down her initial ideas about what she could write about in response to this task.

From these initial ideas, Student A has chosen the first time she saw her baby sister as the special childhood memory she will write about.

Student A has used the flow chart on the facing page to note down her ideas about this childhood memory in the order they occurred. However, this might not be the order she chooses to write them in. For example, to create an attention-grabbing opening, she might begin by describing seeing her sister for the first time and then write the rest of her response as a **flashback** describing the build-up to this moment.

Key term

flashback a scene in a story or film that is set earlier in time than the main part of the story

1. Waking up – sunshine, birdsong, dad shouting, feeling giddy with excitement, wash, dress, rushing downstairs, dad being excited too, radio playing, quick breakfast, no appetite
2. Journey by car to the hospital – frustrated by traffic in town, music on radio, picked up speed on the motorway, heat of summer, windows down, car full of presents, balloons, holding my card tightly, endless stream of questions torturing dad
3. Walking into the hospital – chemical smell, nurses, other visitors, patients milling about, huge size of it, lift full of people all squashed in together, excitement growing with each 'ping' as we reached a floor
4. Entering the ward – buzz of other visitors, holding dad's hand, card gripped in the other, pastel-coloured walls, signs about washing hands everywhere, a loud, crying baby, fit to burst with excitement
5. Seeing my baby sister for the very first time – entering room, seeing mum, she looked tired, small white bundle asleep in a transparent plastic cot on wheels, hushed voices all round, strangers, dad lifting me up, heart thumping with excitement, small red face, so beautiful, black hair, big yawn, unique smell of a newborn child, how light she felt

Activity 1

Look again at the flow chart. For each panel, decide which are the key ideas you think Student A should include in her response. Think about which details will help to show how special this occasion was and how the writer felt about it.

Activity 2

Now look at the writing task below.

1. Make a list of the different events or experiences you could write about.
2. Choose one of these events or experiences and use a flow chart to plan your response.
3. Select the key ideas and details from your plan and decide how you will order these in your writing.

Imagine you are writing your autobiography. Describe a time when you felt afraid.

You could write about:

- where you were and what you did
- how you felt about the experience
- how you feel now, looking back.

Planning a story or personal writing

A useful planning tool when writing narrative fiction in the form of a short story or a personal writing response is to use a 'story mountain'. This can help you to think about the content and organization of your writing at the same time.

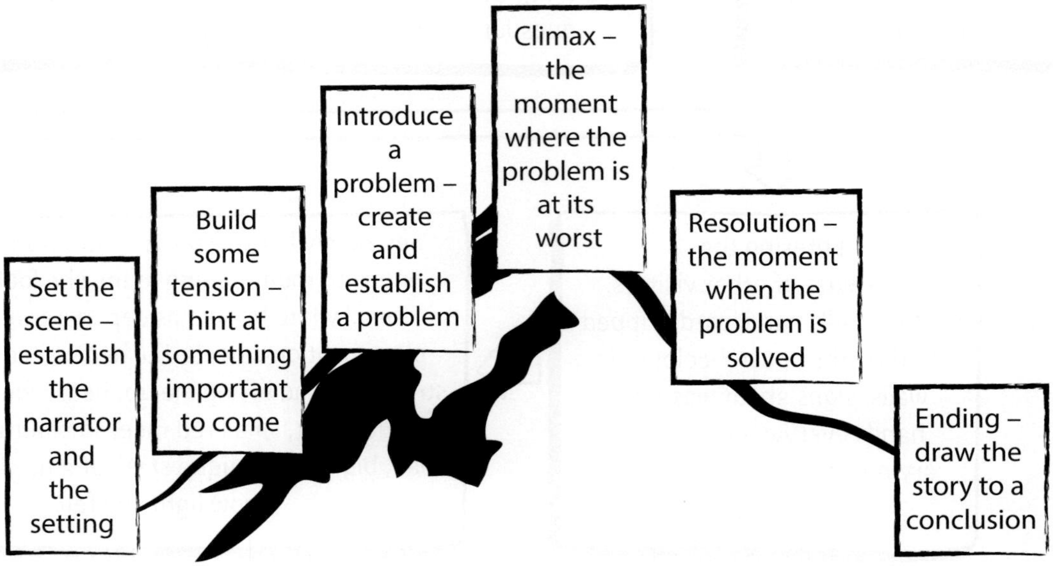

Look again at the following writing task.

The Bully

Use this as a title for a short story or a piece of personal writing.

In your writing you should:

- choose a clear viewpoint
- establish the setting
- explore the experience of the bully or of being bullied.

Key term

frame narrative a literary technique presenting a story within a story

Student B has decided to write a short story and use the story mountain approach to plan his response to this task. Look at Student B's plan on the facing page.

Student B has made some interesting choices in this plan. He has used a **frame narrative** to begin and end the story with a conversation between the grandson and his grandfather, presenting the grandfather's own story about being bullied as a flashback between these opening and closing scenes.

Set the scene – Grandson tearfully telling his grandfather he is being bullied. Shift to grandfather who then tells his grandson a story, from his point of view, of being bullied himself.

Build some tension – Grandfather heading home from school as a child, winter's evening, rain, very cold, sitting on crowded bus, then the boy who is bullying him takes the seat behind him, sound of thunder in distance, very warm, feel nervous, sick, desperate to get off

Introduce the problem – Gets off the bus early, struggling through people, panic stricken as bully gets off too, start to walk faster, bully follows, begin to run, knocking into people, panic increasing as the bully chases after him

The climax – running down street, end up in a dead end, father's words start ringing in his ears, "You must stand up to bullies." Nowhere else to run. Stop. Turn. Face the bully. Decide to make a stand summon up courage and charge at bully.

The resolution – Grandfather explains that seeing the determination in his eyes, the bully turned and fled and never bothered him again from that moment.

The ending – Grandson is no longer tearful but determined to stand up to the person bullying him at the next opportunity.

Activity 3

Look at the writing task below.

1. Decide whether you would write a short story or a piece of personal writing in response to this task.
2. Make a list of the different possible ideas you have for your writing.
3. Choose one of these and use the 'story mountain' approach to plan your response.

The Dark

Use this as a title for a story or piece of personal writing.

In your writing you should:

- think carefully about the form and structure of your writing
- create a suitable tone and atmosphere
- use language in an interesting and imaginative way.

Practising key skills for AO5

When you have completed your planning, you will need to focus writing your response. This will be assessed on two objectives, AO5 and AO6. In this section you will work on the skills you need to do well in AO5, which is divided into two sections.

AO5	• Communicate clearly, effectively and imaginatively, selecting and adapting tone, style and register for different forms, purposes and audiences. • Organize information and ideas, using structural and grammatical features to support coherence and cohesion of texts.

This is about the content of what you write.

This is about how you organize that content.

What are content and organization?

In a piece of original creative writing, whether this is a story, autobiographical writing or personal writing, you need to communicate your ideas clearly to the reader and match your writing to the form you have chosen to write in.

This means using language and structure creatively and imaginatively in your narrative. To assess this, the examiner will look at the way you use vocabulary, grammar and literary techniques to achieve particular effects, as well as the way you establish and maintain a narrative viewpoint. The way you organize and structure ideas in the narrative in order to create deliberate effects will also be taken into account.

Narrative viewpoint

The narrative viewpoint refers to who is telling the story. Autobiographical and personal writing both require you to write a first-person narrative. However a story could be written from a variety of narrative viewpoints, including a **first-person narrator**, a **third-person omniscient narrator** or a **third-person limited narrator**. The viewpoint you choose directly affects the way your readers experience the narrative and contributes to the **tone** created in your writing.

Activity 1

Read the following extract from Student A's short story, which has the title 'The Bully'.

1. Rewrite this extract from a third-person narrative viewpoint. (You might want to make up a name for the character of the narrator.)
2. Compare the two extracts and discuss the effects created by the different narrative viewpoints. Decide which narrative viewpoint you find more effective.

Student A

Bill Bates. The name still gives me shivers to this day although I have not seen him for more than ten years. We were very well acquainted throughout secondary school and I was equally well acquainted and repelled by his disgustingly black, chipped teeth and his spit, which he lobbed involuntarily on my face as he demanded my lunch money, maths homework, seat on the bus or whatever else he simply fancied that day. At 16, he was a gorilla of a man already and I was, no doubt, a mere plaything to be toyed with, making his day slightly more bearable and entertaining and my own one of fear, dread and loathing. No matter where I hid, the unbrushed mop of black hair and the tall, lumbering frame in undersized clothes of my tormentor always seemed to find me.

Key terms

first-person narrator where the narrator is a participant in the narrative, using the words 'I' or 'we' to recount events

third-person omniscient narrator where the narrator is not a character in the story, but can share the thoughts and feelings of different characters with the reader

third-person limited narrator where the narrator is not a character in the story, but is not able to share the thoughts and feelings of one of the characters with the reader

tone the writer's or narrator's attitude, which is implied through their language choices

Read Source text A and Source text B on the facing page and then complete the activities below. Source text A is taken from Maya Angelou's autobiography *I Know Why the Caged Bird Sings* and Source text B is taken from Ian McEwan's novel *The Child in Time*.

Tip

Whether you choose to write your response in the first person or the third person, remember to stick to this. Switching between different narrative viewpoints in your writing can be confusing for your readers.

Key terms

omniscient knowing everything

perspective viewpoint, e.g. a narrator's viewpoint or the viewpoint of the writer

Activity 2

1. For each extract, identify the narrative viewpoint the writer has chosen.
2. Which extract creates the most sympathy for the main character? Discuss the way the narrative viewpoint influences your response to the text.
3. Choose one of the extracts and rewrite it from a different narrative viewpoint, for example, changing a first-person narrator to a third-person omniscient narrator or a third-person limited narrator to a first-person narrator.
4. Share your rewritten extract with a partner. Discuss whether the change in narrative viewpoint changes the way they feel towards the main character.

Activity 3

Imagine you are writing a story which has *The Bully* as a title.

1. Write a paragraph describing a scene where the victim unexpectedly sees the bully. This paragraph should be written from a first-person narrative viewpoint.
2. Now write a paragraph describing the same scene but this time written from a third-person **omniscient perspective**.
3. Compare the two paragraphs. Which do you think is more powerful and why?

Source text A

Extract from *I Know Why the Caged Bird Sings* by Maya Angelou

In this extract, Maya Angelou, who has been living with her grandmother, describes an important moment in her childhood.

Then came that terrible Christmas with its awful presents when our father, with the vanity I was to find typical, sent his photograph. My gift from Mother was a tea set – a teapot, four cups and saucers and tiny spoons – and a doll with blue eyes and rosy cheeks and yellow hair painted on her head. I didn't know what Bailey received, but after I opened my boxes I went out to the backyard behind the chinaberry tree. The day was cold and the air as clear as water. Frost was still on the bench but I sat down and cried. I looked up and Bailey was coming from the outhouse, wiping his eyes. He had been crying too. I didn't know if he had told himself they were dead and had been rudely awakened to the truth or whether he was just feeling lonely. The gifts opened the door to questions neither of us wanted to ask. Why did they send us away?

Source text B

Extract from *The Child in Time* by Ian McEwan

In this extract, the narrator describes the moment he loses his daughter while at the supermarket.

The man with the dog food was leaving. The checkout girl was already at work, the fingers of one hand flickering over the keypad while the other drew Stephen's items towards her. As he took the salmon from the trolley he glanced down at Kate and winked. She copied him, but clumsily, wrinkling her nose and closing both eyes. He set the fish down and asked the girl for a carrier bag. She reached under the shelf and pulled one out. He took it and turned. Kate was gone. There was no one in the queue behind him. Unhurriedly he pushed the trolley clear, thinking she had ducked down behind the end of the counter. Then he took a few paces and glanced down the only aisle she would have had time to reach. He stepped back and looked at lines of shoppers, on the other a clear space, then the chrome turnstile, then the automatic doors on to the pavement. There may have been a figure in a coat hurrying away from him, but at that time Stephen was looking for a three year-old child, and his immediate worry was the traffic.

Setting

When you write a narrative, whether this is a story or piece of personal writing, you need to establish the setting – the place and time where the narrative takes place. The vocabulary you use to describe your setting can help you to achieve deliberate effects, e.g. to create a tense atmosphere or reflect a character's mood.

Activity 4

Read the following extract from Student B's description of a time when he felt afraid.

Look at the vocabulary changes Student B has made. Discuss the impression they help to give of:

- the setting
- the atmosphere
- the narrator's mood.

Student B

The monstrous black gates barely moved as I desperately pushed with all my might against them. A tiny slice of space slowly opened up, making just enough room for me to ~~get~~ squeeze through. A ~~fat~~ bloated full moon glared down ominously from above.

Tip

Look for ways you can weave in details about the setting into description of the narrator's actions such as, 'The monstrous black gates barely moved as I desperately pushed with all my might against them.'

Now read Source text C on the facing page. This is an extract from Anita Desai's short story 'Games at Twilight'.

Activity 5

1. Look at the annotations to explore how the writer conveys Ravi's fear through the description of the shed. Which do you think are the most powerful examples?
2. Look back at the planning you did for Activity 2 on page 180. Write the opening paragraph of this response, drawing on the techniques from Source text C to establish the setting and convey a sense of fear.

Source text C

Extract from 'Games at Twilight' by Anita Desai

Here, a young boy, Ravi, who is playing hide and seek, has hidden himself in a shed.

Ravi shook, then shivered with delight, with self-congratulation. Also with fear. It was dark, spooky in the shed. It had a muffled smell, as of graves. Ravi had once got locked into the linen cupboard and sat there weeping for half an hour before he was rescued. But at least that had been a familiar place, and even smelt pleasantly of starch, laundry and, reassuringly, of his mother. But the shed smelt of rats, ant hills, dust and spider webs. Also of less definable, less recognisable horrors. And it was dark. Except for the white-hot cracks along the door, there was no light. The roof was very low. Although Ravi was small, he felt as if he could reach up and touch or feel anything. What might there not be to touch him and feel him as he stood there, trying to see in the dark? Something cold, or slimy – like a snake.

Repetition through the text emphasizes the darkness and lack of light.

The idea of death and decay is introduced.

The unknown is often more scary than the known.

A sense of claustrophobia is created here.

Heightens the sense of fear; contrasts his previous isolation and the fear this caused him, even though it was in a much more pleasant environment.

All unpleasant creatures associated with terrible things: rats – disease; spiders – witches; snakes – evil.

Tip

Be consistent in the tense that you use in your narrative. Don't switch between past and present tense in the same piece of writing.

Key terms

simile a figure of speech in which one thing is compared to another using 'like' or 'as...'

metaphor the use of a word or phrase in a special meaning that provides an image

personification to present an idea in human form or a thing as having human characteristics

Action, description and dialogue

In your writing, the tense of a verb tells the reader when the action of the narrative takes place. Autobiographical writing is typically written in the past tense, but a story or piece of personal writing could be written in the past tense or present tense. Whichever tense you choose, you need to use powerful and descriptive verbs to make the events seem more immediate to the reader.

Activity 6

Look back at your plan from page 177 for a story or piece of personal writing with the title 'The Dark'.

1. Write the opening paragraph of this response using the past tense.
2. Now write the opening paragraph using the present tense.
3. Compare these paragraphs. Which do you think is the most effective and why?
4. Underline your verb choices. Could you change any of the verbs for more powerful alternatives?

Using imagery such as **similes**, **metaphors** and **personification** can help your reader to visualize the events described in your narrative. You can add to the power of the imagery you use in your writing by including descriptive details that appeal to your readers' senses to help them to imagine the experience.

Look again at Student A's plan for her description of a special childhood memory on page 174. She has now developed her ideas to describe the moment she first saw and held her baby sister using the grid below.

Sense	Idea	Use of imagery
See	black hair	Her hair was as black as a winter's sky at night and exactly like mine when I was born.
Hear	heart beating	The only sound now was that of my own heart which thumped loudly with nervous excitement in my chest like a bass drum.
Taste	Lip balm	The sweet cherry lip balm I wore left a small, faint heart shaped smudge on her forehead when I kissed her.
Touch/ feel	the baby's skin	Although incredibly light in my arms, I held the precious cargo carefully and with all my focus and concentration.
Smell	new born baby	That unique and incredibly intoxicating scent of a newborn child suddenly danced round me and delighted my senses.

Activity 7

1. Which of the examples from the grid do you think Student A should use in her description? Give reasons for your choices.
2. Look back at the planning you did for Activity 2 on page 180. Identify where you can appeal to the reader's senses and use imagery to develop specific details in the narrative.

Tip

Try to avoid **clichés** in your writing such as 'He was as big as a house.' Think about how you can use imagery to surprise and interest the reader and make them look at things in a fresh way.

You can use dialogue to move the action of your narrative forward or reveal something about the characters in your story. Look at the following extract from Student B's story 'The Bully'.

Student B

"I think it's time we talked," Granddad said as he shuffled into his favourite armchair.

"What about?" I asked, keeping my eyes on the red glowing coals of the fire that blazed in the hearth.

"About why I haven't seen you smile for about three weeks now," came the reply.

Key term

cliché a phrase or idea that is used so often that it has little meaning e.g. Love is blind

Activity 8

1. How does this dialogue help to move the plot forward?
2. What do you learn about the characters from this dialogue?
3. Look back at the planning you did for Activity 3 on page 179 where you were asked to write a story or piece of personal writing with the title 'The Dark'. Plan where you will include dialogue in this response.

Openings

When writing a narrative, whether this is a story, autobiographical writing or a piece of personal writing, you need to hook your reader's attention from the very first line. The opening of your narrative should:

- establish the tone of the narrative, e.g. suspenseful, mysterious, etc.
- introduce characters and setting
- raise questions that the reader will want to find out the answers to.

There are a number of ways of starting a narrative. You could use:

- description to introduce characters or the setting and create a sense of mood and atmosphere, e.g. 'The sky above the port was the colour of television, tuned to a dead channel.' (*Neuromancer* by William Gibson)
- dialogue to introduce characters, the setting and situation, e.g. '"Yes," said Tom bluntly, on opening the front door. "What d'you want?" A harassed middle-aged woman in a green coat and felt hat stood on his step.' (*Goodnight Mister Tom* by Michelle Magorian)
- action to create drama and shock or surprise the reader, e.g. 'It was the day my grandmother exploded.' (*The Crow Road* by Iain Banks)
- an intriguing statement to hook the reader's interest and make them want to find out more, e.g. 'It was seven minutes after midnight. The dog was lying on the grass in the middle of the lawn in front of Mrs Shears' house. Its eyes were closed.' (*The Curious Incident of the Dog in the Night-time* by Mark Hadden)
- first-person narration to introduce the subject or theme and establish the main character, e.g. 'Late in the winter of my 17th year, my mother decided I was depressed, presumably because I rarely left the house, spent quite a lot of time in bed, read the same book over and over, ate infrequently, and devoted quite a bit of my abundant free time to thinking about death.' (*The Fault in our Stars* by John Green)

Activity 9

1. Which of the above openings do you find most effective? Discuss which story you would choose to read and why.
2. Look back at the opening paragraph you wrote for 'The Dark' on page 184. What approach did you use for this?
3. Now rewrite this opening paragraph using the other different approaches, e.g. starting with action, etc.
4. Identify which of these openings you think is the best and give reasons for your choice.

Paragraphs

In narrative writing you need to begin a new paragraph when you:

- change the subject or focus, e.g. for a new event, character, action
- change the location, e.g. switching to a new setting
- change the time, e.g. flashback or moving forward in time
- change the speaker, e.g. introducing a new line of dialogue.

You can use paragraphs to control the pace of your narrative.

Short paragraphs can help to speed up the pace of your writing. You can use short paragraphs for action scenes, quick-fire dialogue and to create dramatic impact.

Longer paragraphs can help to slow the pace of your writing. You can use longer paragraphs for detailed descriptions of character and setting or to build tension.

Varying the length of the paragraphs you use can stop your writing becoming one-paced and predictable.

Activity 10

Read Source text D below.

1. The first and second paragraphs are one-sentence paragraphs. What effect does this create?
2. Look at the second and third paragraphs. Why does the writer begin new paragraphs here?
3. Look at the third paragraph again. How could you split this into two paragraphs? What impact does this change create?
4. Look back at your plan for your story or piece of personal writing with the title 'The Dark'. Plan where you will include short and longer paragraphs in this response.

Source text D

Extract from *The Shock of the Fall* by Nathan Filer

Here, the narrator Matt, a young man being treated as a mental health patient on a secure ward, watches another patient, Thomas, trying to escape.

Thomas half ran, half stumbled – wearing his tomato ketchup-stained tracksuit bottoms, and his Bristol City football shirt.

The alarm made a startled, violent sound.

He made it down the slope to where the water feature wasn't working, before being caught by Nurse This and Nurse That, and a Third Nurse who was just that moment arriving to work and still had his luminous yellow bicycle clip on around his ankle. I opened my bedroom window as far as it would go, which wasn't very far – obviously. It was impossible to hear what Nurse This was saying over the shouting.

Structuring narrative

Key term

cohesive device word or phrase which links paragraphs together and links points within paragraphs

When assessing your narrative writing, an examiner will be looking at the coherence and cohesion of your response.

- Coherence is the way you have organized your ideas across the text as a whole, e.g. how you developed the plot or built tension in your writing.
- Cohesion is how you have used **cohesive devices** to make links between and within the paragraphs, e.g. using time connectives to indicate when something is happening.

Time connectives can be placed at the beginning of paragraphs or within them and help the reader to follow the events being described in a narrative. These can be particularly useful in narratives which are chronological in order, such as autobiographical writing. Look at how time connectives are used in the following sentences taken from Student A's description of her special childhood memory

Student A

Instantly my eyes opened, encouraged by the intense sunshine on my face which had penetrated through the curtains.

Soon we were travelling by car in the sweltering summer sunshine, which was a torturous ordeal.

Immediately, a familiar chemical smell filled my nostrils as we walked through the revolving doors and into the main reception area of the hospital.

Eventually we reached the labour ward which was a hive of activity with business-like nurses briskly moving here and there, pushing trolleys stacked with files and medicines and directing bewildered-looking adults to where they needed to go.

Finally I saw her! She was so small and so snug, wrapped tightly in a blanket and the sight of her that day is something I will never forget.

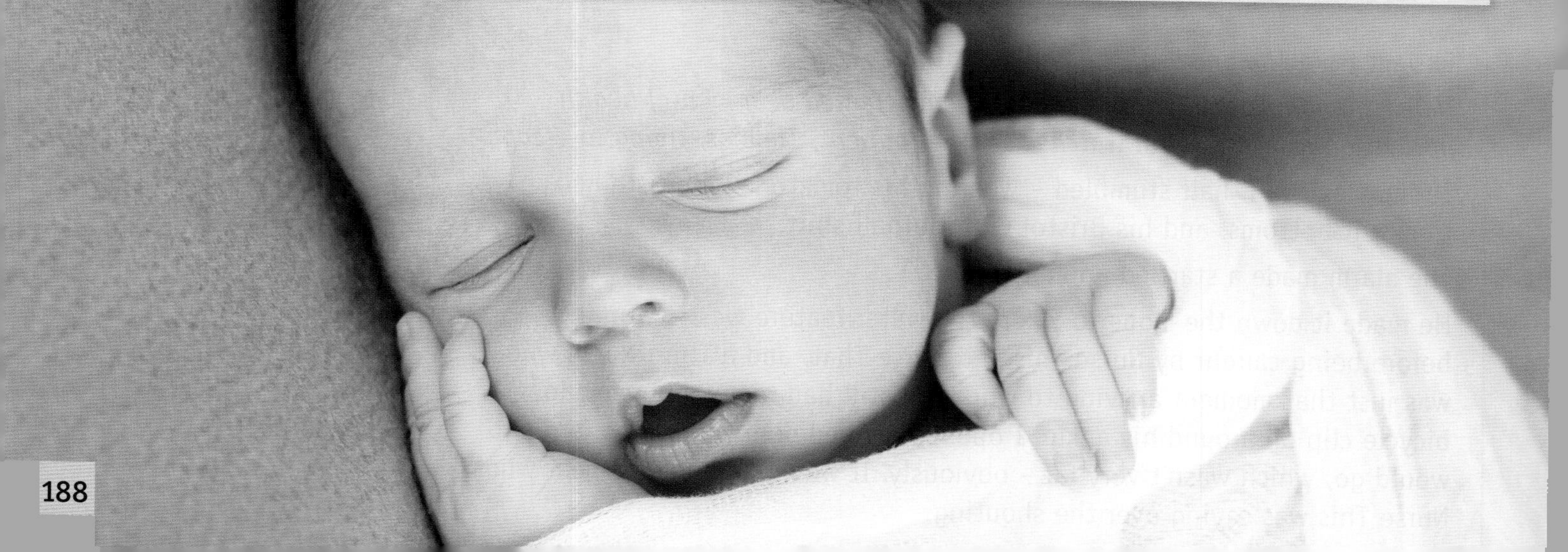

Now look at the cohesive devices Student A has used to link her ideas within the opening paragraph of her response.

Student A

Instantly my eyes opened, encouraged by an intense sunshine which had penetrated through the curtains. On this occasion, there was no need for dad's daily and increasingly angry five alarm calls. Breathlessly bounding into and out of the bathroom, soon I was washed and dressed and tugging at his sleeve as he attempted to eat breakfast, urging him to finish it and get going. He was happy too, so happy he ignored my lack of table etiquette. Swallowing a last tablespoon full of cereal, he eventually acquiesced with a smile. I don't think I had ever been as excited but this day was like no other. This day was special. This day was unique. This was the day I would meet my newly arrived baby sister for the very first time!

- Time connectives at the start of and within sentences direct the reader.
- Adverbs of time at the start and end of sentences help to position the reader.
- Chains of verbs to suggest the various actions.
- Synonyms avoid repetition and emphasize the importance of the event.
- Verbs starting sentences and subordinate clauses add variety.
- Prepositions add clarity.
- Adverbs add more information about how, when and the frequency of an action taking place.
- **Pronouns** at the beginning and within sentences avoid repetition and establish the relationship between father and daughter.

Activity 11

Look back at the planning you did for the following writing task in Activity 2 on page 180. Write the rest of this response using a range of cohesive devices to create links between and within your paragraphs.

> Imagine you are writing your autobiography. Describe a time when you felt afraid.
>
> You could write about:
>
> - where you were and what you did
> - how you felt about the experience
> - how you feel now, looking back.

Key term

pronoun a word used to replace a noun

Practising key skills for AO6

What is technical accuracy?

In this section you will work on developing the skills you need to do well in AO6.

AO6	• Use a range of vocabulary and sentence structures for clarity, purpose and effect, with accurate spelling and punctuation.

The focus here is on how accurately you punctuate and spell, and also how you use vocabulary imaginatively and structure your sentences in a very deliberate way to create specific effects.

Sentence structure

Whatever type of narrative you are writing, whether it is a story, autobiographical writing or a piece of personal writing, you should vary the length and structure of the sentences you use to shape the reader's response and create impact in your writing. Look back at page 96 to remind yourself of the three main sentence types.

As you write each paragraph of your response, think about the sentences you are using. Try to avoid:

- using too many simple sentences in a row as this makes your writing seem simplistic
- repeating the same word or part of speech at the start of each sentence as this will create a repetitive tone
- using overly long complex sentences which are difficult for the reader to follow.

Look at how Student A has used a range of sentence structures to create different effects in the extract from their story with the title 'The Bully' on the facing page. Then complete the activity below.

Activity 1 SPAG

1. Look back at the planning you did for Activity 3 on page 184 where you were asked to write a story or piece of personal writing with the title 'The Dark'. Write this response using a range of sentence structures to create deliberate effects. Think about how you can craft sentences that:
   - add detail and description
   - suggest the passing of time
   - echo the fast pace of the action
   - emphasize a moment of drama or tension.
2. Swap your writing with a partner. Can you identify where they have used different sentence structures for deliberate effects? How successful have they been in your opinion?

Student A

The bus wound its way slowly through the early evening traffic, much too slowly, heaving up the steep hill, past the church, out beyond the outer ring road, heading for the bright lights of the city in the distance.

Commas used to extend this multi-clause sentence create a sense of movement and time passing.

I was beginning to doze off, the heat and gentle rocking of the bus making me succumb to sleep although I tried to fight it. We ground to a halt for the last stop before the high street and then the depot. The doors opened with an icy chill and it was then I saw him. My blood froze.

Short, simple sentence emphasizes this moment of drama and tension.

Terror. It washed over and through me every time I saw him. No matter what I did it was always the same.

ne-word sentence ghlights the sense fear and dread the rrator feels when he es his tormentor.

Fleeing the bus, I ran through darkened streets until finally I reached a dead-end and there was nowhere left to run. I fleetingly thought about scaling the wall but the idea seemed suddenly absurd. I could hear his footsteps behind me as they slowed from a run to a walk. Turning to face him, I scoured the ground for something to protect myself with. I looked up. He stood motionless. He wore a smirk. The panic washed away. My anger erupted.

Multi-clause sentence conveys a sense of fast-paced movement and suggests the narrator's panic.

Short, simple sentences emphasize the tension as the narrator and the bully come face to face.

Punctuation

You need to use punctuation to help you to present the events in your narrative clearly and craft sentences to achieve particular effects. Look back at pages 96–97 to remind yourself of the different types of punctuation you can use and how you can employ the different punctuation marks in your writing.

Remember to think about the punctuation marks you use to demarcate your sentences. Every sentence should begin with a capital letter and end with either a full stop, question mark, exclamation mark or an ellipsis.

The ellipsis is a series of three dots and can be used in narrative writing to:

- indicate an unfinished thought or statement, e.g. It would not be long now...
- indicate a pause or a trailing off into silence in dialogue, e.g. "But I thought you knew..."
- create a sense of tension or mystery, e.g. The door slowly swung open...

Think about when it is appropriate to use the ellipsis in your writing, but try not to overuse this punctuation mark.

Tip

In dialogue you can use a dash to show when one speaker is interrupted by another, e.g.

"But I was going to tell you that we –"

"You don't have to tell me anything. I already know."

When you are writing dialogue in your narrative, you need to remember to:

- put speech marks around the words spoken
- start a new paragraph whenever the speaker changes
- only include the exact words the speaker says inside the speech marks
- put punctuation marks inside the speech marks
- give the name of the person speaking when this would make it clearer for the reader.

Activity 2 SPAG

1. Review your autobiographical writing where you described a time you felt afraid. Check that you have used a range of punctuation, including:
   - full stops, exclamation marks, question marks and ellipses to mark the end of sentences
   - commas and semi-colons to separate clauses within sentences
   - speech marks to indicate dialogue
   - other punctuation marks such as apostrophes, dashes and brackets where appropriate.
2. Now review your story or piece of personal writing with the title 'The Dark' in the same way. Make any corrections you need to improve the accuracy of your punctuation.

Vocabulary and spelling

When writing your response in the exam, you need to make imaginative and creative choices in the vocabulary you use. Try to avoid including commonly used phrases or clichés in your writing. Think about how you can make more creative choices of vocabulary to express these ideas in more original ways.

Activity 3

1. Copy and complete the grid below to change the clichéd phrases into more creative and imaginative sentences. You could use a dictionary and thesaurus to help you.

Example of cliché	Creative and imaginative sentence
It was a dark and stormy night.	Squalls of rain swept across a crepuscular sky.
That was a day I will never forget.	
I was afraid of my own shadow.	
I returned home looking like something that the cat dragged in.	
Dad looked like he was on top of the world.	

2. Add five more clichéd phrases to the grid and suggest creative and imaginative sentences to replace these.
3. Review your autobiographical writing where you described a time you felt afraid. Can you identify any commonly used phrases or clichés in it? Rewrite these to improve them and make them more original.
4. Now review your story or piece of personal writing with the title 'The Dark' in the same way. Make any revisions you think are needed to improve the ambition and precision of the vocabulary you have used.

Tip

When writing in the exam, think about the exact meaning you want to communicate and choose words that express this precisely. Although you should try to spell every word correctly, don't let this stop you from attempting to use more adventurous words. You can make occasional spelling mistakes in the ambitious words you choose and still be awarded the highest level.

Try it yourself

Try it yourself WITH SUPPORT

Look at Student A's complete response to the following writing task. Pay particular attention to the examiner's notes in the margin and the comments which follow.

Imagine you are writing your autobiography. Describe a special childhood occasion such as a birthday party or school trip.

You could write about:

- the things you did and who was involved
- the way that you felt
- how you feel now, looking back.

Student A

Instantly, my eyes opened, encouraged by an intense sunshine which had penetrated through the curtains. On this occasion, there was no need for dad's daily and increasingly angry five alarm calls which it normally took to get me out of bed. Breathlessly bounding into and out of the bathroom, soon I was washed and dressed and tugging at his sleeve as he attempted to eat breakfast, urging him to finish it so we could get going. He was happy too, so happy he ignored my lack of table etiquette. Swallowing a last tablespoon full of cereal, he eventually acquiesced with a smile. I don't think I had ever been as excited but this day was unlike any other. This day was special. This day was unique. This was the day I would meet my newly arrived baby sister for the very first time!

Shortly afterwards we were in the car and heading for the hospital. The hot summer sun made it an oven and even with the windows down and the air conditioning on, it was stiflingly hot and uncomfortable. Cars full of early morning shoppers out hunting for a bargain were causing long tailbacks as we approached the city. Powerful petrol and exhaust fumes invaded my nostrils as a cacophony of car horns screamed their drivers' displeasure. Dad did well to manage all of that and my incessant questions without complaint. Through traffic lights and the city centre, we headed out through the suburbs and eventually onto the motorway, where we picked up some speed, finally reaching our destination: the General Hospital.

Immediately, that familiar chemical smell hit me as we walked through the revolving doors and into the main reception. It was

Time connectives used between and within paragraphs to provide overall structure and cohesion

Interesting opening sente

'This day' repeated for emphasis

Evidence of a more sophisticated vocabulary

Suspense successfully created by not revealing what the special memory is until the end of the first paragraph

Metaphor use for descriptior and to appeal the reader's se of touch

Personificatior used for effec

Alliteration used to appeal to the reader's sense of sound

a hive of people, nurses, visitors, patients in robes, doctors and porters all busily going about their business. Heading straight for the lifts, we arrived just as the doors were about to close, squeezing into the tiny remaining space with our cards, presents and balloons. My excitement was at fever pitch! With each 'ping' announcing our arrival at a ward, I counted as we ascended towards floor eight where mum and the new arrival were waiting for us.

Entering the natal unit, dad's strides had started to lengthen with his increasing excitement, causing me to break into a skipping motion as I desperately tried to keep up. I recall my hands being sweaty and my grip on his loosening as we power-walked towards the room where mum was. Large signs on the wall instructed everyone to 'Wash your hands!' and in each room we passed laughter and the babble of excited talk could be heard. The place was a sea of happy, smiling faces.

Finally we found them! Mum looked tired but she smiled that distinctive broad, beaming smile which always made my heart soar at us as we walked in. I ran straight to her with the gifts and cards.

"Do you want to hold the baby?" she asked after a series of hugs and kisses.

"Yes please!" I shouted. "Oh, yes please!"

Gently she lifted the little bundle out of the transparent, plastic cot and slowly and carefully, as if she held something precious and sacred, she lowered my baby sister into my arms while keeping a protective arm around us both. Immediately, I noticed the black hair which was just like mine when I had been born. She was small, delicate, rosy-cheeked and she was absolutely beautiful. I was utterly speechless. Only one word could describe her: perfect.

I believed she had been sent from heaven and for that reason we called her Angel – although she is far from that these days!

Sentence structure chosen for deliberate effect

Mix of simple, compound, complex and multi-clause sentences add variety and make the writing interesting

Varied sentence starters avoid repetition and make the writing more interesting

Reasonably successful closing sentence

Key term

alliteration the occurrence of the same letter or sound at the beginning of a group of words for special effect

This response would be given Level 5 for AO5 and be placed at the top of Level 3 for AO6. The student could improve this response by:

- using a more ambitious variety of sentence structures more frequently for deliberate effect
- employing a more consistently adventurous vocabulary.

Look at Student B's complete response to the following writing task and complete the activity below.

The Bully

Use this as a title for a short story or a piece of personal writing.

In your writing you should:

- choose a clear viewpoint
- establish the setting
- explore the experience of the bully or being bullied.

Activity 1

1. Identify what is good about Student B's response.
2. Set two targets which you think would improve this response.
3. Use the mark schemes on pages 198–199 to award this response a level for A05 and A06.
4. Which of the two responses, Student A's or Student B's, do you think is best and why?

Student B

It did not take long, just a few encouraging words, softly spoken. Just his usual patient eyes and his assurance that it would be alright, is all it took. And after months, the floodgates burst open, the tears flowed immediately and then the babbling, an incoherent rambling of words hardly sensible and then the rage and the anger and the screaming poured out of me. This is how I broke the news to Granddad that I was being bullied.

Through it all he sat calmly, patiently and listened intently. When I had finished and after a few seconds pause, he spoke…

Let me tell you of a boy much like you who was also being bullied. Me. I was 13 and the bully in our year decided I would be his next victim until I spoke to my father, your great grandfather and he explained to me that a bully is an unhappy person who can only make himself better by making someone else equally unhappy. "Stand up to bullies, son. That's the only way they will stop. You must make them see you are not afraid of them." That's what he told me and so that's what I did. I stood up to Billy Bates.

I'll never forget that night. I had been to band practice at school. That was one of the things that Billy Bates made fun of, the fact that I played the trumpet. Anyway, it was winter and a cold and stormy evening as I headed off to catch the bus into town. Thunder rumbled in the distance and it began to rain as I waited at the bus stop.

After 20 minutes in the freezing cold, it finally arrived. Immediately, I was hit by a wall of heat and the smell of damp clothes as I boarded. It was disgusting! However, I was glad to be out of the cold and finally heading home at long last. I took a seat near the front, trumpet case on my knee and school bag at my feet.

Eventually, I began to doze off despite the constant drone of the engine and the noisy chatter of the shoppers, commuters and school kids who populated the bus. Ribbons of condensation ran down the windows. Slowly, it wound its way through the early evening traffic, much too slowly, heaving up the steep hill, trudging on through the throng of commuters heading home, past the church, out beyond the outer ring road, heading for the bright lights of the city in the distance.

Abruptly, we ground to a halt for the last stop before the high street. The doors opened with an icy chill. I saw him. My blood froze. What was Billy Bates doing on this route?

He grinned instantly when he spotted me and looking like he'd just won first prize at a raffle, he took his seat right behind me saying, "Alright there, me old mate, fancy meeting you here" with a hiss in my ear. I immediately jumped up, panic stricken, and made for the exit doors, squeezing through with a clatter as my trumpet case was slapped by the closing doors. Out in the cold air of night again, I headed off aimlessly, with a shiver of fear running down my spine, too afraid to look behind me, blindly stumbling away in terror.

The blood beat in my ears. The schoolbag and trumpet case were cumbersome. I chanced a quick glance over my shoulder. He was there! My breathing began to quicken and I instinctively began to run. Unfortunately, and in my panic, it was down a dead end...

Trapped. I fleetingly thought about scaling the wall but the idea seemed suddenly absurd. I could hear his footsteps behind me as they slowed from a run to a walk. Turning, I scoured the ground for something to protect myself with. There was nothing. I looked up. He stood motionless. He wore a smirk. I suddenly remembered my father's words, "Stand up to bullies, son" and that's what I did. At that moment, the panic washed away, replaced by determination.

"What happened granddad?" I asked after a few moments silence. "What did you do?"

"I simply showed him I was not afraid anymore," he replied. A few choice words were all it took to make Billy Bates turn and walk away and he never bothered me again.

"So I must stand up to this bully?" I asked.

"Yes," he replied. "You must stand up to this bully, son."

Look back at your completed responses to the following writing tasks.

5 Imagine you are writing your autobiography. Describe a time when you felt afraid.

You could write about:

- the thing that frightened you
- where you were and what you did
- how you felt about the experience.

OR

6 *The Dark*

Use this as a title for a story or piece of personal writing.

In your writing you should:

- choose a very clear viewpoint
- establish the setting
- explore the idea of darkness in a way which is interesting for the reader.

Activity 2

1. Use the mark schemes below to award your responses a level for A05 and A06.
2. Set yourself three targets (two for A05 and one for A06) which you think would improve your responses.

Level	Key words for content and organization (A05)
Level 6 (21–24 marks)	Form – deliberately adapted; sophisticated control of purpose and effect Tone, style and register – ambitiously selected Overall structure – skilfully controlled overall structure
Level 5 (17–20 marks)	Form – confidently adapted; secure understanding of purpose and audience Tone, style and register – sustained Overall structure – controlled overall structure
Level 4 (13–16 marks)	Form – confidently adapted; secure understanding of purpose and audience Tone, style and register – matched to task Overall structure – well-managed overall structure

Level 3 (9–12 marks)	Form – sustained; clear awareness of purpose and audience Tone, style and register – appropriate with some inconsistencies Overall structure – clear overall structure
Level 2 (5–8 marks)	Form – mostly appropriate; generally maintained Tone, style and register – attempted Overall structure – some evidence
Level 1 (1–4 marks)	Form – some attempt Tone, style and register – limited attempt Overall structure – some attempt

Level	Key words for technical accuracy (AO6)
Level 4 (13–16 marks)	Sentence structure – an ambitious range shapes meaning and creates impact Punctuation – accurate; makes writing clear and achieves specific effects Vocabulary – precise and subtle Spelling – accurate; very few mistakes
Level 3 (9–12 marks)	Sentence structure – a wide range used for deliberate purpose and effect Punctuation – consistently accurate Vocabulary – used convincingly; sometimes ambitious Spelling – accurate
Level 2 (5–8 marks)	Sentence structure – a range used and mostly secure Punctuation – generally accurate Vocabulary – appropriate Spelling – generally accurate
Level 1 (1–4 marks)	Sentence structure – simple mostly with some attempt at complex structures Punctuation – some Vocabulary – straightforward Spelling – simple spellings, mostly accurate

Try it yourself ON YOUR OWN

Read the questions below and write your response to **one** of these tasks, applying all the skills you have learned.

5 Imagine you are writing your autobiography. Describe a time when you learned an important lesson.

You could write about:

- something which happened at home or at school
- who was involved and the way that you felt
- what you learned from it.

OR

6 *A New Beginning.*

Use this as a title for a story or piece of personal writing.

In your writing you should:

- choose a very clear viewpoint
- establish the setting
- explore the experience of a new beginning.

Progress check

1. Use the mark scheme on pages 198–199 to award yourself a mark for AO5 and AO6.
2. Use the grid below to help you to assess whether you have met the targets you set yourself in Activity 2.

Focus	Not met	Partly met	Fully met
The response is paragraphed.			
The opening is attention-grabbing.			
Cohesive devices are used between paragraphs.			
Cohesive devices are used within paragraphs.			
Sentence structures are varied for deliberate effect.			
A wide range of punctuation is used accurately.			
Punctuation is used for deliberate effect.			
Vocabulary is ambitious and imaginative.			
Commonly used phrases and clichés have been avoided.			
Spelling is consistently accurate.			
The tone is appropriate for the task.			
The use of tense is consistent.			
The form is appropriate.			
The narrative voice is consistent.			
A range of linguistic devices have been used to good effect.			

Sample Paper Component 01

Section A
Reading information and ideas

Answer all the questions in Section A.
You are advised to spend **one** hour on this section.

Question 1 is about **Text 1**, *Etiquette of the Street.*

1 a) Look again at lines 1–6. Give **two** quotations which show how a gentleman is expected to behave when travelling. **[2]**

b) Look again at lines 7–15. Explain the way a lady's behaviour is expected to change when she receives attention from a gentleman. **[2]**

Question 2 is about **Text 1**, *Etiquette of the Street* **and Text 2**, *Modern Manners: A complete guide to etiquette in the digital age.*

2 Both texts offer advice about etiquette.

What other similarities and differences can you identify between the two texts? Draw on evidence from **both** texts to support your answer. **[6]**

Question 3 is about **Text 2**, *Modern Manners: A complete guide to etiquette in the digital age.*

3 Explore how the writer uses language and structure in this extract to present information and advice in a humorous way.

Support your ideas by referring to the text, using relevant subject terminology. **[12]**

Question 4 is about **Text 1**, *Etiquette of the Street* **and Text 2**, *Modern Manners: A complete guide to etiquette in the digital age.*

4 'These texts show how people's behaviour has changed between the 19th and 21st centuries.'

How far do you agree with this statement?

In your answer you should:

- discuss what you learn about people's behaviour in the 19th and 21st centuries
- explain the impact of these ideas on you as a reader
- compare the ways information and ideas about people's behaviour are presented.

Support your response with quotations from **both** texts. **[18]**

Text 1

This is an extract from Our Deportment *by John H. Young, an etiquette guide published in 1881.*

In Victorian society, men and women were expected to act in certain ways. This extract describes how men and women should act when walking on the street or travelling by public transport.

Etiquette of the Street

The manners of a person are clearly shown by his treatment of the people he meets in the public streets of a city or village, in public conveyances and in travelling generally. The true gentleman, at all times, in all places, and under all circumstances, is kind and courteous to all he meets, regards not only the rights, but the wishes and feelings of others, is deferential to women and to elderly men, and is ever ready to extend his aid to those who need it.

The street manners of a lady

A lady walks quietly through the streets, seeing and hearing nothing that she ought not to see and hear, recognizing acquaintances with a courteous bow, and friends with words of greeting. She is always unobtrusive, never talks loudly, or laughs boisterously, or does anything to attract the attention of the passers-by. She walks along in her own quiet, lady-like way, and by her preoccupation is secure from any annoyance to which a person of less perfect breeding might be subjected.

A lady never demands attention and favours from a gentleman, but, when voluntarily offered, accepts them gratefully, graciously, and with an expression of hearty thanks.

Recognizing friends in the street

No one, while walking the streets, should fail, through preoccupation, or absent-mindedness, to recognize friends or acquaintances, either by a bow or some form of salutation. If two gentlemen stop to talk, they should retire to one side of the walk. If a stranger should be in company with one of the gentlemen, an introduction is not necessary. If a gentleman meets another gentleman in company with a lady whom he does not know, he lifts his hat to salute them both. If he knows the lady, he should salute her first. The gentleman who accompanies a lady, always returns a **salutation** made to her.

Do not lack politeness

Never hesitate in acts of politeness for fear they will not be recognized or returned. One cannot be too polite so long as he conforms to rules, while it is easy to lack politeness by neglect of them. Besides, if courtesy is met by neglect or rebuff, it is not for the courteous person to feel mortification, but the boorish one; and so all lookers-on will regard the matter.

Turn over

Shouting

Never speak to your acquaintances from one side of the street to the other. Shouting is a certain sign of vulgarity. First approach, and then make your communication to your acquaintance or friend in a moderately loud tone of voice.

Etiquette for public conveyances

In street cars, omnibuses and other public street **conveyances**, it should be the endeavour of each passenger to make room for all persons entering, and no gentleman will retain his seat when there are ladies standing. When a lady accepts a seat from a gentleman, she expresses her thanks in a kind and pleasant manner.
A lady may, with perfect **propriety**, accept the offer of services from a stranger in alighting from, or entering an omnibus or other public conveyance, and should always acknowledge the courtesy with a pleasant "Thank you, sir," or a bow.
Never talk politics or religion in a public conveyance.
Gentlemen should not cross their legs, nor stretch their feet out into the passage-way of a public conveyance.

Glossary

salutation greeting
conveyances vehicles
propriety good manners

Text 2

This is an extract from Modern manners: A complete guide to etiquette in the digital age*, an article first published in* The Independent *newspaper on 21 May 2011.*

Modern manners: A complete guide to etiquette in the digital age

When John H Young published his *Guide to the Manners, Etiquette and Deportment of the Most Refined Society* in 1879, it became a bestseller.

After you've read its 400 pages of rules governing everything from napkin use to dismounting a horse, you feel that you could deal with anything day-to-day life might chuck in your direction. If it were 1879. It isn't 1879, though, and while Young presents an idealized version of Victorian life (nowhere does he address "being accosted by a drunkard" or "coping with gout") it's clear that behaviour has changed radically.

For instance, his assertion that you should offer your own reading material to others on a train before settling down to read it yourself is laughably out of step with the habits of modern commuters.

The web is, by any standards, a maelstrom of unhinged lunacy. No one is who they say they are; they hide behind aliases like bubblewrap23 and either insult or stalk you. We really need a new set of rules to help us become level-headed beacons of decency in the internet age – but as far as I'm aware, it doesn't exist.

If John H Young were still alive to see the abuse that's dished out on Facebook between people who are notionally "friends", I think he'd probably tear up his section on "The **Pernicious** Influence of **Indolence**", ignore his own advice about never ridiculing others, and pen a withering anti-guide, detailing the ways in which technology is creating a Most Unrefined Society...

Street etiquette

Mobile communication has revolutionized the ancient art of walking about. When taking a call on the street, one should immediately become oblivious to one's surroundings and saunter about, randomly. When the call is terminated, you must then take a few seconds to assess where the hell you've ended up, before rejoining your original course. Asking for directions is no longer the done thing; instead, consult Google Maps on your smartphone. If Google Maps isn't working, start screaming and praying. Tipping one's hat to acquaintances has, for many years now, been replaced by the act of shouting loudly from car windows. Or repeatedly hollering to a figure on the opposite pavement until you give up on them and continue your journey. Texting while walking can be dangerous. This is manifestly obvious to anyone who has witnessed near-misses with vehicles caused by people jabbing their thumbs repeatedly at a miniature keyboard. Despite this, continue doing it anyway. The odds are probably stacked in favour of you surviving. Just about.

Turn over

Travel and public transport

There are times in modern life where one becomes bored of one's mobile phone ringtone and fancies changing it to something more raucous. The upper deck of a bus is the correct place to explore the dozens of options on offer. As per street etiquette, when speaking on your mobile phone on public transport, pay no heed to those around you. Imagine that you're in some kind of soundproof bubble, allowing you to sound off at great volume. After hanging up, wonder for a moment why it could be that everyone is staring at you. Put it down to the fact that your hair is looking particularly nice today, and make your next call. When travelling on trains late at night with a friend, it's polite to offer them one earpiece of your stereo headphones so you can both have a faintly uninvolving mono experience of the last Adele album. Fall asleep on each other's shoulders, end up stranded at some grim terminus and argue about who should pay for the 30-mile taxi journey back to civilization.

Glossary

pernicious harmful
indolence laziness

Section B
Writing for audience, impact and purpose

Choose **one** of the following writing tasks.
You are advised to spend **one** hour on this section.

In this section you will be assessed on the quality of your extended response, these questions are marked with an asterisk (*). You are advised to plan and check your work carefully.

EITHER

5 Write a speech to be given in a school assembly advising new Year 7 students on how they should behave in school.

In your speech you should:

- explain how Year 7 students are expected to behave
- suggest any problems or difficulties they might face and how they can avoid these
- convince your audience of the importance of following school rules on behaviour. **[40]***

OR

6 Write a letter to a national newspaper in which you argue that modern technology is improving the way that people behave.

In your article you should:

- explain why you think that modern technology is improving the way people behave
- give some examples to support your argument
- convince readers that overall modern technology has a positive rather than a negative effect on people's behaviour. **[40]***

Sample Paper Component 02

Section A

Reading meaning and effects

Answer **all** the questions in Section A.
You are advised to spend **one** hour on this section.

Question 1 is about **Text 1**, *The Rainbow* by D.H. Lawrence.

1 Look again at lines 1–11.

a) Give **two** quotations which show Ursula's feelings about the students she is teaching. **[2]**

b) What do these suggest about Ursula's character? **[2]**

Question 2 is about **Text 1**, *The Rainbow* by D.H. Lawrence.

2 Look again at lines 18–39.

How does D.H. Lawrence use language and structure to emphasize the violence of the encounter between Ursula and Williams?

You should use relevant subject terminology to support your answer. **[6]**

Question 3 is about **Text 2**, *Cider With Rosie* by Laurie Lee.

3 Look again at lines 1–15.

Explore how the writer presents the headteacher and how this influences readers' views about the character.

Support your ideas by referring to the language and structure of this section, using relevant subject terminology. **[12]**

Question 4 is about **Text 1**, *The Rainbow* **and Text 2**, *Cider With Rosie*.

4 'These texts show the conflicts that can exist between teachers and students.' How far do you agree with this statement?

In your answer you should:

- discuss your impressions of the situations presented
- explain what you find unusual about the teachers' and students' behaviour
- compare the ways the writers present the conflict between teachers and students.

Support your response with quotations from **both** texts. **[18]**

Text 1

Set at the start of the 20th century, this is an extract from the novel The Rainbow*, by D.H. Lawrence, published in 1915.*

Ursula Brangwen is a teacher in a mining town in the Midlands. Here she is teaching geography to a class with some troublesome students including a boy called Williams.

Ursula turned to the map again, to go on with the geography lesson. But there was a little ferment in the class. Williams' spirit infected them all. She heard a scuffle, and then she trembled inwardly. If they all turned on her this time, she was beaten.

"Please, Miss," called a voice in distress.

She turned round. One of the boys she liked was ruefully holding out a torn celluloid collar. She heard the complaint, feeling futile.

"Go in front, Wright," she said.

She was trembling in every fibre. A big, sullen boy, not bad but very difficult, slouched out to the front. She went on with the lesson, aware that Williams was making faces at Wright, and that Wright was grinning behind her. She was afraid. She turned to the map again. And she was afraid.

"Please, Miss, Williams," came a sharp cry, and a boy on the back row was standing up, with drawn, painted brows, half a mocking grin on his pain, half real resentment against Williams "Please, Miss, he's nipped me," and he rubbed his leg ruefully.

"Come in front, Williams," she said.

The rat-like boy sat with his pale smile and did not move.

"Come in front," she repeated, definite now.

"I shan't," he cried, snarling, rat-like, grinning. Something went click in Ursula's soul. Her face and eyes set, she went through the class straight. The boy cowered before her glowering, fixed eyes. But she advanced on him, seized him by the arm, and dragged him from his seat. He clung to the form. It was the battle between him and her. Her instinct had suddenly become calm and quick. She jerked him from his grip, and dragged him, struggling and kicking, to the front. He kicked her several times, and clung to the forms as he passed, but she went on. The class was on its feet in excitement. She saw it, but made no move.

Turn over

She knew if she let go the boy he would dash to the door. Already he had run home once out of her class. So she snatched her cane from the desk, and brought it down on him. He was writhing and kicking. She saw his face beneath her, white, with eyes like the eyes of a fish, stony, yet full of hate and horrible fear. And she loathed him, the hideous writhing thing that was nearly too much for her. In horror lest he should overcome her, and yet at the heart quite calm, she brought down the cane again and again, whilst he struggled making inarticulate noises, and lunging vicious kicks at her. With one hand she managed to hold him, and now and then the cane came down on him. He writhed, like a mad thing. But the pain of the strokes cut through his writhing, vicious, coward's courage, bit deeper till at last, with a long whimper that became a yell, he went limp. She let him go, and he rushed at her, his teeth and eyes glinting. There was a second of agonized terror in her heart: he was a beast thing. Then she caught him, and the cane came down on him. A few times, madly, in a frenzy, he lunged and writhed, to kick her. But again the cane broke him, he sank with a howling yell on the floor, and like a beaten beast lay there yelling.

Text 2

This is an extract from Laurie Lee's memoir of his childhood, Cider With Rosie, *published in 1959. Here he describes the headteacher at his school, Miss B, who was given the nickname Crabby.*

She was a bunched and punitive little body and the school had christened her Crabby; she had a sour yellow look, lank hair coiled in earphones, and the skin and voice of a turkey. We were all afraid of the gobbling Miss B; she spied, she pried, she crouched, she crept, she pounced – she was a terror.

Each morning was war without declaration; no one knew who would catch it next. We stood to attention, half-crippled in our desks, till Miss B walked in, whacked the walls with a ruler, and fixed us with her squinting eye. "Good a-morning, children!" "Good morning, Teacher!" The greeting was like a rattling of swords. Then she would scowl at the floor and begin to growl "Ar Farther..."; at which we said the Lord's Prayer, praised all good things, and thanked God for the health of our King. But scarcely had we bellowed the last Amen than Crabby coiled, uncoiled, and sprang, and knocked some poor boy sideways.

One seldom knew why; one was always off guard, for the punishment preceded the charge. The charge, however, followed hard upon it, to a light shower of angry spitting.

"Shuffling your feet! Playing with the desk! A-smirking at that miserable Betty! I will not have it. I'll not, I say. I repeat – I will not have it!"

And indeed there came the inevitable day when rebellion raised its standard, when the tension was broken and a hero emerged whom we would willingly have named streets after. At least, from that day his name was honoured, though we gave him little support at the time...

Spadge Hopkins it was, and I must say we were surprised. He was one of those heavy, full-grown boys, thick-legged, red-fisted, bursting with flesh, designed for the great outdoors. He was nearly fourteen by then, and physically out of scale – at least so far as our school was concerned. The sight of him squeezed into his tiny desk was worse than a bullock in ballet-shoes. He wasn't much of a scholar; he groaned as he worked, or hacked at his desk with a jack-knife. Miss B took her pleasure in goading him, in forcing him to read out loud; or asking him sudden unintelligible questions which made him flush and stumble.

The great day came; a day of shimmering summer, with the valley outside in a state of leafy levitation. Crabby B was at her sourest, and Spadge Hopkins had had enough. He began to writhe in his desk, and roll his eyes, and kick with his boots, and mutter; "She'd better look out. 'Er, – Crabby B. She'd better, that's all. I can tell you..."

We didn't quite know what the matter was, in spite of his meaning looks. Then he threw down his pen, said; "Sod it all," got up and walked to the door.

"And where are you going, young man, may I ask?" said Crabby with her awful leer.

Spadge paused and looked her straight in the eye.

Turn over

"If it's any business of **yourn**."

We shivered with pleasure at this defiance, Spadge leisurely made for the door.

"Sit down this instant!" Crabby suddenly screamed. "I won't have it!"

"**Ta-ta**," said Spadge.

Then Crabby sprang like a yellow cat, spitting and clawing with rage. She caught Spadge in the doorway and fell upon him. There was a shameful moment of heavy breathing and scuffling, while the teacher tore at his clothes. Spadge caught her hands in his great red fists and held her at arm's length, struggling.

"Come and help me, someone!" wailed Crabby, demented. But nobody moved; we just watched. We saw Spadge lift her up and place her on the top of the cupboard, then walk out of the door and away. There was a moment of silence, then we all laid down our pens and began to stamp on the floor in unison. Crabby stayed where she was, on top of the cupboard, drumming her heels and weeping.

Glossary

yourn yours
ta-ta goodbye

Section B
Writing imaginatively and creatively

Choose **one** of the following writing tasks.

You are advised to spend **one** hour on this section.

In this section you will be assessed on the quality of your extended response, these questions are marked with an asterisk (*). You are advised to plan and check your work carefully.

EITHER

5 Imagine you are writing your autobiography. Describe your experiences of a time when someone treated you in an unfair way.

You could write about:

- the situation where someone treated you unfairly
- how this made you feel and the way you reacted
- the way that you feel about this experience now.

[40]*

OR

6 *Breaking the rules*.

Use this as a title for a story or piece of personal writing.

In your writing you should:

- choose a clear viewpoint
- describe the setting
- explore what rules could be broken.

[40]*

Key terms

adjective a word added to a noun to describe it or change its meaning

adverb a word used with a verb, adjective or other adverb to describe how, when or where something happened

adverbial a word or phrase that is used as an adverb and helps to link ideas together. A fronted adverbial is used at the start of a sentence and followed by a comma

alliteration the occurrence of the same letter or sound at the beginning of a group of words for special effect

balanced sentence a sentence where the two halves are parallel or balanced in structure. If the two halves are in contrast, it is called antithesis

clause part of a sentence with its own verb

cliché a phrase or idea that is used so often that it has little meaning, e.g. Love is blind

cohesive device a word or phrase which links paragraphs together and link points within paragraphs

command an instruction, usually written in the imperative with the verb as the first word in the sentence

conjunction word that links words, phrases and clauses

connective a word that joins words or phrases or sentences

coordinating conjunction a word used to join two single clauses of equal importance together, e.g. and, but, because, so, for, or, nor, yet

dialogue words spoken by characters in a play, film or story

discourse marker words and phrases used in written or spoken communication to connect or signpost information and ideas

emotive language words and phrases that arouse emotion

exclamation expresses surprise, shock or amusement and is marked by an exclamation mark. Exclamations do not always have a subject or a verb

explicit stating something openly and exactly

figurative language techniques such as simile, metaphor, personification and onomatopoeia which use words for the effects they create, rather than their literal meanings

first-person narrative story or experience told by someone who is part of the story and action, using the words 'I' and 'we'

flashback a scene in a story or film that is set earlier in time than the main part of the story

frame narrative a literary technique presenting a story within a story

genre a particular kind or style of literature

hyperbole deliberately exaggerated statement

ideas the information, experiences, opinions or arguments in a text

imagery writing which creates a picture or appeals to other senses, including simile, metaphor and personification, and the use of vivid verbs, nouns, adjectives and adverbs

implicit implied but not stated openly

independent clause (or main clause) a part of a sentence that can be used as a complete sentence

interpret to explain the meaning of something said or written

inverted sentence a sentence where the verb comes before the subject

metaphor the use of a word or phrase in a special meaning that provides an image

minor sentence a sentence which isn't complete but which makes sense as a unit of meaning in context

motif an element, idea or theme that is repeated throughout a text

noun a word used to name a person, place or thing

omniscient knowing everything

onomatopoeia words which imitate the sound they represent

past tense verb forms used to describe something that happened earlier, e.g. I drove the car, He climbed the mountain

pathetic fallacy when natural elements such as the weather or the landscape mirror the feelings of a character

personification to present an idea in human form or a thing as having human characteristics

perspective viewpoint, e.g. a narrator's viewpoint or the viewpoint of the writer

present tense verb forms used to describe something that is happening now, e.g. I drive the car, He climbs the mountain

pronoun a word used instead of a noun or noun phrase

protagonist the chief character, or one of the leading characters, in a drama or narrative

question asks about something and is marked by a question mark

reference chain different words or phrases used for the same idea, person or thing many times in a piece of writing, like links in a chain

register the formality of the writing (e.g. vocabulary use, grammatical choices, etc.) which can vary according to the context and audience

relative pronoun a pronoun used to introduce a clause which describes or limits the subject, e.g. what, who, whom, whose, which, that

rhetorical question question asked for dramatic effect and not intended to get an answer

setting the place and time where the story occurs

sibilance the use of the 's' sound at the beginning or within neighbouring words

simile a figure of speech in which one thing is compared to another using 'like' or 'as…'

simple sentence (single-clause sentence) the most basic type of sentence, consisting of a subject and a verb

statement gives information or tells you about something

style the way in which the writer uses language

subordinate clause a part of a sentence which gives more meaning to the main clause, but cannot exist on its own as it is not a complete sentence

subordinating conjunction a word used to join two clauses which are not equal, e.g. although, as, before, once, though, until

synonym a word or phrase that means the same or almost the same as another word or phrase

synthesize draw together information and ideas from two or more texts and explain this in your own words

tense the tense of a verb tells you when the action of the verb takes place (present, past or future)

theme a key idea or issue that the text is concerned with

third-person limited narrator where the narrator is not a character in the story, but is not able to share the thoughts and feelings of one of the characters with the reader

third-person omniscient narrator where the narrator is not a character in the story, but can share the thoughts and feelings of different characters with the reader

third-person narrative story or experience told by someone outside of the story, using the words 'he', 'she' or 'they'

time connective word or phrase used to indicate when something is happening, e.g. firstly, then, afterwards, instantly, meanwhile, next, shortly, later on, that night, the next day, etc.

tone the writer's or narrator's attitude, which is implied through their language choices

topic sentence the sentence that introduces or summarizes the main idea in a paragraph

tricolon groups of three related words or phrases placed close together

verb a word used to describe an action, feeling or state

Acknowledgements

The authors and publisher are grateful for permission to reprint extracts from the following copyright material:

Maya Angelou: *I Know Why the Caged Bird Sings* (Virago, 2012), copyright © Maya Angelou 1969, renewed 1997, reprinted by permission of the publishers, Little, Brown Book Group Ltd, Hachette UK and Random House, an imprint and division of Penguin Random House LLC. All rights reserved.

Iain Banks: *The Crow Road* (Abacus, 2013), copyright © Iain Banks 1992, reprinted by permission of Little, Brown Book Group Ltd, Hachette UK.

Laura Bates: *Everyday Sexism* (Simon & Schuster, 2014), reprinted by permission of Simon & Schuster UK.

Charlie Brooker: 'Poor A Levels? Don't Despair. Just lie on job application forms', *theguardian.com*, 21 Aug 2011, copyright © Guardian News and Media 2011, reprinted by permission of GNM.

John Cleese: *So Anyway: The Autobiography* (Random House, 2014), copyright © John Cleese 2014, reprinted by permission of The Random House Group Ltd.

Roald Dahl: *Going Solo* (Puffin, 2013), copyright © Roald Dahl 1986, reprinted by permission of David Higham Associates Ltd.

Anita Desai: *Games at Twilight, and other stories* (Vintage, 1998), copyright © Anita Desai 1978, 1998, reprinted by permission of the author c/o Rogers, Coleridge & White Ltd, 20 Powis Mews, London W11 1JN.

Daphne Du Maurier: *Rebecca* (Virago, 2012), copyright © Daphne Du Maurier 1938, reprinted by permission of Curtis Brown Group Ltd, London on behalf of The Beneficiaries of the Estate of Daphne Du Maurier.

Stephen Emmott: *10 Billion* (Penguin, 2013), copyright © Stephen Emmott 2013, reprinted by permission of Penguin Books Ltd.

Sebastian Faulks: *A Week in December* (Hutchinson, 2009), copyright © Sebastian Faulks 2009, reprinted by permission of The Random House Group Ltd.

Nathan Filer: *The Shock of the Fall* (Borough Press, 2014), copyright © Nathan Filer 2013, reprinted by permission of HarperCollins Publishers Ltd.

Nicci French: *Until It's Over* (Penguin, 2009), copyright © Nicci French 2008, reprinted by permission of Penguin Books Ltd.

William Gibson: *Neuromancer* (HarperVoyager, 1995), copyright © William Gibson 1984, reprinted by permission of Martha Millard Literary Agency.

John Green: *The Fault in Our Stars* (Puffin, 2013), copyright © John Green 2012, reprinted by permission of Penguin Books Ltd.

Mark Haddon: *The Curious Incident of the Dog in the Night-time* (Vintage, 2004), copyright © Mark Haddon 2004, reprinted by permission of The Random House Group Ltd.

The Independent: 'Modern Manners: A complete guide to etiquette in the digital age', *The Independent*, 21 May 2011, copyright © The Independent 2011, reprinted by permission of The Independent, www.independent.co.uk

Marie Javins: 'Bragging Rights' from Perceptive Travel website, www.perceptivetravel.com, reprinted by permission of the author.

Laurie Lee: *Cider with Rosie* (Vintage Classics 2002), copyright © Laurie Lee 1959, reprinted by permission of Curtis Brown Group Ltd, London on behalf of The Beneficiaries of the Estate of Laurie Lee.

Penelope Lively: *Oleander, Jacaranda: A Childhood Perceived* (Penguin, 2006), copyright © Penelope Lively 1994, reprinted by permission of Penguin Books Ltd.

Andrea Levy: *Every Light in the House Burnin'* (Headline Review, 1995), copyright © Andrea Levy 1994, reprinted by permission of Headline Publishing Group, and David Grossman Literary Agency for the author.

Ian McEwan: *The Child in Time* (Vintage, 1992), copyright © Ian Mc Ewan 1987, reprinted by permission of The Random House Group Ltd.

Michelle Magorian: *Goodnight Mr Tom* (Puffin, 2010), copyright © Michelle Magorian 1981, reprinted by permission of Penguin Books Ltd.

Jack Monroe: 'More than "hunger hurts"', *theguardian.com*, 10 Dec 2014, copyright © Guardian News and Media 2014, reprinted by permission of GNM.

Haruki Murakami: *'A Walk to Kobe'*, Granta Magazine, No 124, Summer 2013, copyright © Haruki Murakami 2013, reprinted by permission of ICM on behalf of the author. All rights reserved.

Redmond O'Hanlon: *Into the Heart of Borneo An account of a journey made in 1983 to the mountains of Batu Tiban with James Fenton* (Picador, 1994), copyright © Redmond O'Hanlon 1984, reprinted by permission of United Agents on behalf of Redmond O'Hanlon.

Michael Parkinson: *Parky: my autobiography* (Hodder & Stoughton, 2008), copyright © Michael Parkinson 2008, reprinted by permission of Hodder and Stoughton Ltd.

Amy Tan: *'Rules of the Game' from The Joy Luck Club* (Vintage, 1998), copyright © Amy Tan 1989, reprinted by permission of Abner Stein on behalf of the author.

Dylan Thomas: *A Child's Christmas in Wales* (Orion Children's Books, 2005), copyright © Dylan Thomas 1954, reprinted by permission of David Higham Associates Ltd.

Julie Walters: *Maggie's Tree* (Phoenix, 2007), copyright © Julie Walters 2006, reprinted by permission of The Orion Publishing Group.

Emma Watson: HeforShe campaign launch speech given at the United Nations, 20 Sept 2014, reprinted by permission of Emma Watson.

Winifred Watson: *Miss Pettigrew Lives for a Day* (Persephone, 2008), reprinted by permission of Persephone Books Ltd.

Although we have made every effort to trace and contact all copyright holders before publication this has not been possible in all cases. If notified, the publisher will rectify any errors or omissions at the earliest opportunity.

Cover image by DrAfter123/Getty Images

p9: wavebreakmedia/Shutterstock; **p11:** Everett Collection Historical/Alamy; **p15:** INTERFOTO/Alamy; **p16-17:** STILLFX/Shutterstock; **p18:** true nature/Shutterstock; **p19:** Stephen Alvarez/National Geographic/Getty Images; **p23:** Pictorial Press Ltd / Alamy; **p24-25:** Trevor Chriss/Alamy; **p28-29:** jadimages/Shutterstock; **p30:** Robert Harding Picture Library Ltd/Alamy; **p34:** Piotr Marcinski/Shutterstock; **p37:** Syaheir Azizan/Shutterstock; **p39:** Robin Marchant/Getty Images; **p40:** Steve Sands/Getty Images; **p44:** robert_s/Shutterstock; **p45:** topnatthapon/Shutterstock; **p47:** Malcolm Fairman/Alamy; **p48:** benjaminec/Shutterstock; **p52:** Corbis; **p53:** Classic Image/Alamy; **p54:** Gustavo Frazao/Shutterstock; **p57:** Lordprice Collection/Alamy; **p58-59:** Denis Burdin/Shutterstock; **p60-61:** Tsuguliev/Shutterstock; **p63:** Thelma Amaro Vidales/Shutterstock; **p65:** Corbis; **p67:** WENN Ltd/Alamy; **p69:** sakkmesterke/Shutterstock; **p73:** Gustavo Frazao / Shutterstock; **p74:** Zhukova Valentyna/Shutterstock; **p75:** Andrew Paterson/Alamy; **p77:** stockyimages/Shutterstock; **p80:** Tatiana_Kost/Shutterstock; **p83:** Robert Harding World Imagery/Alamy; **p85:** Rtimages/Shutterstock; **p86-87:** Navidim/Shutterstock; **p88:** ra2studio/Shutterstock; **p92:** Robert Harding World Imagery/Alamy; **p96:** Jin Jo/Shutterstock; **p101:** Ewelina Wachala/Shutterstock; **p106:** Gergana Encheva/Shutterstock; **p105:** Duncan Davis/Britain On View/Getty Images; **p108:** Heritage Image Partnership Ltd/Alamy; **p109:** AF archive/Alamy; **p111:** AF archive/Alamy; **p113:** Barry Winiker / Getty Images; **p118:** lculig / Shutterstock; **p120:** Mariiii / Shutterstock; **p123:** BestPhotoStudio / Shutterstock; **p127:** Terese Loeb Kreuzer / Alamy; **p133:** Slawomir Fajer / iStock; **p138:** Tyler Olson/Shutterstock; **p135:** Tyler Olson/Shutterstock; **p136:** Photographee.eu / Shutterstock; **p141:** cineclassico / Alamy; **p142:** Kathy deWitt / Alamy; **p145:** Francesco Scatena/Shutterstock; **p147:** Graham Mulrooney / Alamy; **p154:** brizmaker / Shutterstock; **p153:** vovan/Shutterstock; **p156:** trekandshoot / Shutterstock; **p162:** Shebeko / Shutterstock; **p164:** Art_man / Shutterstock; **p176:** ra2studio / Shutterstock; **p167:** Sidarta/Shutterstock; **p168-169:** Flas100/Shutterstock; **p179:** We.photography / Shutterstock; **p180:** BestPhotoStudio / Shutterstock; **p181:** Semmick Photo/Shutterstock; **p183:** STOCKFOLIO® / Alamy; **p185:** bikeriderlondon / Shutterstock; **p186:** Sokolova Maryna / Shutterstock; **p189:** William Perugini / Shutterstock; **p193:** Michael Dechev / Shuttertstock; **p195:** 1MoreCreative / iStock; **p198:** Gustavo Frazao/Shutterstock;